Power Up!

Power Up!

The Guide to Leadership Coaching with Strengths

Gene Knott, PhD, ABPP

iUniverse, Inc.
Bloomington

Power Up!
The Guide to Leadership Coaching with Strengths

Copyright © 2012 by Gene Knott, PhD, ABPP.

All rights reserved. No part of this book may be used or reproduced by any means, graphic, electronic, or mechanical, including photocopying, recording, taping or by any information storage retrieval system without the written permission of the publisher except in the case of brief quotations embodied in critical articles and reviews.

iUniverse books may be ordered through booksellers or by contacting:

iUniverse
1663 Liberty Drive
Bloomington, IN 47403
www.iuniverse.com
1-800-Authors (1-800-288-4677)

Because of the dynamic nature of the Internet, any web addresses or links contained in this book may have changed since publication and may no longer be valid. The views expressed in this work are solely those of the author and do not necessarily reflect the views of the publisher, and the publisher hereby disclaims any responsibility for them.

ISBN: 978-1-4620-4153-4 (sc)
ISBN: 978-1-4620-4154-1 (hc)
ISBN: 978-1-4620-4155-8 (ebk)

Library of Congress Control Number: 2011918534

Printed in the United States of America

iUniverse rev. date: 12/17/2011

What They Are Saying About *Power Up!*

This is a fantastic book. Knott takes us back to the roots of strengths-based coaching, and then leads the reader through the seminal writing of today's leaders in the field. The author uses mnemonic devices and an inviting writing style to introduce powerful concepts foundational to strength-based, positive coaching. A clear, scholarly, science-based approach to the profession for the novice as well as the seasoned coach. Books like Gene Knott's *Power Up!* are bringing a new level of credibility to executive coaching.

—John S. Stephenson, PhD, Executive Coach/Consultant

I immediately started highlighting and dog-earring pages; the book will be greatly appreciated by those of us who attempt to serve as coaches. A positive and potent "strongbox" of resources for anyone working to serve as a successful strengths-based coach, *Power Up!* builds upon existing strength-based research to incorporate key tenets of change models, positive psychology and successful coaching strategies in order to produce a purposeful and practical guide for those interested in facilitating real change.

—Melissa Boyd-Colvin, Leadership Educator and Strengths Consultant

As current research in neuroscience and positive psychology tells us, there is a correlation between positive image and positive action. What we look for, we find; and what we pay attention to, grows. *Power Up!: The Guide to Leadership Coaching with Strengths* is a compelling, insightful collection of real-life stories and techniques for understanding and applying the strengths paradigm—highly recommended for anyone who wants to flourish at work and in life.

—Jen Hetzel Silbert, Co-author of *Positive Family Dynamics: Appreciative Inquiry Questions to Bring Out the Best in Families,* Co-founder & Partner at Innovation Partners International

This book is a gem for coaches, supervisors, mentors and those who want to enhance the quality of their helping relationships. Packed with useful tools, tips, and tales of the coaching trade, *Power Up!: The Guide to Leadership Coaching with Strengths* skillfully guides both the seasoned and beginning coach to an appreciative method of coaching that is truly transformational. Read it and unleash the power of personal strengths!

—Sylvia C. Spears, PhD, former Dean of the College, Dartmouth College

Gene Knott is a master coach, bringing to life the power of strength-based methods in the coaching process. His straightforward approach makes the theory and research easily understandable, with practical activities, insightful stories, and key takeaways in every chapter. Anyone interested in coaching and being part of the strengths revolution will profit from this book.

—Tony Silbert, MSOD, Founding Partner, Innovation Partners International; co-author of *Healing Conversations Now*

CONTENTS

For Nancy,
my strength, inspiration and
role model for appreciation

INTRODUCTION

Power Up: The Guide to Leadership Coaching with Strengths is a comprehensive description of a strengths-oriented, positive professional coaching approach that re-focuses the tenor of transactions for both leader/client and coach, thereby yielding substantially better outcomes. While I am, by no means, a pioneer or sole practitioner of the positivist or strengths approach to coaching, the development of my practice over 24 years has yielded some frameworks and practical approaches that will prove helpful and constructive to any coach.

Power Up gives coaches and, in turn, their coachees or clients—terms I will use interchangeably throughout, a guidebook for implementing coaching with strengths. This is a framework that will alter your way of thinking and the resulting dialogues between you and those you coach. I firmly believe it can enable more certain and more lasting personal growth and development, as it is built on recently emerging evidence from compelling, cutting edge work by both behavioral scientists and management professionals. For those already initiated into the advantages of using strengths, what follows offers a set of reinforcing notions, and a number of expansive tools and techniques for enriching your coaching work. In short, it provides frameworks, guides and tools that can lead to a more satisfying, successful, and rewarding experience in coaching others.

In these seven chapters, first you will find a brief orientation to coaching, including a summary of "the case" for coaching intervention, and an introduction to how I use strengths and the positive framework, an approach some have referred to as appreciative or asset-based. Following that we'll address the key knowledge sets, instrumental and narrative tools, overarching procedures, sometimes knotty issues and necessary boundaries for strengths coaching. I have intentionally chosen not to write here of the related matters of marketing and the logistics for a full time coaching practice, concentrating instead on the actual coaching process itself, using a strengths paradigm. This one-to-one coaching guide is further enhanced with a chapter that explicitly addresses leadership role coaching, considers the vagaries and variances of coaching teams and groups, and suggests how to enroll an entire organization and its culture in a strengths coaching mindset and practice. In sum, this is a *Guide* for the coach who would fortify him—or herself in their coaching role, and look at the same time to use the potency of this approach to empower their supervisees or anyone they coach as clients.

"Strongboxes"

Throughout the book, I have inserted what I call "strongboxes," like the ones at the start and close of each chapter, as well as sprinkled strategically throughout. This familiar term originally referred to a small, rectangular, usually metal box that was stoutly made, had a lock, and was a secure and portable holder for valuables, most often money. This approach to highlighting pertinent quotes and key features of a chapter calls to mind a family story and personal lesson from my youth. My Dad's father, Grandpa Joe, was reputedly a master salesman who, for much of his life, sold major appliances for a small business in the city in western Maryland where I was raised. My parents and I lived for my first few years with him and my paternal grandmother. As a tyke then, I vividly recall seeing him carry into the house each evening a small, metal strongbox containing his receipts—checks and cash—that he'd taken in that day. Each night after dinner, he would sit down with its contents and make an accounting of his day's sales, using it both for record-keeping and to help him set his next day's goals, so my father told me, always looking to better the "take" each succeeding day. He also had a habit of preparing a comprehensive set of weekly objectives for his business life and his family. This set of routine scribbles, along with those daily receipts, found their way to and from home in his dark green strongbox.

I'll seek to mirror that intent analogously throughout this book, as the contents of the strongbox inserts in *Power Up!* are either positive tips, highlights from the section under discussion, or pertinent quotes that supplement the learning to be gained. As their name denotes, the summary ideas, findings, and provocative thoughts to ponder that are contained in the shaded strongboxes are there to help strengthen the reader to carry out better, more effective coaching. Hopefully, they offer others' wisdom, and spotlight key points from the chapters about the use of strengths in coaching, highlighting some specific practices to assist the reader with bettering their coaching each time out.

Language and Memory Aids

Another aid to learning and using the many cognitive devices and tools for coaching that is employed extensively in the core chapters of *Power Up!* is *mnemonics*. Named for the Greek goddess of memory, this category of aids for the mind includes the frequently used recall tool, the *acronym*, where a familiar term is spelled out by the first letters of the main elements in the set or topic under discussion. Our younger years of schooling and tutoring were filled with such devices, including those often found in musical education, biology, and for such rote tasks as remembering strings of numbers or chemical elements. Research on effective training and teaching has noted the importance of structured and organized memory units for improving recall and learning.

Less frequently resorted to, but of equal value, are some *acrostic* devices, wherein complex strings of material are converted to cues for more easily remembered phrases, and even nonsense statements that are notable for their oddity. Colors of the rainbow, bones of the body, musical scales, and many other similar and familiar information bits have been more easily recalled thereby as school kids in our pasts.

Also, numbers may be arranged to align with letters of the alphabet and vice-versa, for any number of memory aids, and this book makes occasional use of some of these devices to make the topics more user-friendly. Finally, there is liberal use of analogy and metaphor throughout *The Guide* to embellish the points being made more indelibly. The language we all choose is central to how we think and represent experience, so it is hoped that these approaches help with application of many of the frameworks and instruments offered in the pages to come.

The learning adventure that lies ahead in *Power Up!* certainly can help bolster the reader's performance as coach. In the end, it also can make for a clientele that is more resilient, better able to lead, more apt to see the positive possibilities in their co-workers, likelier to experience holistic well-being and success, and more capable of flourishing in their own personal and professional lives.

1

Powering Up!

STRONGBOX 1-1: *It is great folly to wish to be wise all alone.*
- La Rochefoucald

Dan *was a newly promoted vice-president of a fledgling tech company, a go-getter as an engineer and team leader in his previous duties—thus the promotion. Yet he sensed that this was a new level of challenge, and he was not sure he was fully ready for the demands of the role. A former colleague, Will, now living across the country, was still on his speed-dial, and Dan called him seeking advice and support. Will was a former coaching client of mine when in a similar situation himself a couple years before, and suggested Dan email me to see about coaching for the first half—to full year of his new role. Like many of my coaches at the outset of our work together, Dan presumed we would be assessing his weaknesses and working on shoring them up, both as they arose in the course of work, and in a more general way. While the assessment part was right, the change of focus to a strengths approach was a surprise, and even a bit off-putting for him in our early sessions, as he was a skilled problem-solver . . . had been as long as he could recall in his 42 years, and this paradigm shift did not come easily. However, in less than 3 months this "quick study" not only had re-framed his leadership mindset, he had become a coach-in-the-making himself, frequently sharing in our talks a hunch he had about how to assist a co-worker with a more asset-focused outlook, or Dan's version of a more appreciative way to get supervisees to move toward their best work. Perhaps even more to his credit, Dan had found the enlarged perspective that now characterized his thinking had also enabled him to become a stronger problem-solver when that vital skill was called on—a common, daily occurrence in the new job and worksite.*

What's in this for you?

This thumbnail sketch of Dan's (pseudonym) experience with coaching is typical of my clients' encounters with successfully engaging their strengths in the service of taking themselves and others toward desired changes. *Power Up!: The Guide to Leadership Coaching With Strengths* is an account of the key ingredients—the reasons and roles, main processes and practices, as well as the tools and techniques, to be employed in the successful practice of coaching using strengths. These pages lay out those vital elements in a very logical order, with easy, practical steps and immediately usable activities, all in a highly readable narrative.

Whether you are a novice to the role, a seasoned coaching professional, a leader seeking help overseeing a project, a line manager looking to get more out of your team, or a mentor seeking to guide a protégé's career steps more surely, *The Guide* has much to offer. One could read select sections of the book for immediate application, or scan and skim for specific types of instrumental assistance. Or, you could thoroughly cover the topics in sequence for a comprehensive learning of the approaches and benefits to strengths coaching. Whatever your coaching objective, there is a new slant or an alternative method for practical adoption to be gained. To sum up, these pages provide a comprehensive exploration of professional coaching using a strengths paradigm, a novel set of perspectives on the practice of coaching, and a creative collection of stimulating, interactive formats and devices for use with those you coach.

Potency Realized

There are at least two definitions in recent use for the phrase "power up." The first, and more familiar, is the notion originating just a few years ago that this phrase meant to turn on your computer, igniting the system to boot up for use, often with an iconic "power" button. A second, more technical form of the phrase involves reference to a "power-up," an element that is used in computer and video games to add benefit by having extra capabilities written into the instructional options accessible for game play. It is a feature designed to enhance the experience, to make it more robust, and thereby more enjoyable. Both of those meanings pertain to the use of that phrase for this book's title. It is at once intended to invite readers to join in, to empower their coaching practice, and to refresh their engagement with it through a set of powerful constructs. It lends itself also to the idea of a coach assisting another to use the power of their own strengths to grow, and to reach new heights of achievement and satisfaction.

The ideas of becoming more powerful, of growing in one's areas of expertise, and gaining greater mastery, all by leveraging one's very best talents to reach new heights and excel are core to this book. Not only is gaining power critical, but helping others to become more empowered is the essence of both coaching and good leadership. The word "power" in contemporary parlance has several meanings germane to our topics here. For example, a strength can be amplified, i.e., successfully multiplied by itself to a level that is a higher quantity, a factor called a power. And, a power is also defined as a skill, an ability, capacity, or faculty one possesses and uses at a high level of competence. Further, power denotes the ability to influence others either emotionally or attitudinally, a theme very relevant to our strengths discussions throughout the book. The term "power" can also signify the measure of a lens to magnify an object or image, very much akin to our thoughts about the use of strengths to see optimal and positive means of improvement and finding success. Finally, the word is sometimes used to connote a personal capacity that is designed to enhance one's effectiveness, influence or position. All of these can be construed as relevant applications of the term as we seek to understand better the potency of coaching as magnified by the use of strengths.

This book is addressed to any in that growing vanguard of coaches who are plying their craft or looking to polish their practice—whether it is for a single employee, a full client organization, or for multiple coachees in diverse settings. The ideas and activities in these pages offer a helpful set of inputs to those in leader positions at any level who seek to coach their associates. If your goal is to enhance productivity through and purpose, this book can help. If you value the rewards that come most readily through a respectful, relationship-driven work compact, this framework can point the way. And if you are dedicated to execution through engaging others via agile leadership, be sure to read on.

> **STRONGBOX 1-2**: *Primary coaching objectives are performance enhancement, leadership development, managing poor performance, talent and succession planning, for "on-boarding" new employees, and change management.*

Serendipity

I frequently get the opportunity to train groups of professionals to be coaches, and when we begin, one of the first things I ask them to do is share with another trainee their recall of an earlier coaching experience. I start this exchange saying that, by "coaching," here, I mean "*. . . any experience where you were aided by someone's guidance, instruction, or reflection to perform better or to re-consider an attitude or belief.*" This could have been for an intrapersonal or decisional awareness, a transaction with another, or regarding some skill. Most of us can relate to numerous instances of this, e.g., a scholastic, athletic, vocational, driver's education, or musical coach who offered such assistance at some earlier point in our development.

Afterward, I ask them to think about what makes it a memorable experience still, usually years, and often decades later. The discussion that ensues almost always identifies the extraordinary feelings of empowerment and a caring relationship that accompanied the coaching experience. They routinely cite the connection, and the learning experience itself, plus the lingering quality of those "lessons." Almost universally, each person can state vividly how they were enabled to grow, to stretch, and to find perspective.

People consistently describe those attributes, despite telling coaching stories that vary greatly in focus, context, and age at the time, as well as method of coaching. Always a powerful early memory, it continues to have meaning for practically all who engage in the recollection of it. And, I often have found it a useful way to initiate early conversations with new individual coaching clients as well. The following personal coaching audit in verse gives just a sampling of the variety of coaching experiences one may have in their life span:

Coaches All!
Life's lessons,
Sticking still:

Walk, ride, assert:
Mom, Dad, Myrtle.

4

Write, speak, sing:
Jacqueline, JP, Mercedes.

Throw, swing, slide:
Dad, Roy, Rick.

Drive, work, plan:
Mom, Dad, Eric.

Shoot, pass, jump:
Mac, Crow, Shad.

Study, learn, teach:
Donna, Ellis, Lots.

Counsel, consult, train:
Jimmie, George, Skip.

Care, love, parent:
Gramps, Nancy, K & G.

Console, compose, finish:
Patients, families, mentors.

So much more, and
So many to thank . . . Coaches All!

Why is it that coaching in all those guises is such a universally appreciated and often dramatic experience? I suspect it's simply because we all have an abiding appreciation for those moments when we felt cared about, even when that caring may have been exhibited by a gruff-seeming elder, yet someone who took the time and effort to offer us a better way to go about things. And, of course, we are grateful for the nudge, clarification, or just plain cathartic opportunity to re-think a situation or viewpoint that the coaching exchange provided. That is the essence of coaching, and the reason for this book: to offer a set of ideas, principles and instrumental frameworks for helping others in a way that they will experience as a positive and potent approach to doing so.

Personal Evolution

For nearly twenty-four years at this writing, since the late 1980s, I have been coaching executives, entrepreneurs and leaders in organizations of many varied kinds and sizes. My purpose has been to help them grow as leaders, to make better decisions, to stretch their skill range, and to strengthen their personal and professional talent and asset bases. This first evolved from an almost accidental chance to advise the leaders of two separate companies where I was hired as a management consultant and trainer. Once into the coaching role, I found it both intriguing and rewarding, particularly in terms of my new learning and an alternative use of my expertise, providing an additional pathway for delivery of service. As new coaching opportunities arose, the range of organization types and leader issues and personalities also widened, enriching my practice, deepening my coaching repertoire, and enhancing my effectiveness as well. I had also been a licensed clinical psychotherapist before that, and some self-education and formal coaching training, along with practical experience had helped me achieve some level of success in what was still a part-time endeavor for me.

Then, in the mid-90s, a serendipitous set of confluent opportunities changed my paradigm and my professional direction for good. It was in that period, over the span of just fourteen months, that I was asked to lead a campus-wide training and organization development effort at my university workplace, and used the occasion and role to expose myself to some newly emerging concepts and pioneers. In the space of just over a year, I had a weeklong training in Appreciative Inquiry with David Cooperrider, and became certified as a multi-course facilitator with the Covey Leadership Center's offerings. Following that, I had learning opportunities with the Co-Active Coaching paradigm at an OD Network conference, and later in a weekend seminar with Ben Dean of MentorCoach.

The net effect of all those experiences was transformative in terms of how I viewed individual and system-wide behavior change. It led to a radical shift in how I sought to consult with organizations, and to coach individuals. The evolution of the strengths movement, along with positive psychology's overall development in that same period further steeled my resolve and helped me acquire a set of new perspectives and approaches for my work with clients. In sum, I had a personal paradigm shift, and it has led to a more satisfying and successful way of coaching, one that has been more effective in every way, both for me as coach, and for my very diverse clientele.

> **STRONGBOX 1-3**: *Coaching is a (usually) short-term relationship between professionals aimed at sharing perspective and (occasionally) advice, using reflective dialogue.*

In the next several chapters, I will be detailing the ways in which I have come to coalesce these frameworks, and show how their various contributions make for a dynamic and highly useful coaching model, one that has delivered optimal results, both for me and for those I coach. I feel strongly that these materials and ideas will be compelling for you, too, and can lead to meaningful professional practice additions, perhaps even across-the-board alterations in how you work with and coach others.

Power Up! offers a different mental map from the majority, yet a kind of approach that has seen a growing number pursue it. It is one that promises to modify beneficially the nature of the coaching role, and thereby improve the outcomes of coaching transactions. We'll begin with a brief look at what professional coaching has come to be in this second decade of the new millennium, as well as an examination of the potentiating benefits of strengths in the coaching process. This will help you to understand better this growing and dynamic role, and the emergent profession dedicated to it. A more detailed look at the recent developments in professional coaching as a global field can be found in the Appendix at the end of the book's chapters.

In just the past two decades, the world has embraced the field of non-athletic professional coaching in a big way, and with many variations. Coaching has moved from a narrow, infrequent and usually one-sided event confined to the corner office, to where it has become an integral practice throughout the organizational and corporate mainstream. The appeal of a helpful relationship with a mentoring guide, and the many ways that such an advisor can help ensure growth and change, already have led to many seeking out a professional coach, prompting the exponential growth of the burgeoning field of coaching in a relatively brief time span. Rare is the organization these days that has not seen the gains to be had, or experienced the "goodness of fit," that a coaching relationship can have for its employees at many levels.

Coaching Today: A Snapshot

There are almost as many definitions of coaching as there are distinct publications about the topic, and as yet, none has risen to become *the* standard for the field. So, let me offer briefly my own opinion about what is involved, incorporating what, in my view, are the best and most parsimonious thoughts from all the others.

First, and most broadly conceived, coaching is a (usually) short-term relationship between professionals aimed at sharing perspective and (occasionally) advice through reflective dialogue. There are arguably about a half-dozen distinct categories or types of coaches in the field:

- *Executive* coaches who address the interests of executives and those on track for advancement in leadership roles
- *Management* coaches who mostly focus on the improvement of supervisee performance. This and the next type, peer coaching, are sometimes regarded as coaching associates in an attempt to eliminate the notion of rigid tiers of hierarchies
- *Peer* coaches, who are co-workers outside a supervisory relationship, often in separate work units, and devoted to a very specific agenda or a broad array of coaching targets
- *Life* coaches, who have a wide range of interests in helping coachees enhance their lifestyles, or general well-being
- *Career* coaches, whose focus is solely on helping clients find appropriate or more satisfactory employment
- *Niche* coaches, a growing segment of the profession whose clients all share a vocational field, such as law, computers, engineering, etc.

While I have had some experience with each of these segments, my primary focus has been with executives for over a decade now. Increasingly, professional coaches specialize in one of these areas, or at most, a couple related ones, such as management and executive coaching. Peer coaching differs in that it is a largely internal arrangement within an organization. In peer coaching, those who coach have had some introduction or even some formal training in coaching processes, and are seen as adept at creating this type of collaboration with other employees. Usually they do so to assist with new employee adjustment to the organization, for a specific skill acquisition, or to help with a particular role transition. I will have more to say about modes or formats for coaching later in the book.

When considering the uniqueness of this book on coaching, the use of a strengths (a.k.a. positive or appreciative) framework is the most significant, major addition to the picture. In short, strengths coaching operates out of a positive framework to assist in the growth of desired performance traits and decision-making acumen by the client.

When I am asked—usually by prospective clients, managers, or HR directors—what is the bottom line for coaching, my "elevator speech" reply goes something like this: "The coaching process is about <u>changes</u>. By that, I mean it helps clients alter their actions, senses of self-worth and self-efficacy to new, higher levels. It does so by giving them support and tools for improving their relationships with others—a foundational feature of optimal leadership cited throughout the literature. That, in turn, increases the fiscal and human capital bottom lines both additively and through avoidance of dysfunction and turnover—desirable outcomes for any organization. So at all three levels—self, relationship and organization, coaching is a solid path to improvement, success and excellence, and a true 'win-win-win' proposition!"

> **STRONGBOX 1-4**: *Typical reasons clients give for seeking coaching include time management, career development, business decisions, relationship management, and finding family-work balance.*

The International Coaching Federation (ICF) noted recently that over 16,000 coaches were affiliated with them, while the IAC or International Association of Coaches, another professional group, listed over 13,000 affiliates as of mid-2011.[1] Nearly twice that combined number have become external, "hang out my shingle" professional and business coaches globally. These significant and growing numbers of coaches are operating successfully, especially in the US and Canada, the northern and westernmost European countries, and the urban centers of Asia. Fairly dense penetration and low ratios of coaches to employees already exist in North America, the UK, Ireland, Japan, Korea, Germany, Brazil, South Africa, Australia, and the Scandinavian countries.[2] This doesn't even begin to count the myriad internal coaches—managers and leaders who have been trained minimally or merely pressed into the role of coaching for some organizational goal, usually performance improvement. Dozens of credentialing organizations have emerged just in the past couple decades to help fill the demand for this kind of supportive aid. Like it or not, participant or not, coaching has evolved over the last twenty years to be an omnipresent force in private and public organizations, in both the for-profit and not-for-profit sectors of the working world.

Scores of universities and independent organizations now sponsor certificate-based coaching education ventures, and the ICF just recently celebrated its twentieth year of existence. In the same time frame, a parallel pan-European development has seen the European Mentoring and Coaching Council grow to similar size representing coaches in dozens of countries. There are also at least a dozen professional coaching periodicals currently in print, and more online, all dedicated to the coaching profession. Conferences are held around the globe annually that seek to spread both the techniques and the benefits of coaching. Consulting firms that used to let coaching fly under their radar, now tout their extensive menu of coaching interventions, and often have entire staff units devoted to the practice of coaching, and frequently also to training coaches. Further, many publishing houses now have separate coaching categories with dozens of offerings, and new titles emerging regularly.

Recent statements in several professional journals in the field declared that people in pursuit of personal growth and/or professional improvement have made coaching omnipresent. Most organizations in the private sector, and a large and rapidly growing number of not-for-profits have sought and found the advantages of such intervention programs. Recent reports of mind-boggling figures like 600%+ returns on investment, nearly 20% annual growth, and multi-billion dollar revenues in the United States alone, all speak to a large, thriving, and expanding field. The Hay Group, a global management consulting firm founded in Philadelphia 65 years ago, noted in a 2009 report for the ICF, that the majority of the Fortune 500—nearly three out of four so-designated organizations, have developed or contracted for extensive coaching programs, many instituted at multiple levels of leadership in their company.[3] British coaching leaders have cited an even higher penetration of coaching in business, reaching as many as 80% corporations and organizations there.[4] As I noted earlier, for those interested in a more detailed exploration of the state of professional coaching today, I have included an Appendix to these pages that offers just such an expanded set of survey research details.

> **STRONGBOX 1-5**: *The range of coaching arrangements is broad: from brief project lifetimes, to ongoing compacts over years, with most averaging half to a full year in duration, often being renewed at a later time for another issue.*

While a comprehensive summary linking all the disparate findings about coaching's developmental evolution today is probably not feasible, some themes and trends are readily notable. They include these observations:

- o Coaching is a rapidly expanding enterprise tool across the globe, with both internal and external coaches deployed widely
- o It is used at many levels in diverse types of organizations, with higher penetration the further one ascends the organization ladder
- o The larger the company, the likelier coaching is available and used
- o In descending order of frequency, the primary objectives for coaching are learning & development, focal remediation, on-boarding, high-potential talent development, and succession planning
- o Though not consistently or well measured, most sponsors and coaching clients have evaluated coaching as a positive process with moderate to high return on investment
- o There is no single model or credentialing body recognized as <u>the</u> standard, and both purveyors and user groups are inconsistent about whether there are preferred or desired coach backgrounds and credentials
- o The majority of coaches, nearly three out of every five, are not formally certified by anyone for the practice, but helping skills training, and/or relevant business experience are viewed as highly desirable, with experienced, well-regarded coaches finding favor, especially as external and executive coaching providers

○ Coaching is done mostly in-person and via phone, using other electronic supplementation, with three, six, and twelve month arrangements the norms for a coaching compact.

I'd also summarize all this pictorially using a racehorse comparison that I'll expand on later. For now, over a decade into the new millennium, suffice to say that professional coaching has emerged galloping full force as a relatively young, but rapidly maturing field, and shows no signs of breaking down. In fact, new coaches, clients and coaching paradigms are being developed at a rapid pace. Much of that development is in spite of limited theory and even more sparse research to point the way to a readily unified and regulated professional field.

How has all this come about so rapidly and in such a widespread fashion? The need for faster access to input and support, and for quicker turnaround for decisions also have helped nudge coaching firmly into near ubiquity in the business and professional culture-at-large. Further, more modern and expanding methods for communicating have enabled coach and client to see and hear one another more easily in both individual and group contexts. Now, more than a decade into the 21st century, expanding internet, cloud-based, and telephonic options are showing the way to a virtual face-to-face coaching scenario. All this harkens to a new wave of coaching vehicles for tomorrow, and that future is imminent. The promise that coaching holds for us all is stirring and encouraging, and in the next chapter we will look at the exciting elements that have forged this dynamism.

| *STRONGBOX 1-6: Dwell in possibility.* | *- Emily Dickinson* |

2
Coaching's Promise

STRONGBOX *2-1: No pleasure is comparable to standing on the vantage-ground of truth.*
- Francis Bacon

Leona *was CEO, co-founder and business partner with her spouse in a modest, yet thriving regional accounting services company in a nearby state. She had attended a coach training program I had done for a professional association a few months before, and contacted me later to inquire about some help with her professional path. She had reluctantly and painfully come to the conclusion that she didn't want to continue what she was doing—neither the role nor even being in the business at all. After a couple sessions of sorting through whether she was being "impulsive and imprudent"—her words—we set about the task of determining her more natural strength base to decide what was in her best personal interest going forward. We also discussed how she might best go about withdrawing from her business without hurting it or her marriage; no easy feat. Through nine months of concerted effort, first in weekly, and then biweekly sessions, including several face to face, Leona arrived at an affirmation of her decision, a new direction that she felt enthused to explore, and a set of plans implemented throughout our coaching time for removing herself from her former business without a lot of collateral damage. The key to her success in using coaching so well for a complicated situation was her ability to use reflective inquiry and to listen to her own "voice" non-defensively in the process of re-routing her career and life. No small factor in this was the confidence she grew to feel about the better match of her new choices with her perceived and measured strengths.*

Despite its age, or more precisely, coaching's relative youth as a field—some have traced its modern origins to the end of the Cold War period, and in contrast to the older, traditional practice of performance coaching found in large corporations, surprisingly little research has been published about coaching's frameworks, techniques and efficacy. A recent spurt of effort to measure key variables in the coaching process has been seen, and several organizations have produced Return on Investment (ROI) estimates that range from good to very impressive.1 Yet the field is still quite nascent regarding research and published evidence along the lines of that old mantra asking about best practices in help-giving: "What works with whom, delivered in what manner, by whom, where, and when!"

There are a couple very general categories of frameworks for coaching that might be called the "process" model and the "person" model. The former addresses the conduct of coaching, while the latter is framed around the characteristics of the client. Each has features that overlap, and either form can be applied in the service of a number of coaching niches, from career and life to professional, executive and performance coaching. Most often, the personal format is used for life, wellness, career and performance coaching, while process paradigms dominate when professional or executive coaching are pursued. Again, elements of each are frequently seen no matter who the client is, what their role may be, or their purpose for seeking coaching. The approach used is also influenced by the preference of the coach for work style or coaching strategy.

British psychologist and coaching scholar Jonathan Passmore wrote in 2007 of what he called an "Integrative" model of executive coaching, an eclectic framework that sees the coach operating seamlessly and simultaneously across six levels or "streams," as he labeled them.2 These include (1) *developing*, and then (2) *maintaining* the coaching relationship, followed by a trio of streams focused on desired change—(3) *behavioral alterations*, as well as conscious or (4) *mindset cognitions and unconscious cognitive changes*, such as emotional or motivational ones. The model concludes with attention to the critical (5) *surrounding context* that includes both coach and client issues, and finally, important topics like (6) *ethics and organization culture*. The International Association of Coaches has a program based around a process model they call "The Masteries," a set of nine competencies deemed necessary for quality coaching in any niche.3 Many of these features and some of the same inspiration, such as the intelligent use of emotions, the insights of Edgar Schein's consultative process writings, the use of readiness for change assessments, and the importance of mindset—find exposition here in this book as well, albeit in a different and more expansive light.

Empiricism and Evidence

Those attempting to make the case for coaching have frequently cited the paucity of empirical evidence available to support the sizeable anecdotal data for coaching effectiveness.[4] This is especially so at the matching variables level, where lack of controls for randomness, and unclear reasons for relationships might easily confound any cause-and-effect picture. Many argue instead for using a foundation that grounds their work as coach in current best practices, while still calling for more and better empiricism.[5] Some have urged the field to see evidence-based practices for coaching as a general type of intervention, distinguished from actual specific practices one employs in coaching another. So far, the literature for general qualitative gains far outweighs that for any distinct practices, largely because the latter is much more complex and tedious to measure while controlling for the several cogent variables in the coaching paradigm. Thus, the knowledge amassed to date offers the coach some help, but is far from a comprehensive set of theories and technical practices. Suffice to say at this time that most coaches who have received formal training in any model are practicing based on some behavioral science helping framework, and, as a result, their psychological-mindedness and grounding in such a general foundation is an important minimal criterion for qualification as a coach.

I grew up about a half mile from a thoroughbred racetrack at the county fairgrounds. Once a year, for a week or two, the site would host pari-mutuel horse racing. What impressed me most viewing that scene as a young boy was the size, speed and power, as well as the beauty and grace of the horses. I mention this again here because I think it provides a metaphor for the field of coaching today, and particularly its research foundation compared with its practice. Specifically, I see the upper body of the horse, a greater than thousand pound animal, as like the fast growing and robust planet-wide practice of coaching. It is already a force for improving business practices and practitioners, and yet it rests atop still spindly foundations (the four legs akin to coaching theory, research, process and experience). In comparison to that powerful upper body (practice), the scientific basis of coaching (the empirical evidence likened to the spindly legs) is meager still, but that has not impeded it from growing rapidly and widely.

As so often occurs in a field's development, practice outpaces empirical support, and often the generation of theory as well. I could extend further the equine comparison of this shaky reality for the evidence for coaching effects, since I learned awhile back that two- and three-year old horses—the prime racing ages, are literally jeopardizing their lives and futures in each race because their leg bones do not usually mature fully until they are nearly four years old. Accurately and reliably dating the age of horses is yet another compounding problem, but I'll end this line of comparison here, hoping the main point has been made clear: a sizeable coaching industry has evolved and spread quickly of late, and is still in its relative youth, resting atop what are so far limited bases of measured evidence and solid scholarship.

> **STRONGBOX 2-2**: *Among the many correlates of positivity in the workplace are greater productivity, engagement, retention, & teamwork.*

Despite this, let's look at what does exist, as the following is quite encouraging. California-based coach David Drake has proposed the following four overlapping types of knowledge that all play into the quest for holistic mastery as a coach.[6] They are:

o *Foundational* knowledge that covers the evidence-based background of guidelines and formats for the coaching relationship

o *Professional* knowledge that includes the competencies and approaches used in helping another from a coaching perspective

o *Self*-knowledge, referring to the personal developmental acumen of the coach and the growing savvy about themselves as they proceed over time

o *Contextual* knowledge, which is the expertise and professional wisdom gleaned from experience and learning that a coach employs to understand the client's systemic issues & goals.

Drake's model of types of coaching knowledge contends that the full picture cannot be obtained for coaching without address of all four, and he refers to them as levels or types of evidence for the coach's worth, as s/he moves from a basic coaching role to one of mastery bordering on artistry. He asserts further that this type of evidence-based coaching practice is a step on the pathway to shoring up the science of the coaching exchange as well. To paraphrase his rhetorical root question: Isn't this the quintessential art and purpose of coaching—helping clients get to the heart of their issues, while relying on their core values, their meanings of life, and their desired legacies?

In a 2009 presentation to the Institute of Coaching conference at Harvard, Australian scholar Anthony Grant noted the basic outcomes of some early research on coaching's efficacy.[7] He cited these summary findings from his University of Sydney work group:

They found coaching has shown positive psychological benefits, including mental health improvements, and reduced anxiety, depression and stress. It also seems to work most effectively with a solution focus and insight-based action planning, rather than simply through self-reflected learning of even short-term (several weeks) duration, and is effective in both individual and group formats. They also found that coaching can yield gains for both workplace well-being and for adapting to organization changes, and has durable positive outcomes lasting for at least a half year. Services rendered by coaching professionals may be superior to that by (even trained) peers, he noted. And coaches-in-training may enhance the effects of that exposure on learning. Finally, he reported that efficacy can be measured using a variety of both quantitative measures and qualitative ones that use grounded, proven behavioral theory bases.

Korn/Ferry, the international consulting firm, sponsored a meta-analysis of the executive coaching effectiveness literature that was published and available before 2009.[8] This research process involves a combining of multiple sets of previously published data for analysis that arrives at a summative conclusion, and the study by Kenneth DeMeuse, Guangrong Dai, and Robert Lee, yielded the following observed highlights:

- Coaching worked, i.e., the meta-analysis demonstrated that executives made moderate-to-large gains in skill and/or performance. Individuals using self-ratings who experienced the coaching themselves reported having experienced stronger effects than did others who rated them for coaching's impact.
- Coaching affected a wide array of individual and organizational outcomes, such as individual skills and behaviors, team

performance, productivity, employee job satisfaction, and some business outcomes measures.

- Some research suggested that coaching had the most positive impact when tied directly to specified coaching objectives.
- Coaching returns varied from situation to situation, and even led to negative outcomes in some circumstances.

The final part of their paper on those results may prove of more worth in future studies, as they enumerated a list of analytic areas for further evaluation of coaching effectiveness. These include:

- Deciding whether the purpose of the coaching evaluation is summative or formative evaluation, recommending ongoing assessments of the latter type, and a summative one at the end of the coaching engagement.
- Deciding whether the criteria used to measure coaching effectiveness is ROI, or linked to coaching objectives, including individual gains versus organizational indices.
- Asking what is the level of rigor of the coaching evaluation, i.e., the research design criteria employed to assess coaching outcomes?
- Determining whether the coaching objective was developmental or remedial, and the content was skill acquisition and behavioral change or unconscious discovery and deep learning.
- Looking at what was the character of the interaction between the coaching methods employed with the coaching content itself. In other words, evaluating the outcomes by purpose, content and type of coaching as well. They suggested that one of several available "stage" models of coaching be used as the conceptual framework for grounding the analysis.

STRONGBOX 2-3: *When I dare to be powerful, to use my strength in the service of my vision, then it becomes less and less important whether I am afraid.*
- Audre Lorde

Coaching Frameworks

Several pioneers and exponents of a consistent process approach to coaching have paved the way for today's practitioners. From Graham Alexander & Sir John Whitmore's linear process model GROW (Goal, Reality, Option & Will or Way) to a more recent variant, Jack Zenger and Kathleen Stinnet's FUEL model (Frame the conversation, Understand the situation, Explore the desired state & Lay out a success plan), basic coaching progression templates abound. The Columbia University (NY) Coaching program, one adapted by the FranklinCovey Company's coaching division, lists a set of nine competencies by which they certify coaches, using these three overarching processes: *Co-create a Relationship, Assist with Meaning-Making,* and *Help Others Succeed.* Marcus Buckingham's company refers to a three-phase executive coaching model—Assess, Act, and Evaluate. And Robert Bacal's OUTCOME model for managers that coach (Objectives, Understanding, Take stock, Clarify the gap, Options generation, Motivate to action, and Enthusiasm & encouragement), and several more like it, all use a linear or recursive developmental model. This approach goes from coaching around a set of objectives and delineating the circumstances of the issue or project, to exploring paths to improvement and learning, and finally, to assessment of effect. Indeed, multiple contextual frames are crucial perspectives, and one researcher, Otto Laske, found evidence for efficacy from three generic coaching processes that he labeled "supporting and guiding attention, envisioning outcomes, and enacting new behaviors and experiences."[9]

The *7-D framework* for strengths coaching that I will be explaining is similar to the behavioral and developmental constructs found in these formats. Yet, I believe it offers a more comprehensive model for both micro- and macro-applications, i.e., it applies to both the single session, and to the overall experience with the coaching client. A few other models for coaching also employ their formats for both the entire coaching arrangement as well as in every single coaching transaction or session.

Before proceeding next to strengths and the three "knowledge sets" of coaching that form the practical core of this book, I feel it is important to delineate a bit more clearly what I think coaching entails from the comparative perspective of other helping processes. I offer these observations from having spent decades in most of the arenas below, particularly as coach, counselor or therapist, instructor, and consultant.

I tend to view coaching as residing somewhere between the formal, one-to-one helping process of counseling, and that of the consultant. Coaching has already been depicted here as assisting another in their professional development dealing with personal decision-making, work-related choices and role-based change. As such, it is distinct from counseling in a few ways: For instance, coaching seeks to use the client's declaration of interest for setting the agenda for dialogue, while the counselor often sets the focus diagnostically after hearing the presentation of the client's issues. And, while both roles employ similar communication exchanges as relational tools, in coaching it is more akin to collaborating—a mutual process of relative equals, whereas the counselor seeks the counselee's willingness to confer and to confide in her or him, which is not expected to be a reciprocal dynamic. Thereby, the role of coach borders more on that of consultant process-wise, while the counselor confers with their client in a more authoritative role relationship that Edgar Schein argues is always unequal and one-down. More will be said on that in the coaching skills chapter.

Historically, the relationship between coach and client always has been more collaborative and mutual, and regards the coachee as expert, while counselors are often sought for their expertise. Both are involved in confidential expository transactions, with the traditional difference also being seen in the primary "remediation of deficit" context of counseling versus the major focus on growth, learning and development of strengths implicit in the present approach to coaching.

Another distinction is in the nature of the help provided, with coaches rarely making unsolicited suggestions for action, preferring to help clients arrive at their own solutions, while counselors frequently offer behavioral change recommendations. The coach's "now-to-tomorrow" context also is different from the usual "past-to-present" focus of the counseling dyad. Some theorists would argue that they are complementary approaches.

In addition, the coaching compact is usually for a fixed, brief period of time, and the content of dialogue from session to session may vary greatly. Counseling has a fairly singular focus over time, which could be months to even years, in some cases. A final key difference resides in the fact that most coaches are working with clients on their professional lives, whereas counselors usually are helping people primarily with their personal emotional and relational issues.

To sum up strengths coaching from this comparative aspect of the helping roles and processes, the coach borrows from several related helping role skill repositories, most certainly those of the consultant and the counselor. Good coaching outcomes emerge from finding a process that borrows from each for positive effect. In doing so, the distinctions described make for a unique combination of features for the coaching process that fits it in that niche between them, while distinguishing coaching as its own specialty.

The Evidence Conundrum

A cherished mentor of mine from graduate school was famous among us students for his particular style of questioning during classroom presentations and thesis or dissertation defenses. In fact, he had a pair of near mantras that he would utter routinely in those settings; they went like this: "How do you know you are making a positive difference?" . . . and . . . "Show me the data!" His frank and prudent obsession with our replies to those two queries helped all of us become both clearer thinking scientists and better clinical practitioners and administrators. In an article in the *Harvard Business Review*, authors Jeffrey Pfeffer and Robert Sutton incisively made the case for similar interventions in our workplaces.[10] They urged more allegiance to a true evidence-based practice of good management, urging leaders to foster enculturation of the linked quartet of practices that follow:

1) Encourage and reinforce continuous learning by all employees, particularly those in key decision-making roles.
2) Always seek supporting data for any suggested change or compelling claim.
3) Collectively examine the logic behind any evidence presented, not limiting that to quantitative data.
4) Encourage risk-taking in the form of small pilot experiments to see if the proposed idea has verifiable "flying capacity" in your own setting.

The Ken Blanchard Companies have gathered some self-reported qualitative evidence of coaching's perceived effects from thousands of employees in hundreds of client organizations over the past decade, and they report the following aggregate outcomes:

First, there was improvement in teamwork (77%), interpersonal relations (67%), job satisfaction (61%), quality (53%), and productivity (48%). Further, these outcomes were grounded in measures that were yoked directly to desired business results, not just superficial level gauges of satisfaction with the coaching experience itself. The net effects on that score, too, were also impressive: Eighty-six per cent of participants agreed that they had received significant benefits from the coaching programs, 90% cited the coaching process as a good time and resource investment by them and their company, and 92% reported a high degree of satisfaction with the coaching received.[11]

Dianne Stober, Leni Wildflower, and David Drake also have urged adoption of an evidence-based approach to coaching, in lieu of stronger empiricism at present in the field.[12] Their three-legged stool of a base for that seeks to cull evidence from (1) coaching-specific and related research, (2) from the coach's own professional disciplinary training, and (3) from an appreciation of the unique talents, features and characteristics of the client being served. Stated alternatively, they advocate for use of *the best available knowledge, the practitioner's expertise, and the client's preferences* in the exercise of an evidence-based coaching practice. In her University of Texas at Dallas course, Stober has taught coaches to understand and use the best practices drawn from four somewhat distinct approaches to coaching that she calls the *humanistic, behavioral, integrative*, and *systemic* frameworks. Appreciating the various contributions from each framework to how one conducts coaching can enlarge the coach's understanding of the client's world and its many contexts.

> **STRONGBOX 2-4:** *Current evidence-based coaching combines use of the best available knowledge, the coach's process and experience base, and the client's preferred focus.*
> — *Dianne Stober*

It's clear that the coaching field currently lacks *universal* constructs, definitions, processes and proofs, despite its near omnipresence in business, and its growing application in other arenas. The 2008 Dublin Global Convention on Coaching was an attempt at such collaboration on drafting those overarching tenets, but so far the yield has been mostly agreement on what still needs to be agreed to! Witness the Convention's need statement for the field, enumerated prior to the gathering, all of which are insightful consensus goals:

1. Establish a common understanding of the profession through creation of a shared core code of ethics, standards of practice, and educational guidelines that ensure the quality and integrity of the competencies that lie at the heart of our practice.
2. Acknowledge and affirm the multidisciplinary roots and nature of coaching as a unique synthesis of a range of disciplines that creates a new and distinctive value to individuals, organizations and society. To accomplish this we need to add to the body of coaching knowledge by conducting rigorous research into the processes, practices, and outcomes of coaching, in order to strengthen its practical impact and theoretical underpinnings.
3. Respond to a world beset by challenges for which there are no predetermined answers by using coaching to create a space wherein new solutions can emerge. In doing so, we are stepping into the power of coaching as coaches and inviting our clients to do the same.
4. Move beyond self-interest and join with other members of the Global Coaching Community in an ongoing dialogue to address the critical issues facing our field.[13]

Those present in Dublin documented several objectives they called "stakes in the ground," for achievement by 2010. The fact that they are not yet in place a year later as hoped is testimony to the complexity of the field, its global reach, the many economic and political influences on it, and the multi-disciplinary nature of coaching's roots and rudiments, many of which were cited previously. A series of conferences recently begun in Europe have attempted to jump-start and reconsolidate this effort, and the ICF and EMCC have agreed to a joint venture aimed at the same outcomes.

In summary, the current reality is that neither the boundaries nor the portals, whatever they are and however many there should be, have yet to be promulgated succinctly and convincingly for the field as a whole. This is a developmental pattern previously seen in the 20th century in many emerging disciplines. Take, for instance, then-APA president Martin Seligman's acknowledgement a decade ago that, after decades of finding its way, psychology has only recently helped generate more than a dozen standards of practice for treating mental illnesses and symptoms.[14] These days, he seeks to identify what eventually led to that significant outcome, and to apply it similarly to an understanding of what happiness, mental health, and well being are, beyond the mere absence of sadness, illness or strife.

At this point in time, the pulse of evidence for coaching primarily has a "best practices" beat, with the economic benefit data regarded as strong and positive, despite little agreement on either what to measure for coaching outcomes, how to do so, or how to link specific practices with them. Meanwhile, the encouraging feedback from clients and their supervisors about the impacts of coaching also is very positive, citing widespread impact from the practice, despite being mostly reliant on value statements and qualitative assessments by recipients and sponsors. We learned almost by rote in graduate school some version of the basic conundrum of helping research that goes like this: "What works with whom, under what conditions, using what practices, and why?" The kernels of some truly exacting research into answering that timeless riddle as a coach are just beginning to come into place. So we should see more and better evidence start to appear in the next several years to inform and support good coaching practice. In the meantime, the cautionary message that all clients need to be given offers assurance that they are being coached by a trained professional with the ideal combination of behavioral science and role-related experience and understanding, grounded in what are the existing best practices for the field.

> **STRONGBOX 2-5**: *Concentrate on your powers, not your problems.*
> *- Paul J. Meyer*

Coaching with Strengths

For the strengths coach, as Carol Kauffman, head of Harvard's Institute for Coaching noted, positive psychology is "the science at the heart of coaching", providing both theoretical and practical buttressing, and a stout evidentiary foundation.[15] This meme of personal strengths has been harnessed to the benefit of coaching for several years now, as its promise has been realized across the globe, and in formal and informal settings alike. Examine this impressive summary list of diverse research findings about the benefits of a positive outlook and behavior in accord with that:

Personally, a positive attitude and reflective action are associated with higher creativity, pro-social behavior, altruism, health, longevity, happiness, emotional flourishing, resilience, joy, life satisfaction and sense of fulfillment, motivation, resourcefulness, and optimism.

In the workplace, it related to better productivity, retention, engagement, income, advancement prospects, attendance, coworker relationships, teamwork, customer service ratings, supervisor evaluations, and sick day experience.

So, focusing on one's strengths in all the corridors of life we traverse can make for a more rewarding experience, more enjoyable transactions to work with, and greater yield of desirable outcomes for individuals, their relatives and coworkers. This is the case more often than when one employs the traditional strategy of solely attempting mainly to remedy deficiencies and solve existing problems. It is also a tailor-made advantage for strengths coaching and for working with clients open to this paradigm.

Be clear that no one in the strengths or positive psychology fields is arguing for an avoidance of weaknesses or disregard of deficits. Rather, the specific approaches to these problem-framed issues are what differ in an asset-based paradigm. Lest those new to a positive approach to improvement and change see it as an ostrich-like avoidance of facing that which gives pause, let me briefly highlight how this approach is different from traditional problem-solving formats.

First, that which is not working is a key barometer, a vital alert to us that something is amiss, and to begin to focus effort on finding what is better. And, once it is apparent that change is needed, the approach promoted herein departs from that which has been conventional for decades. The difference is contained in where we look for improvement: With the positive outlook, we are asking ourselves to examine what really works for us, what has found success in the past—the lever of our very best outcomes. It really is a matter of seeking the optimum first, then using that which is deemed faulty as a signal for what to look at for desired change, preferably through appreciating how things would be at their best in that arena. This differs fundamentally from looking at what's wrong and seeking a remedy in four very basic and crucial ways:

(1) In that paradigm we tend to spend our time and energy becoming steeped in what hasn't worked, acquiring in-depth expertise about

what's wrong. (2) This approach leads to a "fix" that is, at best, limited and temporary, as it will be akin to a band-aid, not a re-engineering to incorporate what we do best, that which is founded on our strengths. (3) This way of going about change-seeking founders because it is likely to mean we change in a transitional rather than a transformative way, more like greasing the wheel rather than finding another conveyance for moving things toward excellence and desirable completion, grounded in our strongest suits. (4) In my experience, and that of the many appreciative practitioners who have experienced the difference and written about it, the process of exploring change through the lens of positive assessment and planning fortifies that which is most rewarding and least contentious in our cooperative ventures. Rather than re-sowing the seeds of conflict and, at best, tweaking the weakness, we can use an asset focus in place of a deficit focus to alter the way we go about our business, finding a truly affirmative re-direction.

In the next chapter, we'll answer the reader's likely question "Why Strengths?" by looking at the influences that have converged to make appreciative, strengths-focused, and asset-based approaches the most compelling, fastest growing and exciting frameworks for coaching today.

> **STRONGBOX 2-6:** *Power based on love is a thousand times more effective and permanent than one derived from fear of punishment.*
> *- Mohandas Gandhi*

3

Strengths & The Positivity Revolution

> **STRONGBOX 3-1:** *There is little difference in people, but that little difference makes a big difference. The little difference is attitude. The big difference is whether it is positive or negative.* — *W. Clement Stone*

Will called a couple years after I had first worked with his small company, a regional medical billing service and durable medical goods provider, back when they were initially trying to expand. Now they were twice their original size and he felt they were being challenged to embrace more fully the shift to electronic media, both for infrastructure processes and for marketing emerging product lines. He asked if I might assist him with ascertaining the next level of growth feasible for his organization, a $3 million revenue generator in its field at the time. We used his own history and the prior lessons of building on the group's strengths to recalibrate the prospects for their desired future, and instituted a coaching compact for him for six months. Will made excellent use of our time by having me serve as a sounding board outside the company to help him shape and sharpen the vision he was crafting for their next 3 to 5 years. Will has since attributed their ability to anticipate industry direction and to plot a fitting growth curve in large part to the prudent use of coaching, and sticking to their strengths-based operating philosophy.

———

Most college and professional teams in major sports have employed for some time now a staff specialist called the "strength coach." S/he is responsible for the maintenance of a conditioning regime and expansion of strength-building by team members. Not surprisingly, most head coaches of those teams have reported significant gains in performance and durability from such additions, to the point where strength (not strengths) coaches and their work are now well-paid fixtures in those organizations.

In a world where seemingly small differences in preparation and self-confidence often are rightly seen as difference-makers, coaching often catalyzes those differences. In other words, being in optimal condition as the head of the team or organization by using a strengths lens to appraise heritage, current demands, and future desires, can lead to greater success and higher levels of performing. So, practitioners of strengths coaching can be seen as personal strengths (not physical strength *per se*) "aides." Their impact can be significant, is often impressive, and usually proves vital to the improvement of most coached managers, leaders and other professionals at many levels and across diverse areas of human endeavor.

Personal & Professional Strengths

As the strengths movement generally has evolved, a number of related, yet somewhat distinctive aspects of what "being strong" entails have been developed, including identifying and fortifying abilities, character, and talents. So, let's examine briefly the ways in which that has occurred, and the resulting distinctions. First, we should acknowledge the several angles from which strengths are viewed, including values and character, transactional and intrapersonal capacities, as well as skills and technical expertise that people possess to a high degree.

Just what are personal, non-physical strengths, and how can we measure, appreciate, enlarge, and use them beneficially? Perusal of dictionaries yields a fascinating and telling array of types of strength, from physical to cognitive, and from potency to effect, as well as a range of measures and labels for them. Words like *power, potency, force, vigor,* and *might* appear as synonyms, and, in a bit of a paradox for our consideration of strengths as positive entities, many dictionary references regard a strength as an ability to deter, reduce, or withstand a force! Even a majority of our idiomatic language has adopted that stance about being strong. Consider phrases like "coming on (too) strong," or "using strong language" or "having a strong stomach, or even the metaphorical "strong as an ox" (bear, bull, lion, etc.)." So, there is an etymological tradition of viewing strengths usage as a countering agent, and even a somewhat overdone behavior.

When coaching a client about strengths, we are focusing together on their capacities, not merely to fend off reactively, but to be proactive with assets, the attributes that make them more capable of positive action. We are not looking mainly at withstanding some force or event. We are looking to personally *play with* those strengths, accessing their best assets, *play to* them when working with and relating to others, and *play on* all of them collectively when exercising strengths across the organization as a whole.

> **STRONGBOX 3-2:** *Hide not your talents, they for use were made. What's a sundial in the shade?*   *- Benjamin Franklin*

The following terms and their meanings come from an extensive and growing literature in the positive psychology and strengths areas, from working directly with many different kinds and styles of leaders, and from coaching clients and teams on their strengths over the past two dozen years. Deviating from the earlier basic word meanings, strengths scholars have derived slightly different applications. For instance, Alex Linley of CAPP, the British-based Center for Applied Positive Psychology, in his book *Average to A+*, defined a strength as a "pre-existing capacity for a particular way of behaving, thinking, or feeling that is authentic and energizing to the user, and enables optimal functioning, development and performance."[1] He regards strengths as having three core parts:

performance—how good we are at something;
energy—how much energy we get from doing them; and
use—how often we get to act with them.

His group's *Realise2* strengths assessment instrument also divides the sixty strengths they measure into five overarching "families" or clusters: *Being, Communicating, Motivating, Relating and Thinking.*

Psychologists Martin Seligman and Christopher Peterson have referred to "character strengths" as subsets of universal virtues, while intentionally not defining strengths *per se* outside of that complementary framework.[2] They have compiled an encyclopedic set of descriptors of each of the twenty-four character strengths that are sub-divided into six discrete virtues they have culled from the literature. These virtues, which have been verified cross-culturally as universal, are:

Knowledge: cognitive strengths that fuel the pursuit and use of knowledge;

Courage: emotional strengths that exercise the will to succeed in the face of opposition, external or internal;

Humanity: interpersonal strengths that involve nurturing, tending and helping others;

Justice: civic strengths that motivate building a strong community life;

Temperance: strengths that guard and protect against excess, and

Transcendence: strengths that build connections to the larger universe and provide meaning.

The Gallup Corporation writers have parsed the terminology quite differently, regarding a strength as ". . . the ability to consistently produce a positive outcome through near-perfect performance in a specific task."[3] They offer practical examples such as the ability to consistently recommend the perfect products and services for a customer's needs, or the ability to always meet your family's grocery needs on a tight budget. Further, they consider a strength to be composed of these three subunits:

(1) *skills*—basic abilities to perform fundamental steps of a task, such as operating a computer. Skills are not thought of as natural attributes, rather they need training and practice to be fully acquired.

(2) *knowledge*—what you know, such as game rules or scientific facts, like awareness of historical dates. This, too, is not seen as natural, and requires both formal education and informal learning.

(3) *talents*—natural ways of "doing the ABCs"—the Affective, Behavioral and Cognitive performance parts of our unique repertoires. This involves things like motivation, emotional intelligence and social skills. Talents are thought to be special parts of who we are, and to have emerged somewhat naturally or unintentionally, rather than via training or learning, and we each are felt to have these special, personal talents within us. The Gallup model gives primacy to talents, and urges development and recognition of those as emergent strengths.

Meanwhile, the basic definition of a strength promoted by Marcus Buckingham is "the physical or mental power that makes somebody strong," or simply "that which makes me strong."[4] This is the most straightforward description of a strength, and represents a helpful and forward-thinking shift from the conventional "that which I am good at," to a more progressive, accessible, and inviting concept.

> **STRONGBOX 3-3:** *Success is achieved by developing our strengths, not by eliminating our weaknesses.* — Marilyn vos Savant

Finding your STAR

Since I view these varying descriptors as somewhat similar to one another in practice, and most clients are not finitely attuned to those differences, I have put the acronym *STAR* to use for some time now in discussing with clients the assorted elements of positivity and their related personal faculties:

The *S* is for <u>Strengths</u>, which are the empowering personal features one has developed to a high level, including both viewpoint or outlook, and a positive propensity.

The *T* is for <u>Talents</u>, the capabilities and skills one possesses as a complement of inherited and developed abilities, and which often originate from genetics or social habituation.

The *A* refers to <u>Assets</u>, one's special enabling characteristics, including physical and cognitive gifts, and facility with certain 'tools', such as electronic, musical, artistic, or mechanical ones, in addition to the key and inimitable personal asset of one's own mind.

Finally, the *R* refers to <u>Resources</u> that are available to a person, such as economic means or physical access to particular material goods, providing distinctive resourcefulness.

A simple four-item questionnaire derived from the STAR acronym is printed in the Tool Set section for use as an alternate early form of strengths inquiry, in place of a more instrumental approach to strengths determination, or to supplement such.

Dennis Saleebey, now an emeritus professor of social work at the University of Kansas, has long been an advocate for the use of strengths in both training providers and treating human service and social work clients using the lens of strengths. The 2009 edition (the fifth since 1992) of his basic text for the field views the essentials of strengths as captured in the acronym *CPR*.[5] Here, *C* stands for competence, capacities and courage. *P* refers to promise, possibility, positive expectations, and potential. And the *R* symbolizes resilience, reserves, and resourcefulness. The introductory writing in this text is a very thorough, grounded and compelling argument for the use of strengths in human service work alongside that of Seligman's original psychological proposals, expanded in his newest writings.

Marcus Buckingham, the prolific strengths author and speaker mentioned earlier, uses the acronym SIGN to help others think about what his view of a strength is. In this mnemonic, the *S* stands for Success, the *I* is for Instincts, the *G* is for Growth, and the *N* is for Needs.[6] Put alternatively, and in respective linear order, to help identify your strengths, you might focus first on what you find yourself doing well in a recurrent way, then on what are the activities you find yourself drawn to do repeatedly. Next, he would urge you to recognize the areas where you shine and flourish, and finally, to note what fulfills you in consistent and satisfying ways. He believes that success comes from paying attention to the appetitive satisfaction of our instinctual, growth-seeking behaviors and the need-fulfilling endeavors we undertake.

> **STRONGBOX 3-4:** *The four types of strengths are Primary, Auxiliary, Complementary and Contextual ones.*

Types of Strengths

My experience with my coaching clients over the years has also shown me that not all strengths are equal or used in similar ways. In my practice, I have come to note a number of <u>types of strength</u>, each relative to the others, and fairly uniquely employed by each person.

For example, what some have referred to as key themes or signature strengths is similar to what I call *Primary or Lead strengths*. By that, I mean they are the main ones that a person employs both to function at their best and to build up their capacity to excel. They are the aspects of their performance that come to characterize them, and enable them to stand out, to enlarge their abilities to succeed and to be an exceptional performer.

Then there are some less often used, yet still important strengths that I view as *Auxiliary*. In this case, I mean they are literal companion ways of being and acting that fortify a person's primary gifts and abilities. For example, a person strong in *analytic* ways often employs an auxiliary strength such as their *deliberative* talents to reinforce one another. Thus, *Auxiliary* strengths are supportive or supplemental to the Primary or Lead strengths.

A third form, a *Complementary strength*, is that which balances the tendency of one strength, say for instance, *belief or valuing*—a strong interest in core principles, with, for example, an *empathy* and openness to differing opinions and views, thus avoiding tunnel vision and exclusion of differences. So this pattern sees a less frequently used strength completing a pattern with one that has affinity, and together they make a more potent pair.

I refer to a fourth and final type of strength that is even less frequently expressed as a *Contextual strength*, drawn on situationally to address a specific need that is outside one's usual "best" styles, talents or ways of being. Perhaps a person who is usually reserved or not well connected to others will encounter a relationship or situation that calls on them to be a *relator*, to exhibit a willingness and capacity for engaging a coworker more personally and intensely, perhaps even with an intellectual and affective intimacy not easily or often employed. This is the most difficult type of strength to engage, and to appreciate, and the least often seen of the strengths, but it can be a way of broadening one's other strengths and abilities.

There is also the matter of weaknesses or non-strengths, which entails recognition of those features of one's repertoire that see rare expression, or more likely, infrequent competent expression. They are the attributes that we have little passion or aptitude for, and which no amount of reasonable practice is likely to lead to them elevating to the level of a strength. These are rarely targets for growth, and most of us have a fairly clear, even innate sense of what these are, and how far outside our circle of potentially powerful capacities these lie.

This discussion of strengths types also brings to mind the classic psychological concept that distinguishes a "state" from a "trait." This long-standing behavioral science distinction sees a *state* as a response to a situational stressor or stimulus, while a *trait* is viewed as a behavioral tendency exhibited across time and in a number of varying situations. In strengths coaching parlance, we seek first to have clients identify and optimize their use of *traits*—naturally occurring talents developed and used routinely (Primary/Lead or Auxiliary), as opposed to those lesser strengths (Complementary and Contextual ones) that occur not naturally, but more often in response to recurrent situational demands.

As noted earlier, the many labels and euphemisms that apply here and are utilized by various researchers and writers, including *strengths, talents, assets, gifts, preferences,* and similar others, all convey the positive nature of their contribution. I generally tend to refer to all of them in discussion with clients and trainees simply as strengths, and define them collectively thus: *Strengths are one's unique set of ideas and behaviors developed and used to optimal effect.*

In case you are thinking of this as too simplistic—seemingly the "just call out your strengths and go build on them" approach—I will try to clarify below what might be involved in building a repertoire of strengths that have clarity, breadth, depth and consistent expression.

> **STRONGBOX 3-5:** *Strengths are basically one's unique set of ideas and behaviors developed and used to optimal effect.*

Attaining Mastery and Expertise

If we really weigh the evidence, it is easy to arrive at the observation that none of us is truly a "generalist". By that, I mean the strengths literature and practicing with it as a foundation for performance inevitably lead to the following related observations: If we really consider the evidence about strengths, we come to appreciate that we are each specialists in any undertaking, with our own set of somewhat unique assets and ways of using them. In my experience, those who come to be regarded as generalists in any setting are usually the colleagues who constantly strive to enlarge their sphere of strengths, deepening their primary ones in the process. To the extent they succeed in stretching their repertoire of strengths, we come to appreciate that breadth as approaching a wider range of capacities than the rest of us may possess or use. Also, the vigor of a complement of specialists in any team endeavor is why scholars are constantly calling for diverse membership on work teams, to ensure different viewpoints and complementary capabilities, thus making for a well-rounded and highly resourceful work group.

The work of Anders Ericsson of Florida State University and his collaborators is of particular relevance here.[7] It addresses both the issue of becoming expert, i.e., highly skilled at something, as well as the importance of employing expertise in the coaching and mentoring roles to assist in building high competence and strength. First, they cite the summary evidence that, except for body height and size, few exclusive limitations prevent anyone from developing expertise in most domains in which they seek to excel. Their specific argument is that there is no evidence at present for innate constraints on extraordinary levels of expertise being acquired by most of us. Further, they note that there are no native limits on the possibility of gaining expert level capabilities—fortified strengths over time for most—if certain basic conditions are met. And that is where the bar elevates! Those conditions include extended periods of deliberate, coached or orchestrated practice that leads to both cognitive and physiological adaptations requisite for enhanced performance. This means that improved usage of skills entails not just time on tasks or simple practice duration, but also graduated enhancement and timely, expert feedback. This is attained best via knowledgeable counsel, advice or coaching assistance that accelerates the learning process. They state that motivated and targeted efforts to improve in areas of concentrated skill building have the greatest potential for helping individuals attain expert level capacity. Also, these are likelier to be skills and actions, rather than viewpoints or character traits.

Further, they note that access to improved learning environments, motivational support, dedicated resources for learning and practicing, are all important. So, too, is sustained, supported engagement in those deliberate practices that fortify one's skill sets, all of which contribute to the achievement of expertise. This includes not just repetition of instructed behaviors, but it also involves iterative refinement—step-wise improvement, reflective problem-solving, and graduated levels of challenge and cognitive development. In short, it calls for a scaffolded approach to mastery. In summary then, I think Ericsson and company argue well and clearly that their evidence supports two principled practices that are also promoted in this book: the progressive development of one's chosen and acquired strength areas of performance, and the relevance of coaching to accelerate that process.

> **STRONGBOX 3-6:** *Imagine that the possibilities of the future are greater than the disappointments of the past and the challenges of the future.*
> *- Thomas Jones*

A Web of Strengths

I'd like to introduce here an amateur's metaphorical note from arachnology, the study of spiders, which a university colleague introduced me to some time ago. More specifically, I want to concentrate momentarily on the origins and uses of the intricate creation we know as the spider's web—millimeter for millimeter one of the strongest, most resilient of creations. It will serve, I think, as a very apt comparison for the ideas of strengths usage and specialization.

Apparently, spiders spin their silky webs for different purposes based mainly on their predilection for safety, transport, and predation, i.e., their preferred use of the web for self-protection, mobility, and to capture food! Evidently, web-spinning spiders use this miracle of nature to trap insects because they have poor vision for hunting, yet keen sensors for any movement by trapped prey on their web. Web networks also help some small spiders to travel long distances. In an extreme example, the web material is strong enough that we humans have adopted it as raw material for fishnets and woven handbags.

Spiders have <u>seven</u> pairs of "spinnerets"—glands on their abdomens that produce the silk for web-spinning. Each is differentiated for one of six different kinds and purposes of silk-making, with two sets going to making the crucial and foundational orb spiral lines. The core strength of a web is from that pair of spinnerets that produce a fast-drying liquid made up of protein crystals and amino acids that anchors the web. These particular strands are stronger than steel strands of the same thickness (.001 to .004 mm.) There are even specialized capabilities for making different kinds of strands among web-spinners that vary according to their environment's demands and the nature of their survival drives.

To my mind, here is a natural set of analogies for strengths and the use of them: This minute creature finds unique strength in its ability to create an environment that serves its needs and that of its community. It can spin this elaborate and highly organized web in a matter of minutes to hours, depending on size, and the web's tensile might is impressive and amazingly versatile. There is even greater specialization among these eight-legged creatures for different types of web spinning, depending on use and habitat. The orb web's spoke-like wheel arrangement is the most common, and, even if destroyed, can be replaced in short order by these prolific and efficient silk-spinning arachnid engineers. The result is not just a strong web, it is truly a web of strengths!

This extraordinary skill set has all the main <u>strengths</u> features that we seek to employ ourselves, as do our clients, and they serve the larger society's needs as well. These include a <u>talent</u> for spinning, an innate <u>ability</u> to architect and tailor its responses to its environment, a combination of silk-making and web-crafting <u>assets</u> and physical <u>resources.</u> This extraordinary array of strengths that it expertly deploys makes possible a life-sustaining and cleverly capable environment for the spider and its community. If the spider was to try being an amphibian like a frog, or a bird capable of soaring, it would not be playing to its particular set of strengths and would miserably fail both itself and its biome. Thus it is with us humans and using our strengths both intrapersonally and in our relationships.

> **STRONGBOX 3-7:** *It sometimes seems that intense desire creates not only its own opportunities, but its own talents.* - Eric Hoffer

Strengths Pioneers

Let's explore the origins and nature of some of the bellwether agents of the strengths movement a bit more in depth to fully appreciate the emergence of this framework. Dating back nearly two decades ago, and over the course of several years, with the publication of a series of strengths books, the work of Donald O. Clifton and his associates came to the attention of the management world. Clifton, hailed as the "Father of the Strengths Movement" by the American Psychological Association, was a pioneer in the modern fields of personnel survey and management data gathering with Selection Research. Later, he acquired and, for many years, chaired the Gallup organization, growing it into a worldwide powerhouse in its field. In the process, Gallup has developed immense databases and refined sets of characteristics that Clifton came to call "personal strengths." With *Soar with Your Strengths*, and *Play to Your Strengths*, Clifton, Paula Nelson and their associates at Gallup led the charge to champion this new paradigm in the work culture.[9] They are rightly credited with being the first to give us an appreciation of what empowers people to excel and to find success, using new awareness and learning focused on their strongest personal characteristics and interpersonal assets. Since then, the

StrengthsFinder tools and a later series of books from Marcus Buckingham, Tom Rath and others at Gallup have really clicked with professional and public audiences.[10]

The inherent logic and appeal of this positive approach has grown exponentially into a movement that has expanded in scope and in the variety of strengths approaches available today. For example, Case Western Reserve, Penn and Michigan have all established themselves as academic centers of positivistic scholarship and practice. And, Marcus Buckingham left Gallup after 17 years there, and since has also fashioned a successful corporate publishing and speaking enterprise of his own that has scored with the working public. In Europe, Alex Linley and his colleagues have pioneered similar work and have found like success in that area of the globe, centered in the UK.

In the mid-1980s, a creative grad student at Case Western Reserve University's Business School in Cleveland sought his mentor's assistance and blessing to pursue an unusual line of thinking that became the roots of Appreciative Inquiry (AI).[11] David Cooperrider launched a movement that is viewed not so much as a method, but a philosophy—one that acknowledges the insights of all members of an organization to collectively identify the character and origins of their "best" work and most passionate vision. Based on that shared insight, through inquiry into assets and possibilities, they seek new ways to map a better, more desirable future. AI's influence has expanded in quantum ways, and the precepts foundational to it have renewed the prospects for a more positive approach to team, organization, and community-wide development.

> **STRONGBOX 3-8:** *All human virtues increase and strengthen themselves by the practice and experience of them.*
> *- Socrates*

A groundbreaking leader of the shift from deficit to asset framing and the frequently cited "Father of Positive Psychology," Martin Seligman of the University of Pennsylvania was one of the first to call for a redirection of psychology's concentration on the aberrant and ill, to a recognition of the huge promise of fostering positivity.[12] Early, notable psychology pioneers like William James, Abraham Maslow and Carl Rogers teased out the early roots of the positive psychology canon, yet the field as a whole had not stopped to examine the centrality of its work and the bent of its scrutiny of human behavior. So, Seligman's clarion call for redirection toward that which works has come to represent a transformative moment for behavioral science and its applications. One blogger referred to this some time ago as a compelling invitation ". . . to swap looking for what's wrong for finding what's strong!"[13]

The work of Seligman collaborator and measurement guru Christopher Peterson of the University of Michigan also was part of the early scholarship in the field, and he helped establish the focus on values and character strengths as an arm of positive psychology and the strengths movement.[14] He and Seligman, along with the Gallup writers, have championed the measurement of personal strengths, and used separately the notion of top five or signature strengths as a worthy and practical focus for the major unique assets each person has. With measured sequence dictating order, relative strengths can vary widely from any one individual to another. It has been calculated that over a quarter million possible combinations can be found from administering the Gallup StrengthsFinder's 34-item instrument. This also explains why narrowing the focus to one's top five themes, groupings or signature strengths might be helpful for the subject or client tested to achieve some manageable perspective about feedback.

Ann Arbor, Michigan also has been the setting of an influential strengths-centered site for application to business arenas, in the Ross Business School at the University of Michigan, where Peterson and his colleagues have a dynamic program dedicated to what they call Positive Organizational Scholarship.[15] He and Robert Quinn, Jane Dutton, Kim Cameron, Nansook Park and others there have been generating a wealth of research, as well as programmatic uses of positivist applications to organizational leadership and managing. Their efforts have spawned a wide-ranging and impressive cohort of management scientists, writers and researchers, all devoted to the employment of evidence-based strengths applications in the workaday world. Their "best self" paradigm and activities are intuitive, insightful, well composed and highly effective approaches to delving into strengths by examining what one is about when functioning at their very "best."

About fifteen years ago, Mihaly Csikszentmihalyi, the guru of "flow"—the state of being that athletes call being "in the zone," along with Seligman, Peterson, and a cadre of like-minded scientists, practitioners, and researchers, directed their energies toward a science of human behavior at its best. They posited a belief system geared to nurturing one's ability to thrive, not just to remediate deficits or avoid mental dysfunction.

Initially, Seligman, Peterson, the Mayerson Foundation—sponsor of the Values in Action Institute, Sonja Lyubomirsky of U Cal-Riverside, and Dan Gilbert, as well as Tal Ben-Shahar, both at Harvard, have used the lens of "happiness" to explore positivity, and this has proved to be a rich vehicle in the quest for appreciating positive psychology's contributions.[16] Lyubomirsky has focused her work on *the How of Happiness*, her recent book title.[17] She has received multiple awards over the past two decades to study the nature of happiness, and to examine what activities sustain and nurture felt happiness. Gilbert contributed an insightful voice to this aspect of strengths, with his book *Stumbling On Happiness* being an early, provocative voice ensuring a broad and open-minded examination of the origins and elements of what makes us feel happy.[18] Ben-Shahar teaches a wildly popular course on the topic to nearly a thousand students at a time. He also has published several books of helpful perspectives and activities for appreciating happiness and expressing gratitude.[19] Another early and clarifying exponent of both happiness and human flourishing is Jonathan Haidt, a University of Virginia psychologist. His books *The Happiness Hypothesis,* and *Flourishing* (with Corey Keyes), look at the wisdom literature and past civilizations' contributions to our heritage, contentment and vitality.[20] The moral ground is his forte, and he seeks to keep us honest with ourselves in order to be and live in harmony with each other. His forthcoming book addresses the costs and conflicts engendered by righteousness, particularly as manifest in both religion and politics. These are not mainstream strengths or exclusively positive palettes, but his literary painting with them affords us thoughtful scenarios for considering the applications of our most powerful exertions.

> **STRONGBOX 3-9**: *It is not in the pursuit of happiness that we find fulfillment, it is in the happiness of pursuit.*   - *Denis Waitley*

Another of the trailblazers examining the origins and correlates of positive thought and behavior in our culture is Ed Diener of the University of Illinois, who has been a major force in American psychology for the topics of subjective well-being (SWB, for short) and Quality of Life. Diener's extensive scholarship has helped us come to understand what the role of positive relationships is in felt competence and success, as well as appreciating the roots of happiness and the correlates of satisfaction with life.[21] His many writings on positive psychology topics include a

1995 canvassing of the entire prior psychology literature that showed a ratio of seventeen negatively focused studies for every positively focused piece of published research.[22] This kind of awareness helped lead to a questioning of direction and a revolutionary shift toward assets and away from dysfunction. His work offers the strengths coach a solid grounding in both cognitive and affective self-appraisal, as well as the pursuit of felt success in all realms of living, including international views of SWB; it is well worth examining.

More Recent Contributions

Recently, CAPP's Alex Linley and a quartet of his co-researchers noted for coaches the key findings of their research into strengths' benefits. Their summary shows that people who use their strengths report being happier, more confident, less stressed, more resilient, and having higher levels of self-esteem and energy, compared with those who do not lean in that direction. The strengths-inclined also appear to be likelier to achieve their goals, to perform better as they are more engaged at work, and are more able to develop and grow as people.[23]

Seligman has recently written in *Flourish*, of his rethinking of the happiness focus as too simplistic, and he now endorses instead the more complex and comprehensive goal of well being.[24] He notes the four factors he feels the literature has pointed to as positive and planful pathways to that goal: *thought, engagement, accomplishment and relationships.* In this revisioning, Seligman promotes his PERMA format for conceiving of the roots of well-being. In it, P stands for Positive emotion, E is for Engagement, R refers to Relationships, M is for Meaning, and A is about Accomplishment. The book is a novel, interesting and provocative one, with lots of anecdotal examples, real life and real world applications, and research referents.

Another helpful voice in the strengths and positive psychology literature has been Robert Biswas-Diener, who has followed in his father Ed Diener's footsteps in this direction, and has added a significant component to the global perspective of the field. His co-written books with Ed Diener and with several others (Ben Dean, Alex Linley, etc.) have helped illuminate the applications of positive psychology to both personal happiness constructs, and strengths-based coaching efforts.[25] A resident of Oregon, he is also a key figure in CAPP—the UK-based Center for Applied Positive Psychology. Biswas-Diener's book *Practicing Positive Psychology Coaching* is a recent, rich contemporary resource for us in the strengths coaching arena.[26] I am especially impressed with his expansion of the ideas for developing strengths to include what he calls a "Positive Diagnostic System," and also with the more evidence-based cautionary and contextual boundaries he urges positive psychology coaches to employ in their practices.

Dennis Saleebey, a long-time proponent of a strengths perspective in helping and human service professions, has listed a half-dozen "principles" of a strengths perspective, which I shall paraphrase here, as I feel they are a very useful viewpoint for the strengths coach to weigh and use.

1. Every person, group, family and community has strengths.
2. Negative experiences may be injurious, but they may also be sources of challenge, opportunity and eventual growth.
3. None of us truly knows the upper limits of the capacity to grow and change, and therefore we should take all aspirations seriously.
4. We who care for others in any role serve them best by collaborating with them.
5. Every environment is "resource rich."
6. Caring and a context of compassion and hope are necessary and foundational to a strengths perspective.

These guiding assumptions and frameworks for understanding are indispensable to the integrity and successful conduct of a strengths coaching practice, and I urge readers and trainees to consider them seriously and discuss them frequently with clients, as they can help inform our work in truly vital ways.

Thoughtful and inventive contributions in the areas of *asset-based thinking, socio-emotional intelligence, and positive emotions* also are available to augment the strengths approach, and they have each added critical and supportive aspects and solid scholarship to our understanding of how personal strengths can be accessed and built upon. Here we'll delve briefly into what each has offered to our appreciation of positivity.

Kathryn Cramer & Hank Wasiak formed a publishing and consulting partnership in the early 2000s that generated a series of books conveying the nature of gains to be achieved through using a positive lens, using what they called *asset-based thinking*.[28] Their series of *"Change the Way you See . . ."* publications, and more recent Guidebooks (on Innovation, Appreciative

Coaching, and more coming) offer a very clever and useful set of readings and complementary activities and tools for the strengths coach.[29]

STRONGBOX 3-10: *Never apologize for feeling. When you do so, you apologize for truth.*
                                                                    - Benjamin Disraeli

---

The relationship of emotional intelligence to effective strengths coaching seems somewhat intuitive, given that self-awareness, sensitivity to others, and relational skills in any dyad would seem to be givens for a successful practice. Indeed, publications from Daniel Goleman, Cary Cherniss, Richard Boyatzis, Jane McKee, Peter Salovey, and the people at *Six Seconds* and *TalentSmart* among others, have provided both empirical and insightful theoretical bases for the relevance of EQ—as emotional intelligence is sometimes referred to in shorthand.[30] Thus, sensitivity and relatedness are key building blocks both for an effective coaching relationship, as well as for any client's ability to improve their work team's collaborative foundation and achieve desired productivity.

Empathy, a central feature of an emotionally intelligent leader's repertoire, is a forceful predictor of positive job performance and peer admiration, according to a recent report from the Centers for Creative Leadership. Their study of the relationship between empathy and job conduct also showed that it was an even higher-rated feature of good management in cultures with paternalistic, stratified or high-power/ distance beliefs, that is a frequent descriptor of western work settings.[31] The lack of adequate empathy skills contributes significantly to why research shows that half of all managers today are regarded by peers, subordinates and bosses alike as poor performers. Coaches, too, must have finely tuned empathy skills in order to assist clients in this crucial domain of professional practice. These intra- and interpersonal strengths are crucial to coaching in any role relationship. We will examine this empathic "helping" construct as it applies to the strengths coach's capacities in the Skill Set chapter, and look at a pair of assessment tools for Emotional Intelligence in the Tool Set section after it.

Barbara Frederickson, a former associate in the POS group at Michigan, and now at the University of North Carolina at Chapel Hill, has established a solid base for the use of positivity (also the title of her 2009 book), and its fit for the strengths coach working with emotions is a marvelous one.[32] Her "broaden-and-build" approach is pivotal to both enhanced positive assessment, and to finding resilient resources, particularly in the face of disappointments or seeming setbacks. She found that people who experience and express positive emotional states also are more open-minded, including being willing to take reasonable risks, and they report having better relationships with others. Her compelling findings about resilience and the broaden-and-build phenomena, even in the wake of witnessing the trauma of 9/11/01 in New York, embellish this notion as a crucial new awareness about human hardiness and recovery. We'll look at this set of understandings again when we discuss mindset.

> **STRONGBOX 3-11:** *Knowledge of what is possible is the beginning of happiness.*
> *- George Santayana*

Measuring Strengths

With such variety, even among similar approaches, how can anyone sort out their strengths and know how to assess them? Several major instruments have been developed thus far for assessing personal strengths. These include the CSV, which looks at the six virtues and their related twenty-four character and value strengths from *Appreciation to Zest* mentioned earlier, that is in an assessment available from the VIA Foundation & the University of Pennsylvania.[33] It is an extensive and well-researched instrument, with many questions by which to sort out one's preferred character strengths. This site actually has a number of varied topical assessments, including brief instruments for love, optimism, and happiness, all of which can be taken free of charge, simply for allowing your inputs to become an anonymous part of their large and growing database.

There is also the StrengthsFinder, now in version 2.0 for the business and public sectors, and its cousin, StrengthsQuest, adapted for the higher education community.[34] Each offers a format for measuring and elaborating thirty-four strengths from *Achiever to Woo*, and both originated with Gallup as begun by Donald Clifton. This organization has both a global presence, and over three million profiles of the StrengthsFinder, with nearly a million of the college version in their data collection to date.

The Marcus Buckingham Company has developed their own alternative strengths profiling device that is a thirty-four item, multiple choice, situational response survey that generates an assessment of outstanding strengths among nine roles for the worker in a business setting. This new format, called *StandOut*, reportedly has been beta-tested on over a quarter million subjects since late 2009, and is newly released in final form. It provides an in-depth depiction of the worker's strongest two roles, as well as an amplified discussion of their use, a reflection on what the two in combination may yield, targeted strategies for using them, and a separate framework for assaying an entire team's role combinations. This very affordable ($15—US for the individual test) applied tool is the newest web-based offering in the strengths pantheon.[35]

There are also the sixty strengths ranging from *Action to Work Ethic* as promulgated by the Centre of Applied Positive Psychology (CAPP) in the *Realise2* instrument from the UK.[36] This resource site also has a number of related instruments and helpful tools for coaches and those curious about strengths, including a framework for using the measures to assess team strengths.

All of these, the big players in measurement of strengths, have significant psychometric research and huge databases behind them, and have amassed collectively a vast number (Gallup alone has over three million) of measured profiles from across the world. All of the instruments mentioned above are self-report forms using similar frameworks for narrowing the descriptors most often cited by the test-taker over a series of iterations and comparisons.

The Myers-Briggs Type Indicator (MBTI) is a very widely used personality instrument that a number of organizations have relied on dating back nearly fifty years, although not for determination of strengths themselves.[37] It yields a set of preferences from among four pairs of Jungian typological concepts: Introversion or Extraversion, Intuition or Sensation, Thinking or Feeling, and Judging or Perceiving. From this set of inclinations for taking in the world and making decisions, up to sixteen type combinations can be derived, and those yield different interpretations and recommendations for behavioral adaptation.

The DiSC profile, now in its 3rd generation, is also often used in training and pre-employment settings, and for leadership coaching, and has a lengthy history and a substantial psychometric base undergirding it.[38] The DiSC classifies a person's four quadrants or dimensions of preferred styles from among Dominance, Influence, Steadiness and Conscientiousness, and graphs a matrix of relative assertiveness and openness in doing so. My one reservation with this instrument is that its report format is too frequently negative in tone, often "either-or" sounding, and tempts the recipient to see its findings as prescriptive and not descriptive interpretations. As it, too, is a personality style instrument, and not a strengths assessment *per se*, like the MBTI, its use for the strengths coach may be limited, especially at the outset of coaching. A newly published variant using the DiSC framework derives information on leader style preferences from among eight described dimensions of leadership, and seems particularly suited to leader coaching objectives as one set of data for consideration, albeit with the same cautions noted above.[39]

These instruments are measures for assessing adult strengths, and there are also rich programs for exploring and growing school age children's assets. One is the now fifty-year old program of the Minnesota-based Search Institute, originally sponsored by the Lutheran Church in the United States, and now a private, nonprofit and broadly funded endeavor to enhance family, community, and school experience through the development of what they call the "40 Developmental Assets." This is a set of twenty internal and twenty external factors and traits that are building blocks for empowering and supporting youth in their efforts at fostering values, identity, learning and related competencies. Their programs, materials, and operating principles can be explored at the website that is listed in the Endnotes for the chapter.

In addition, the past few years have seen publication of two other very usable applications of strengths assessment and engagement for youths in Gallup's Clifton StrengthsExplorer assessment and parent-led program for early teens, plus Jenifer Fox's *Your Child's Strengths*, a curriculum and set of imaginative activities for kids, with emphasis on adolescents.[41]

There are some other popular ways that strengths are sometimes assessed in coaching: either through (structured) interviewing, or use of some combination of other instrumental assessments, often using existing marketplace psychometric items, or even just face valid, coach-crafted, simple assessments. Rarer is the use of a coach as observer to discern strengths over time, yet that can be accomplished even better by a modified multi-rater activity using numerous observers. We'll look in more depth at some instruments and resources for these approaches in the later "Know What" or Tool Set chapter.

Next in *Power Up!*, we will consider a number of relevant frameworks for a coaching mindset. These are some worthwhile places where evidence for what works and what matters in coaching can be found at this time. More critically, these perspectives are not just central to the practice of coaching itself, they also encompass the major themes that coaches are tasked with mastering in both their daily coaching and career development work.

> **STRONGBOX 3-12:** *Use what talents you possess; the woods would be very silent if no birds sang there except those that sang best.* - Henry Van Dyke

4

"KNOW WHY": MINDSETS

> **STRONGBOX 4-1:** *Our circumstances answer to our expectations and the demand of our natures.*
> *- Henry David Thoreau*

Helen was an experienced and talented executive, someone who had routinely found doors wide open and receptions warm and enthusiastic for her in a three decade-long professional life that she alternately labeled 'blessed' and 'charmed.' I had met her a few years before when we both served as volunteers for a statewide project to increase literacy. Indeed, her career trajectory had been rocket-like and stellar for nearly 30 years. Now she was making a leap into self-ownership and entrepreneurial life, and she felt a bit uncertain and anxious. We began coaching with the twin overall objectives of ensuring a solid new venture launch and assisting her with the shift from a very large to a very small company. In this transition, she also was going from having command of a wide range of resources and a diversely talented staff, to heading a three-person shop at the outset. We spent a number of sessions teasing out issues of timing and ambivalence over the dedication she had to this new nearly solo enterprise as a private consultant. Building on her rich font of strengths and deep experience in related corporate fields, Helen found both resolve and strategy for her leap of faith, and the skills to move from delegator to doer in so many new tasks. Her evaluation at the end of our year's work reflected great appreciation for the role that coaching had played in what she felt was a very successful transformation to independent professional and businesswoman.

———

In these next 3 chapters we will deal respectively with the central knowledge sets of "Know Why" or Mindset, "Know How and When", or Skill set, and "Know What"—a varied Toolset to use for strengths coaching. For this format, I drew on Peter Vaill's definition of learning that involves the following three forms of change that the renowned management educator used in his classic 1996 book about leading in permanent whitewater.[1] His statement appears below in Strongbox 4-2. This three-part nominal framework also was popularized by Stephen R. Covey as a comprehensive model for what a professional leader or manager needs to consider to grow in their work role.[2]

We are going to speak first here of multiple mindsets or perspectives—what some call "mental maps," i.e., frameworks for viewing the way people function optimally, as well as the current state of knowledge relevant to human behavior, relationships and organization development. It presents a wide-ranging overview of diverse themes and core pieces of up-to-date information useful to coaches assisting their clients. These include learning, motivation, goal-setting, expectations, and many more highly relevant subjects. In fact, these topics are written about here as a result of the inputs from my clients over the years. They represent the most common and noisome arenas of challenge for my coaches over the past two-dozen years.

Then, in chapter 5, we'll explore the primary skills that allow for expert delivery of coaching services, and examine how to understand better and use both performance and relational skills as strengths coaches. This is followed in chapter 6 by a series of more than three-dozen dialogical tools for the strengths coach to use in their practice. That is necessarily the longest section of the book in order to accommodate the variety and relative length of some of the tools. Finally, in a seventh and closing chapter, we will look at applying coaching to groups, teams and their leaders, as well as how to implement coaching as a culture-changing business enterprise in whole organizations.

This chapter of *Power Up!* offers strengths coaches a simultaneous set of perspectives, and a number of diverse professional development opportunities. It does so by gathering a wealth of fairly contemporary human behavior and management findings for adoption in practice that also suffuse the range and depth of knowledge and pertinent information in the quiver of coaching frameworks.

STRONGBOX 4-2: *Learning is the changes a person makes in himself or herself that increase the know-why, and/or the know-what, and /or the know-how the person possesses with respect to a given subject. - Peter B. Vaill*

Embedded Learning

I saw a variation of the following riddle at a workshop some years ago, and want to suggest you try to solve it yourself. Below is a string of letters. By removing seven letters, you can reveal a common, familiar word in what is left. The letters are not otherwise scrambled, so the word will be apparent after you do so. Try it for a minute, covering the solution below.

SCOEVAENLCETHTIENRSG

If you have solved it without looking further, you already know that the key to doing so was to shift from the common mindset that heard or read the instructions as saying remove <u>only 7 letters</u>, not remove the words "seven letters!" The latter instruction aptly understood would reveal the word "coaching" (see below). Thus, changing your mindset to the literal instruction enabled you to see it differently and find the solution.

Solution: SCO~~EVAENLC~~E~~TH~~T~~IEN~~R~~S~~G

Once the notion of an alternative mindset is grasped, openness to other views and pathways to problem-solving become nearly automatic. For example, now that you've been exposed to the previous rebus-like word puzzle, now try the following one. It asks you to determine the word, phrase or saying depicted below:

4S9A2F8E3T6Y5

If you saw the familiar phrase "Safety in Numbers" represented in the puzzle, you are like the majority of people who, having been cued to an alternative mindset, can even translate the paradigm to a slightly different one. That is the wonder of modifying mindsets!

This idea of shifting mindsets is also as simple and as clear as noting the changing use of language in the culture over time. For example, in the early days of radio, this pre-modern communication miracle was referred to as the "wireless," a shorthand name originally given to Guglielmo Marconi's telegraphy invention in the late 1800s. Today, that same term evokes instead a picture of a location or function that enables easy access to the internet without a direct wired connection. A colleague of mine recently mentioned another example that he'd heard in a seminar on generational differences, where the presenter held up a rubber sandal that the audience readily identified using the term "flip flop." The facilitator then asked the audience if they recalled or knew what that was originally known as when it first appeared in the marketplace decades before as footwear for the beach. He said they were called "thongs," which conjured up the image of a quite different piece of clothing in the mind's eye of those in the room!

Coaching Mindset

For many years, author and speaker Joel Arthur Barker has taught about the features and importance of understanding paradigms, borrowing on Thomas Kuhn's and others' writings on the topic over the last 50 years.[3] Barker defined a paradigm as similar to a mindset, i.e., it is a mental map, a pattern or model that does two essential things: it defines our thinking about and labeling of boundaries, and it suggests ways to behave within those boundaries. Strengths coaching itself is just such a paradigm shift, offering a fairly new model and commensurate ways of acting in light of the reframing it calls for. Let's look at some of the pertinent paradigms or recent models—the major mindsets for our consideration in this strengths coaching context.

We'll begin with what might be called a general "coaching mindset." This is a fundamental set of competencies and outlooks that are minimally necessary, though far from sufficient just in themselves, for effective coaching. Here, in no particular order, is a list of the dozen I consider to be basic to the strengths coaching role:

o   A willingness to help others learn & succeed
o   A related dedication to the developmental growth of coachees
o   An appreciative mentality that sees capability and possibility first, not deficit and need for remediation
o   An understanding of strengths and their application dynamics
o   A basic grounding in principles of human behavior and relationship-building practices
o   High level listening, facilitation, empathy and inquiry skills
o   An awareness of the dynamics and nuances of change and transition
o   Respect for differences and tolerance for variant paces

o Standards of confidentiality, privacy, and ethical treatment
o Openness to learning and to deepening skills as a coach
o A set of flexible, appropriate coaching skills and tools
o Ability to use the lessons, not the details of prior experience

I advocate for new coaches-in-training to conduct an assay of their own attributes and motivations for the role, perhaps using the list above as a guide for the audit. One possible way to do so for a strengths coach would be to gauge one's relative strengths by grading (A, B, C, etc.), rating, or scaling (1, 2, 3, e.g.) each, drawing on the higher assessments and the lessons from reflecting on how they came about to enhance those that currently don't measure up as quite so solid.

STRONGBOX 4-3: *Coaching mindset, competencies and values are foundational to the optimal practice of coaching with strengths.*

The 7-D Approach

The primary coaching framework I want to share is what I call the *7-D Strengths Coaching Model*. Coaching typically proceeds through a number of steps that ensure both a thoughtful and comprehensive approach to the client's agenda for coaching. These include both micro- or session flow, and the overall macro-process of the coaching contract, the specific terms of which are decided at the outset. This is the core of the coaching dialogue. In my practice, as well as that of many others, this is usually in weekly or biweekly sessions over the course of 6 months or a year. However, I am finding more variety and flexibility to our arrangements in the past couple years, as work life logistics have become more malleable, and the clients' needs and interests have changed in accordance with those shifts.

The following seven complementary processes provide a thorough, sequential pathway for strengths-focused change conversations:

Declare: selecting what is to be dealt with in the coaching session or overall relationship

Define: a goal statement that focuses on what the desired end is—usually the change s/he seeks

Distinguish: looking at what, in the client's appreciative appraisal, are the key features of the situation, including their relevant applicable strengths

Differentiate: exploring possibilities for alternative directions, choices, and decisions

Develop: planning for the logistics of the pathways chosen

Decide: choosing concrete and optimal ways of implementation, including a timetable

Determine: assessing progress on the declaration and using that information for a next cycle

This is actually both a mindset and a tool. Reading through the meanings and sequence of these serial frames for the strengths coaching scaffold, you will note a few things to commend the model:

First, it suggests a framework that allows both individualization of content and a consistent, goal-oriented process for working together. Similarly, it does so in a logical and helpful sequence of frames that flow naturally, and systematically ensure comprehensive cognitive mapping. It begins with the client' s *Declaration* of desired focus for the session, and their attempt to *Define* the goal, hoped for change or improvement sought. This also honors the preference to have the coachee direct the agenda as it fits their ongoing or emerging interests, needs and wants. Another related plus for the model is the thoroughness with which it enables a useful and complete dialogue—both on a topic or issue, and for the duration of the coaching relationship. The three middle Ds, *Distinguish, Differentiate,* and *Develop*, assist with three related steps of expansive thought and analysis. Then, as a wise person once observed, a decision is not fully made until it is implemented, so the next step in the 7-D process is to *Decide* when to make the change and how to bring it about. Lastly, it uses shared evaluation (*Determination*) to appreciatively assess the session's process, and to close and simultaneously to lever that outcome to renew the process, if so desired.

Let's walk through a prototypical session's flow: After some opening pleasantries, and clarifying the available time for the session, I usually ask the client to tell me about an example of having been at their best, using their strengths optimally, since we last spoke. An alternative opener I use at times asks for a client to name one gratitude they hold for an experience in the interval since our last session. This sets a positive tone for the dialogue to follow, and helps them appreciate their recent experiences, thereby helping avoid a potential "glass half empty" or negative dominant mindset.

Following that short exchange and affirmation, I ask for their *Declaration* for the session, which is simply a statement of what the client would like to talk about and work on in the current session. We then proceed together with *Defining* what it is they want to do with the matter or issue named, and we talk out the particulars of the declaration and the desired goal for our coaching conversation about it.

The next three aspects of the session, *Distinguishing, Differentiating, and Designing*, are serial and linked attempts to discover (1) the background and characteristics of the situation or issue to be dealt with, while also (2) briefly and quickly moving through history to present status about it. Then, (3) we try to ascertain what might be the best circumstance for the change sought, the features of any plausible improvements, again drawing on the client's self-knowledge and strengths.

Following that, the next to last step is *Deciding* which of the possible choices for desired change seems to be the most promising and feasible, and then choosing how and when to begin to bring it about.

Finally, arranging how to *Determine* the success of the implemented plans for reaching the desired goal are discussed, and an evaluation plan or rubric is devised and implemented. I usually end with a short exchange about what we call *"the 3 Ps."* I ask for a numerical, verbal, or symbolic (hot to cold, lead to gold, etc.) assessment of the session's *Process*, its *Products*, and their *related Progress* on strengths usage and growth. This gives us a session-centered, ongoing appraisal of the client's experience that is useful to appreciating change and guiding improvement.

> **STRONGBOX 4-4:** *The 7-D Model—Declaring, Defining, Distinguishing, Differentiating, Developing, Deciding, Determining—offers a comprehensive template for both a thorough coaching session and the overall compact.*

If this is an initial or early session, I will usually talk about some strengths and suggest a self-appraisal instrument for him or her to use and bring to our next session. And, at various points as appropriate, I will employ either another type of strengths assessment or a strengths usage instrument (see the Strengths Index and Strengths Spotting devices in the Tool Set section). Often, to capture and optimize teachable moments about their strengths throughout our weeks of work, I will help them conduct a short appreciative reflection, either from their experience or on some aspect of relevant literature that has been prompted by the discussions we have. This usually takes only a couple minutes, and maintains a positive tone for our conversations as well. Beyond that, the majority of any session sees the client doing most of the talking, and the coach leading the inquiry and offering feedback, adhering generally to the 7-D pattern described.

Coaching Compact

This is also *a model for the entire coaching relationship*, and mirrors a comprehensive framework that also works very well for the total compact. Where it differs is in the use of the 7 Ds as a reflective appraisal that is usually done to some degree as we go along, and then again at the close of the coaching compact as a fully discussed retrospective summary evaluation. Using the 7-D framework for the full coaching contract assessment would look like this:

Declaring: a restatement of the overall reasons for seeking coaching assistance at the outset, usually months before. This often has morphed some as we proceeded, but rarely to a markedly different overall set of objectives for coaching.

Defining is the aspect of the 7-D model that calls for a post-hoc appreciation of the ways in which we went about our collaboration, and particularly an examination of the reflective methods the client has come to know about, be exposed to repeatedly, and usually even acquired themselves.

Distinguishing refers here to the shared afterwords we exchange about coaching contexts and how they have translated to the client's worlds outside the coaching dyad.

Differentiating involves a retrospective look at what worked particularly well for us, what particular strengths were tapped and even amplified.

Developing calls up a reflection on the specific takeaways, the general and key lessons learned in the course of coaching, that the client feels have become valued and active parts of their own repertoire, and often also parts of how they coach others.

<u>Deciding</u> is the phase of the review that explores the landscape of change that we undertook, and what special and noteworthy components of the experience are lasting behavioral shifts and cognitive reframings.

<u>Determining</u>, the final phase, seeks to share the overall feedback for each of us in reflection on the relationship in light of the desired objectives and goals at the outset. It often uses some visual and verbal scaling or rulers, as well as qualitative assessments, usually reflecting more broadly on the earlier "3 Ps—the Process, Products, and Progress on strengths and coaching." This is exceedingly valuable to both of us, as it provides reinforcement for the practices each of us wants to carry forward and repeat. I occasionally use instrumental methods here, and yet, the discussion about the full compact itself is what is most valuable, with any instrumental feedback mainly providing common data and language for part of our evaluation.

Overall, the 7-Ds afford the client (and coach) a dynamic, progressive system of comprehensive analysis, reflection and assessment for strengths-based dialogue. Over the years that I've been employing this model, clients have routinely cited its user-friendliness, completeness, and appreciative character. The elaboration of each of the seven steps or phases may appear complex on first reading, but most report it was an easy model to follow and a seamless one to use, with little appearance or feeling of numerous discrete parts. It takes some rehearsal, but coaches I've trained have found it both helpful and facile to work with in their coaching endeavors. Over time, the 7 Ds have proven to be a powerful, thorough framework for optimizing the coaching experience for both parties.

> **STRONGBOX 4-5**: *The goal is to balance a life that works with a life that counts.*
> *- Peter Block*

The Sevens

The use of this set of seven related steps in the 7-D process may beg the reader to question, "Why seven?" Earlier process models cited were usually shorter, mostly having four or five steps. More than a half century ago, in a paper that is a classic in the field of psychology, George Miller of Harvard wrote of finding in his series of memory studies that seven (+/-2) seemed to be the consistent mean upper limit of human recall for items of information stored in short-term or working memory.[37]

Two recent, separate books dedicated to the subject of the primacy and popularity of the number "7," one by Jacqueline Leo and another authored by David Eastis, may help explain part of the draw of that number of steps or phases to the 7-D model.[38] Leo calls seven ". . . the brain's natural shepherd, herding vast amounts of information into manageable chunks." It seems more than coincidental that, across history and throughout literature, the number 7 appears so prominently and recurrently. Only 3 and 10 are used and cited as much in all fields! Recall, for example, the 7 days of creation, the 7 days of the week, the 7 primary colors, the 7 seas, 7 continents, 7 notes of the musical scale, 7 wonders of the world, 7 deadly sins, and 7 ages of man, just to mention some of the better known out of dozens of examples.

Recent research (see Blenko et al in EndNotes) also has shown that 7 is the optimal number of members for a group to come to a decision, suggesting that for each additional member over that number, there is a 10% decline in the likelihood that the group will arrive at a decision, zeroing out at 17! Seven is the number between 1 and 10 most often guessed, the number that is most often rolled when two dice are tossed (every sixth roll), and the opposite facets of each dice cube add up to 7. From Aristotle's 7 Ethics to Covey's 7 Habits of Highly Effective People, it is everywhere in literary history, and often signifies a special and important set or collection of items. Even a cursory review of the writings and findings of others cited throughout this book will underscore the special place of this number in our world.

To summarize, seven is a commonly used numerical organizing tool, and offers several advantages for ensuring a comprehensive consideration of any set of principles. In the case of the 7-D coaching process model, it has emerged over time and trial as a fully comprehensive and readily remembered set of steps for the coaching sequence.

Coaching Values

Related topically to a coaching mindset in both nature and importance is a set of values—core beliefs and vital attitudes that underlie the practice of coaching. I would include these ten, listed in alphabetical order, not by importance. I'll elaborate briefly on each, after naming the set:

Abundance
Caring
Consistency
Honesty
Humor
Optimism
Patience
Responsibility
Tactfulness
Trustworthiness

Abundance is the view that "there is enough to go around, enough for everybody!" It means we don't have to start by looking out for #1, an attitude that makes our exchanges contentious, competitive and tense. That latter kind of "scarcity" mindset suggests our actions and worldviews are tempered first by a self-serving approach to others, to relationships with them, to objects in our world, and to the situations we have to negotiate daily. Such a self-centered perspective is counter to a positive view of everybody and everything, and without abundance, strengths coaching is hollow, false and untenable. I'll say some more about this particular item at the end of this segment.

Caring is a cardinal attitude in the repertoire of any helping professional, and in the case of the strengths coach, it refers to a fundamental belief in the community of humanity, a sense that we are all related, and are naturally impelled to show concern for others and their wellbeing. Such basic compassion is a hinge on which the front door to strengths coaching must pivot.

Consistency speaks of the continuity of attitudes and behaviors the coach must bring to the client dialogue over time and when contending with a number of differing issues, questions, feedback opportunities and transactions. Being there fully "present," and being the same professional with a palpable set of values and clear standards for comportment over time and topical variance are minimum requirements for consistent, effective and ethical coaching.

Honesty suggests a candor and forthrightness that must permeate the coach's feedback and questions to the client, indeed the entire communication process with her or him. This quality of truthfulness and sincerity goes far toward making the relationship an effective one that can make a positive difference for the client. When combined with "tactfulness," they make a dynamite duo!

Humor is that sense of humility, foible and perspective that admits to our common humanity and our ability to find perspective in all we see and do. It is the paradoxical contrast that enables us to truly find and use our strengths by seeking the many sides and contexts of experience and thinking. As the credit card commercial said, it's "priceless!"

Optimism is the attitudinal platform and belief framework that says "change in anything is possible, and I can be its agent." Some equate it to hope, which is a belief in possibility, and as such, it is a cornerstone of a positive outlook, and a necessary viewpoint for strengths coaching. Psychologists refer to our "explanatory style" in this regard, with some looking at possibility not limitation, and others leaping first to the direst explanation for how things might or must be. It originates from the same root as the word "optimum," meaning we seek the very best, not the least, of our capabilities in all we do. As Emily Dickinson's famous poem suggested, hope ". . . perches in the soul" and "never stops at all" . . . it's just there for the using at our discretion.

Patience is a quality of change agency that acknowledges the client is in charge of him- or herself and their agenda, and so the pace and process through which they attain their goals must be honored. Respecting the client's ways actually is *the* elemental means for a coaching relationship to have any positive effect, in my experience.

Responsibility is that aspect of coaching that makes for logistical flow, a kind of accountability and planning commitment that recognizes what is the coach's territory, and what is that of the client, and how they might beneficially converge. It means being available, punctual, flexible, and reliable, and consistently so. It also encompasses the ethical practice of coaching, to be enlarged on later in the book.

Tactfulness is recognizing the other person's vulnerabilities and their sensitivity when offering feedback and through consistently viewing them as a person, not just a client, a manager, or whatever role they hold. It means giving them opportunity for forthright reflection from a position of neutrality, or better, of real strength in the prospect of fuller self-efficacy. It means the coach doesn't cut their emotional legs out from under them, and conveys the essence of alternative views they might consider without weakening them emotionally.

Trustworthiness—literally being seen as worthy of one's trust—says to the client that you will be coaching from what Peter Drucker often referred to as a dual position of power: that you will do the right thing and you will be competent in its execution! Being trustworthy is an essential ingredient for candor and the bottomless confidence that s/he can tell you what is real for them, so that with it you might facilitate their desired changes. Stephen M. R. Covey, eldest scion of the 7 Habits guru, calls it the quality that changes everything, and argues convincingly that trust is not just the most moral path, but it is the fastest and least costly way to do business and to realize our personal and shared goals.[4]

This compilation of values and beliefs is a minimal list—necessary, but perhaps insufficient—yet foundational to both ethical and effective coaching. It includes the major baseline mindsets for a coach using a positive paradigm, one who approaches her/his work and client with a pro-social outlook. The coach possessing and practicing with these mindset attributes will look to build on basic talents, and will hold a view toward further possibility, even on top of high positive capacity and assets. Not surprisingly, these traits are also commonly represented in the various catalogs of strengths mentioned earlier, and published by major researchers in the past twenty-five years. These values speak of a client-directed and mutually paced coaching collaboration with shared enjoyment and expansion of strengths, the hallmark of this approach.

> **STRONGBOX 4-6**: *What you risk reveals what you value.*
> *- Jeannete Winterson*

Abundance

I want to expand on this topic from our prior list of Coaching Values. That prolific and ubiquitous author "Anonymous" is credited with the following statement: "The optimist sees the donut; the pessimist sees the hole." The implicit concept of abundance noted in that quote reflects both an appreciative mindset, and a worldview that characterizes effective leadership and enables willing, productive collaboration.

Too often the competitive nature of some of our role models and revered heroes (think pro sports) makes for a loud and highly visible cultural benchmark of "win-lose," with its related belief that for me to win, you (or someone) has to lose. Those bumper stickers that say "second place is the first loser" are recent cultural icons emblematic of that. This kind of thinking is a major reinforcement of a scarcity view, and represents a strong, omnipresent counter to an abundance mindset. Let's examine it more intensely:

The first three general meanings that the dictionary lists for the word "abundance" are (1) a more than plentiful quantity of something; (2) a lifestyle with more than adequate material provisions; and (3) a fullness of spirit that overflows.[5] Reflecting on this trio of definitions, one is led easily to see them as corollaries of one another, with each a condition that can influence the other.

If we start with the proposition that our mindset usually dictates our subsequent action, then the perspective that "I not only have enough (of whatever), but there is also enough to go around . . . for everyone," leads to employment of one's talents in <u>all</u> arenas of living with that overflowing fullness of spirit. It is a way of thinking that couches all activity in the ideal of service and servant leadership. By contrast, a mindset of "scarcity" leads inevitably to a competitive and self-centered way of thinking and interacting, creating followers who, at best, are reluctant to engage, and, as Barbara Kellerman suggests in her marvelous book titled *Followership*, at worst can promote opposition or even sabotage.[6]

Worldviews

Along with the skills to be discussed in the next chapter, and the tools offered here, the mindsets discussed hereafter make for a complementary resource base that can help ensure an effective, positive difference-making coaching experience.

A promising place to start examining this topic of mindset further is in the work of Carol Dweck, a Stanford psychologist who has explored the nature, qualities and correlates of *Mindset*, which is also the title of her 2009 book on the subject.[7] In looking at this aspect of cognitive behavior, Dweck has determined that either of two primary dispositions or mindsets characterizes each of us. The first she calls *fixed*, and is the view that ability, intelligence and all that they promise are <u>static</u> sets of traits. A person inclined to see their world through those eyes observes all behavior as immutable and locked in—the way things just are and must be! People with this mindset believe that capabilities, attitudes and intellect are fixed attributes, i.e., birth-given and inflexible traits, and they see little that anyone's efforts can do to alter that.

This contrasts with the other viewpoint where people see those features of themselves and others as developmentally influenced over the lifespan, and therefore, they believe in and possess a *growth* mindset. Dweck believes strongly, and has data to back up her assertion, that future success is not so much a function of any current level of achievement or any particular single competency. Rather, it is a result of the general life orientation one has and the related approach they bring to efforts to change or learn in light of that adopted viewpoint. Further, she notes that mindset is not a function of personality, level of education, intelligence *per se,* or skills, and despite being fairly stable over the short term, it is open to influence and change with new inputs. This latter finding meshes well with the knowledge that changing experiences, acquiring new personal data, if you will, is what alters attitudes, not the other way around, as once was believed by behavioral scientists and the public.

Additional aspects of understanding mindset Dweck espouses include an appreciation for each of us falling somewhere on a continuum of these two types, with the distribution looking more like a bimodal, U-shaped curve, with approximately equal representation in most populations. Dweck also noted that it is common for each of us to hold some parts of both mindsets, allowing for a *growth* mindset for one skill or capability (likely a perceived strength), and a *fixed* one for a different, less potent competency (a probable felt weakness).

The basic worldview we hold is a key ingredient in how we function, as what we see, or in this case, how we have come to view our world, sets us up for how we choose among options, and decide on courses of action or reaction. This, in turn, leads to a loop of sorts where we then get what we expected or have expectations for. If it's a *fixed* view, then it's usually a set up for failure, disappointment and self-blame, as that lens suggests we are unchangeable. If it's a *growth* belief we hold, then the possibilities for improvement are practically unbounded, and effort itself becomes prized, not solely or mainly the goal or the achievement itself.

In the contrarian words of photographer and motivational speaker DeWitt Jones, "If we believe it, then we will see it!" His popular video program, "Celebrate What's Right with the World," is a visual paean to the growth mindset and possibility way of thinking, as it lays out helpfully the merits of a positive vision.[8] This obviously contrasts starkly with the conventional "seeing is believing" mindset that is a cultural standby, literally reversing its order. This has enormous implications for coaching, as the prospect of improvement and learning is implicit in the coaching relationship. Thus, obstacles are seen more as welcome challenges to a positivist with a growth mindset, and feedback is just that, valence-free information, not criticism, with effort rewarded, and not in vain. Others' achievements are seen as helpful, even inspiring, and the idea that "Those who can, do," has become "Those who believe they can are likelier to find a way to succeed." In some ways, these findings about mindset are an independent cornerstone of the strengths philosophy, and a foundation of any coaching practice using such a perspective.

STRONGBOX 4-7: *If you think you can, you can, and if you think you can't, you're right.*
- Henry Ford

Perhaps most central for us to this arena of mindset is the strengths or asset framework and belief system itself. The positive view of people, their relationships to one another, and the circumstances or situations they encounter and contend with, is the foundation of coaching in the manner that this book promotes. The abilities to grow and stretch, to choose and decide, to succeed and excel, all seem to get better when we have an outlook of abundance, not scarcity, one of possibility, not daunting problems in life's key encounters. I particularly like the asset-based approach authors Kathryn Cramer and Hank Wasiak's take on this, using what they call their S-O-S framework for *Self, Other* and *Situation*.[9] I, too, see them not as portents to <u>distress</u> as the international signal letters suggest, but to <u>de-stress</u>. They are the windows to using a positive worldview, not allowing the pursuits of life to overstress or depress us, or relegate us to a fixed belief system. The habitual ability to positively engage our emotional and social selves in all roles and relationships is a critical capacity for self-efficacy, and achieving our goals in any human enterprise. Finding such resilience is also frequently the subject matter of coaching.

The Power of Expectations

Daniel Pink has written of a related mindset phenomenon in his book *Drive*, about the matter of human motivation.[10] His excellent synthesis of the research on this subject is noteworthy in part, he feels, because the real data, long available, has largely been ignored outside of academic circles. His review borrows much from the lengthy scholarly outputs of University Of Rochester scholars Edward Deci and Richard Ryan, the seminal voices in behavioral science re: motivation. In their comprehensive scholarship on what they call "self-determination theory," they challenge and qualify the unitary view of motivation that prizes only external, contingency rewards, asserting the primacy of intrinsic motivators.[11] In fact, they have good data to show *negative* effects issuing from such standard "motivators" as threats of punishment, deadlines, and critical evaluations. Even tangible rewards such as money, prizes and time are found wanting in most cases.

The emergence of the knowledge worker era means that most of us are engaging in work that is fundamentally different in context and style from that of our predecessors and forebears. Ryan and Deci cite the fundamental need of modern employees to be autonomous rather than controlled (think assembly line vs. IT workers). Further, they note that positive feedback is superior to negative feedback, in that only the former increases intrinsic motivation, the energy source for the modern worker's efforts. On a historical continuum, they note both the shift from "control and compensate"-type mindsets to that of internalized regulation of drive to perform and succeed. Add to that autonomous sense of being while on task, the need for relationship, plus both felt and externally perceived competence, and you get the complex of motivators that impel us to engage and excel. They even have data showing that attention to these can lead to greater displays of understanding, learning, creativity, change adoption, physical and psychological health, and well being!

Pink's collated work offers their bellwether motivational parsing, plus several other critiques of the conventional belief in the "carrot & stick" approach to solely rewarding behavior with external forms of gratification, like money and status. He writes that the research clearly shows what impels people to do their utmost is a deeply felt desire for self-direction, buttressed by a wish to learn and create, and thereby to enhance the nearer and farther reaches of their world. One leadership seminar participant of mine recently called this the "3 Cs of Motivation": the Challenge of work that allows demonstration of personal Competence and makes a larger Contribution. This aligns well with the oft-noted finding that people engage in work when they feel included and appreciated, when the work itself has meaning and worth for them, and if they also can find some autonomy or self-direction in doing it. In other words, mastery and excellence come out of a crucible of appreciation and strengths stirred by a belief in the worth of what is being undertaken. Using a similar tone, Rajeev Peshawaria has suggested that engaging workers more intensely is a matter of helping them to see *RED*, and that's good![12] By that, he means that there are three things that motivate people at work—the nature of their *Role*, the quality of their work *Environment*, and their opportunities for *Development*. This mirrors well some of the tenets of self-determination theory, and the larger prevailing wisdom on motivation as summarized in Pink's book. The contributions of Deci & Ryan and their disciples in self-determination scholarship have rearranged the motivation landscape for followers, managers, supervisors, leaders and coaches, and we are all the better for it.

Ken Thomas has also added to this mindset recently, citing the evolution of management beliefs and practice from one of compliance and dependency in a work culture focused on simple extrinsic rewards to a more egalitarian and intrinsically motivated dynamic for workers specialized for knowledge and relative autonomy.[13] His second edition of *Intrinsic Motivation at Work* spells out clearly the recent history of the evolution of the worksite and leader-follower dynamic. His paradigm considers favorably the quartet of engagement-fostering characteristics he labels *meaningfulness, competence, choice* and *progress* as imperative features of both purposeful working and effective manager-associate relationships. Appreciation of these pathways to commitment and productivity are crucial lessons for knowing what truly moves people to perform and dedicate themselves on the job, no matter the level of responsibility. A recitation on this point that I heard some time ago in a training seminar simply states, "Without inclusion there is no caring, and without involvement, we get no commitment!" Think about the implications of that kind of mindset for managers and leaders, and for the people they supervise and call on to be followers!

> **STRONGBOX 4-8:** *Modern-day employees are motivated by finding meaningful purpose, positive relatedness with others, a sense of autonomy and self-direction, and the opportunity to master their craft in the work itself.*

For us who coach, and particularly those of us doing so in a positivist vein, the overall lessons in this set of related principles are clear and compelling: Clients in any professional role will seek to excel when they find ways to eke their own 3 Ms out of the experience—*meaning (in the work itself), mastery (of both their craft and the relationships involved in a team or organization),* and *self-management (in the process).* This offers a critical lesson about what will move associates on our work teams to contribute their very best. That also applies <u>both</u> to the coaching relationship and to the client's goals for change and self-improvement. We can help them improve optimally when we enable them to find their own very best ways of achieving those ends—their most powerful paths, using their unique sets of strengths.

Another contributor to thinking about asset-focused coaching is Ellen Langer. She notes in her latest book, *Counter-Clockwise,* that we can even adversely affect both morbidity and lifespan by clinging to limiting, negative beliefs and patterns of thinking and behaving.[14] Her findings led her to urge us all to adopt more of a possibility mindset, one that reinforces a positive outlook toward surviving and thriving, and that fosters behaviors that recognize and regulate the intimate effects of mind on body. Her previous writings have focused on the creativity-squelching effects of mindless thinking, but here she documents the more telling physical limitations of such a mindset. For coaches, the understanding that elevating our positive expectations can have huge payback for our health experience as well as our work contributions is a bonus.

Grit

An additional theme to ponder in the arena of motivation and accomplishing one's objectives is the recent emphasis on the characteristic of "stick-to-itiveness." Angela Duckworth, a positive psychologist at the University of Pennsylvania, has looked extensively at this matter of undaunted persistence toward goal achievement. Her research and writing have gathered around a central concept she refers to as "grit," originally drawing on the classic John Wayne film title.[15] She defines it as "perseverance and passion for long-term goals," and feels our culture's emphasis on the intellect and our innate gifts versus personal single-minded effort has kept us from appreciating the role grit plays in accomplishment. While such drive involves other traits and behaviors, it involves more than just the self-discipline to stay the course in the face of diversionary temptations. It is an unwavering commitment despite all manner of foreseeable and unpredicted obstacles and costs. As Webster's dictionary notes, grit is a firmness of mind or spirit that includes unyielding courage in the face of hardship or even danger.[16] And while some might see such bravery as being exhibited in the service of others, at base it really is a self-serving drive to attain a dearly held goal. From interviews with successful professionals across many fields, and using instrumental assessments of this quality, Duckworth and her co-researchers have found grit to be a real differentiating quality of those who succeed, and especially those who excel, particularly at a level that might be called "world class."

Winifred Gallagher also writes convincingly in *Rapt* of that power of "grit," that she regards as the tenacity and pluck often called for in the face of setback or seeming adversity. Her reading of the literature on the matter led her to suggest it is a vital component of focus, of keeping one's attention on their overarching purpose, and one of the major keys to that kingdom. And while grit is not exactly high intelligence well applied, she sees this tenacity as a partial explanation for the notable mean population IQ surge of twenty-five points in the past half-century.[17] Endurance over time, coupled with a passion for a single outcome—call it grit or whatever you choose—may be a critical component of succeeding in any arena of life, whatever other talents, resources or tools one possesses.

Martin Seligman also has promoted the importance of that character trait called grit in *Flourish*.[18] He emphasizes the role of effort in succeeding, and acknowledges the findings of his protégé, Duckworth, while theorizing that achievement is the product of skill times effort in any persistent pursuit. He also notes this kind of determination is the probable explanation for how those who become the giants in any field of endeavor do so, despite having few unique or common advantages, and despite often encountering many impediments on their route to success.

This take on what moves and impels us to excellence is a quite useful reflection for the strengths coach, as it is grounded in a set of observations that can speak to any of us who are concerned with both the long haul and the passionate pursuit of desired accomplishments. Citing and using this information should be a useful lever for coaching, as many of the presenting concerns of clients are right on this mark.

Goal-Setting

Related to the motivation literature is the large body of information about setting and achieving goals. Helping clients with this pivotal activity requires a clear understanding of the fundamentals of good goal-setting, i.e., the science behind the overabundant rhetoric of it. Gordon Moskowitz and Heidi Grant, in their edited compilation called *The Psychology of Goals,* offer such a foundation.[19] The themes that are recurrent in all the contributors' chapters in this thorough text, which they originally wrote to create a resource for their classroom teaching at Lehigh, are these four:

1. Most goal-driven behavior seeks to resolve our tensions in the daily challenges of fitting into our environment and making choices between desirable outcomes and feasible ones. In other words, we constantly select goals to pursue based on assaying *feelings* and *values* tempered by *desired results* and *opportunity* for them to be realized.

2. Goals enable us to build a template for making sense of those four frequently confounding influences in our complex world. They do so through offering a structure for considering what provides senses of both *autonomy* and *meaning.*

3. Such a framework lends direction to the many major and mini-choices we use to focus our thoughts and actions, both in the many moments daily, and over the longer haul.

4. Finally, we need to have an awareness that our drives and impulses operate at more than one level of consciousness, often creating conflict for us in terms of time and energy expenditure for pursuit of the goals that compete for those limited resources.

One of these editors, Heidi Grant (now) Halvorson, has added the following related notions on one of her blogs.[20] When dealing with stalled or derailed goals, goal-setting research suggests two strategies: First is to get very specific when articulating goals, including detailed specs—exactly what, under what conditions, by when, and how attained—for what it is you want, not merely what is good enough that you might settle for it. Second is what is called "mental contrasting," a literal internal dialogue about the realistic challenges that lie in the path, weighed against the gratifications of overcoming them. This can more reliably lead to what she calls "experiencing the necessity to act," a personal and intrinsic resolve to make the necessary efforts to get the job done!

This seemingly obvious topic really is a crucial one for many of my clients, and repeated studies and polls have shown the direct links between financial performance and job satisfaction with employee goal awareness and execution. Brian Tracy is a well-traveled and highly reputed speaker and author. In his short, pointed books called *Goals!* and *Eat That Frog*, he urges productive people to be focused on their highest priorities, to concentrate on their top goals.[21] He notes that only a few (3%, he states) successful people do so, including writing them down for constant direction. He, too, has a seven-part model for achieving goal-directed success. In describing those, he accentuates the importance of a positive outlook, accessing one's top talents, and maximizing personal power. Self-motivation for goal attainment is not rocket science, he asserts, but a systematic and positive mindset for accomplishing our vital purposes does seem feasible, necessary and desirable.

Anoher good resource for personal goal-setting is the book of lists and activities in sixteen life goal domains that positive psychology coach Caroline Miller & co-author Michael Frisch titled *Creating Your Best Life*.[22] Based in some solid research on positive psychological interventions and the essential elements of effective goal-setting for one's personal and work objectives, the tools and writing here make this worthy of a place on the strengths coach's bookshelf.

Four Classical Effects

The allied themes of goals, expectations, and motivation also suggest a brief consideration of the following four classical "effects" from the professional literature of medicine, management, and education, each of which offers a minor twist on similar mindset phenomena, related to self-determination and expectancy theories and research findings. They are the *Placebo, Hawthorne, Pygmalion* and *Pareto* Effects.

Placebo Effect

The first of these is the notion of "placebo," the long-used covert sham medical treatment that draws on a patient's expectation and positive regard for symptom relief and healing. Some have minimized this and regard placebo as really "remembered wellness," not some apparent mystical pathway to symptom-reduction. Whatever it is, placebo is a powerful force in the arsenal of healers and their patients, and accounts for as many as one in three patients' reports of improvement, and perhaps as much as half the relief or improvement experience—especially medication-assisted benefits.[23] All this is due apparently to the potency of a positive expectancy mindset. While coaches are not prescribing substances for healing, they can and should take full advantage of the placebo effect when talking with clients about outcomes and capabilities.

For instance, I find it useful to couch my remarks about a client's behavioral outcomes in terms that are possibility-driven, not problem-focused. We also can find more than just salutary gain in noting the difference between the classic "glass half full vs. glass half empty" conundrum when conferring with a coachee about their capabilities and realistic expectable results. Similarly, the opposite of this version of expecting the best is the *nocebo*, a less well-known effect described as "expecting adversity." While placebo effects have long been the subject of research, dispute, debate and speculation, especially regarding their operating mechanisms, few will contest that there is such a dynamic, and that it is critical to many people's ability to experience gains. It is in the germ of the strengths approach to employ the placebo effect to helping clients to reframe pessimism or cynicism about their efficacy in some desirable action. Expecting good outcomes is simply, yet powerfully visualizing the best result for oneself, and is an important part of the strengths coach's arsenal for helping others find the best perspective and most optimum outcome possible.

Hawthorne Effect

From 1927 to 1932, a series of experiments at the Chicago suburb of Hawthorne's Western Electric plant gave rise to a phenomenon labeled the Hawthorne effect.[24] While actually studying what changes in working conditions and environment would yield in improved productivity, Elton Mayo and his fellow researchers, including TQM guru Joe Juran, uncovered an unexpected, overarching finding. The lasting serendipity of that six-year program was the finding that any of their specific changes were far less impactful than the general notion that people tended to work harder and produce better whenever they experienced what was being done as "paying positive attention" to them and their needs. Another key awareness was that encouraging and using upward communication, instead of solely relying on top-down informing led to the perception of being heard, appreciated, and responded to. These early findings about workplace motivation have persisted in some form ever since, and offer a clear, historical and enduring example of the power of mindset.

Pygmalion Effect

The next of this quartet to be cited here is the set of lessons from nearly 500 separate research studies gathered under the heading of the Pygmalion Effect or Principle. Robert Rosenthal and Lenore Jacobsen first experimented with the influence of beliefs on how people were treated back in the 1960s in California elementary school settings, and later in work environs.[25] The primary finding of this body of research on mindset's power is that people (teachers, supervisors, etc.) will interact with others, and even evaluate their associates' performance based on their regard for them, mediated by their expectancy mindset, even when that evaluation is based on hearsay or misinformation. Major concepts from this work include the premise that we <u>cannot</u> act inconsistent with our expectations and beliefs, and our actions toward others always influence their performance either positively or negatively, never neutrally or not at all. Thus, our expectations may appear to become self-fulfilling prophecies, explaining the name *Pygmalion* for the effect, based on the mythological story popularized by George Bernard Shaw in his play and on the screen in "My Fair Lady." The cycle of this effect follows: first, we form expectations, then we communicate them, which leads to them being matched behaviorally, and seeming to become true as predicted. Along with management gurus Douglas McGregor at MIT, and Chris Argyris at Yale, the Pygmalion scholars provided clear and continuing calls for appreciation of the climate and culture of a classroom or work group. They have enabled us to see vividly how these are two elusive yet potent variables in the creation or modification of people's behavior based solely on their mindset.

Pareto Effect (a.k.a. 80/20 Rule)

The last of this set is an oft-cited phenomenon first popularized after WWII by quality expert Joseph Juran, who attributed the origin of what was sometimes called the "law of the vital few and trivial many" to an early 20th century engineer and pioneering economist named Vilfredo Pareto. Pareto once observed that, in his native Italy, 80% of the wealth rested in the hands of just 20% of the populace, and he replicated that finding, or near approximation of it, in a number of other countries he studied. Since then, frequent references to that statistic have arisen in a broad range of fields and observations. For instance, there is broad support for the belief that 20% of activities yield 80% of worthwhile outcomes. And Juran's initial application in the 1940s was that 20% of the defects in a product chain or process accounted for 80% of the problems impacting manufacturing. Also, about 20% of products are responsible for 80% of receipts, as in supermarkets and many product sales environments. Similarly, about 20% of salespeople reportedly generate 80% of the sales in a product or service enterprise. And how about the modern idea that 20% of websites contain 80% of the useful information in any search? Electronic messaging analysis firm Ferris Research reported that only 20% of the information we store electronically will ever be revisited, leaving 80% just taking up e-space.[26] Richard Koch, the frequent writer about this "principle," has penned the summary statement of it, thus: "We find that the top 20 percent of people, natural forces, economic inputs, or any other causes we can measure typically lead to about 80 percent of results, outputs, or effects."[27] Finally, I'd suggest most readers will find 80% of what they will come to value and usefully retain in just 20% of a book such as this!

There is even a relevant near 80/20 finding in the historic origins of the strengths movement. Shane Lopez, a Gallup affiliate at the University of Kansas, noted the work of Elizabeth Hurlock in the 1920s as an early study citing the benefits of a strengths approach. She showed a greater than 70% improvement for math students receiving praise for their efforts, compared to a 19% improvement figure for those criticized for their work.[28] This effect or "law" has relevance in our strengths discussion because we have already seen that just a few talents or areas of strength are responsible for the majority of effective, joyful, engaged contributions from any of us. In other words, our few strengths are really the "mighty," and account for the largest positive contributions we are likely to muster. Expressed another way, if we identify and employ our top strengths in delivering our best efforts at work, or in any endeavor, we optimize the outcome to somewhere in the vicinity of the 80/20 ratio. So, focused on the 20% that matters! Our primary strengths will give us the greatest yield and return on investment.

All of these mindset pioneers, from Pareto, Mayo and Juran to today's scientists and their interpreters, like Dweck, Pink, and Deci & Ryan, have provided us with a solid, deep and broad basis for using strengths to foster desired change, and especially for doing so through coaching.

> **STRONGBOX 4-9**: *Satisfaction lies in the effort not in the attainment. Full effort is full victory.* - Mahatma Gandhi

Clear Communication & Learning Conversations

This same kind of mindset power is depicted well in a very frank and creative book about clarity in transactions in the workplace, titled *Clear Leadership*, written by Gervase Bushe, a Canadian organization psychologist, and recently out in a 2nd edition.[29] Bushe offers an insightful analysis of how we often communicate in the workplace based on the influence of omnipresent "mental maps" we have created for others' actions and styles. Avoiding use of those maps, and using instead (his) clear communication guidelines could lead to consistent clarity and truthful, trusting transactions in any workplace. This theme of communication covers a variety of dynamics and behaviors, and is omnipresent in my coaching dialogues, although not in every session, just on practically all clients' lists of improvement objectives. My own experience over the years in consulting and in coaching has led me to believe that most of us are not really unskilled in one-to-one communication. Rather, we are unpracticed at using good principles. What often gets labeled "poor communication style" is actually poor dialogue habits. The mindset that underlies errant, hurtful chatter instead of candid, civil discourse usually seems to be focused on talking, not on listening. It comes partially from thinking of the correspondent speaker as a competitor for some nebulous victory in the exchange. Frequently, the perception of relative status or position beclouds any attempt to relate openly to a co-worker or peer, never mind a perceived superior or direct report, as the language of the workplace labels us. On this, the most common ground for conflict, practicing communication in a clarifying way as Bushe depicts it, would go a very long way to avoiding discord, misperception and non-productive days in the workplace.

Coming from an appreciative framework Bushe gained as a doctoral graduate of Case Western Reserve University, one outstanding feature of this view is the idea of "intersubjective truths." This is just a formal way of saying that we can openly agree to disagree, still appreciate and respect one another, and facilitate our business while not introducing gamesmanship to our interactions. This perspective is a rare one in the office, classroom, or boardroom today, and calls for a positive change in how we view one another when we communicate, in order to bring about a more satisfying and effective way of transacting. Simple though it sounds, if our teams and organizations were to widely adopt the practices and perspectives Bushe shares, there would be both greater productivity and far less acrimony in the workplace as a whole. It's that straightforward and could be that game-changing! I've tapped Bushe's insightful thoughts on the idea of a "learning conversation" for an exercise called *My 4 Strong Selves* to be found in the activities chapter. Regular practice of those four behavior sets seems to me to be a near universal prescription for all our relationships.

Choosing & Deciding

In any client's change consideration, the work of transforming and transitioning entails a key dynamic: deciding which among several paths has the most merit, and then choosing that new path. From the Garden of Eden scenario to the thousands of daily choices and decisions each of us makes, the challenges of choosing have daunted humankind forever. And, there is no lack of writing to ponder on the topic for those inclined to seek guidance in this crucial process, which is also the penultimate of the 7-Ds in my strengths coaching model. What follows is a sampled exploration of some helpful inputs from the extensive recent literature on choosing and deciding from among a set of options.

Decision Rubrics

Jonah Lehrer has written wisely about decision-making in *How We Decide*, an engaging book on the title subject.[30] Early on in it he dispatches the simplistic paradox attributed to Plato that sees reason and emotion as steeds pulling us and our actions in often opposing directions. More recently, late 20th century cognitive scientists proposed their version of the mind as machine, specifically as computer, thus further cementing the idea of the primacy of reason, never quite abandoning Plato's ancient idea of rational superiority. With the advent of complex neuroscience and using modern technologies, current evidence supports the emotional brain model, a position that endorses what Lehrer calls the most crucial axiom of the decision process: the brain that can't feel, can't make up its mind! That emotions are critical to deciding and selecting from diverse choices is now the vibrant research foundation for a rapidly expanding neuropsychology of decision-making. We know today that the unconscious brain does some sorting before we are cognitively aware of having to choose, integrating memory and visceral emotions into a rapid and reliable, often consistent pattern of deciding. In other words, our feelings help us to decide, and make us both better and more consistent decision-makers, able to choose options more in concert with our truer selves. Based on the present state of knowledge about how our mind works, Lehrer has constructed a simple framework for helping us assess the general nature of a problem's demands. By his analysis, there are three main types of problems:

First are *simple problems* calling on rational thought. And, even though they seem or sound simple, sometimes they have their own complexity, such as hard-to pin down variables to discern and choose among. He says they are best attacked through a logical process of sorting and selecting, based on uncomplicated, personally validated criteria, with little time spent dwelling on them. Next are *novel problems* that can benefit from scanning our memories to find similar properties by which to compare and benchmark prior decisions and their outcomes. The last of the trio he labels *complex problems,* and he feels these warrant a faith in our experience-born intuitive selves, the part of us that calls up the wisdom of prior familiar events and challenges allied with a rational assessment of the particulars of the complexity before us. And while there is much more to how the mind functions in reasoning toward a decision, his basic approach is a helpful model for a first pass at sorting our choices at a macro-analytic level.

Lehrer concludes his interesting narrative by urging that we reflect on our talents (and flaws) as a preamble to making better decisions, by seeing who and how we really are. Strengths coaches can second that idea heartily, and uniquely can bring a specialized portfolio of aids to assist their clients with both the routine and extraordinary choices and decisions they face.

> **STRONGBOX 4-10**: *"More is often less" when considering options for a decision; too many choices can lead to difficult deciding.*

Choosing as Art

Another useful set of considerations for decision-makers comes from Sheena Iyengar, who published a relevant and enlightening book on the subject of choice recently, titled *The Art of Choosing*.[31] A short summary of her diverse research applications in this area is probably not possible, so I will highlight here what seems to me to be most relevant to strengths coaching.

After surveying the biological origins of choosing, Iyengar describes choice as a central feature of our creative selves, a complex medium through which we construct all aspects of our lives. A student of Seligman's while at Penn's Wharton Business School, she has looked into optimism and religion, then later at Stanford she began to examine culture's influence on choice-making. Now a scholar at Columbia University in New York, she has become recognized as a leading light on the complexities of choice overload effects. That refers to the finding that having too many options from which to select, i.e., having more choices, may be worse under some conditions. Current thinking has translated Iyengar's and a number of like-minded behavioral economists' work into a practical application that recognizes the boundaries of deciding from among numerous options. The collective, common wisdom today cites three to seven choices as optimal for the human brain to process under most conditions, and for most decision-making topics and circumstances.

Iyengar also has explored the impact of *context* on choosing, ranging from tragic, "no good solution" decisions, to racial dating preferences, as well as the limits of freedom on choice as it affects public welfare and impacts motivation, just to name a few areas studied.[32] From all of these, she and her collaborators have learned of two distinct yet interconnected "systems" resident in us, by which we process information and arrive at decisions. The first is called the "automatic" system, because it operates outside our conscious control, and is a relative of our primitive brain that recalls prior stimuli and experience, and usually acts for us and before we can consciously compute how to act on our own desires.

This contrasts with the "reflective" system that is not moved by sensation, but by our rational mind, and is more under our aware control. It calculates more variables in weighing a choice, and examines far less rapidly the elements of prior experience, present attention and future possible consequences, in coming to a decision. Which system prevails or rules is determined by a range of factors, including available time and freedom to choose, reflective capabilities, and judgments of morality, as well as environmental influences, physical capacities, and self-regard. So-called heuristics or "rules of thumb," Iyengar writes, are vital tools in the pursuit of optimal choice, and she identifies a handful of such guidelines for our consideration:

The first is, where possible, delegate choice-making to those with expertise, or at the least, seek expert input to weigh in our decision-making. Next is to identify smart default options, including opting out, saying "no, thanks". Another is to minimize the number of options with a reasonable process for narrowing choices, and where possible, to avoid adding options for consideration. We apparently do better most of the time with a low number of choices than a surfeit of them. We are also advised to minimize choices laden with negative emotions where possible, as they can harbor considerable psychic pain, and may interfere with clear deciding. Further, it is advisable to find ways to categorize options, and to discuss decision-making frameworks and support mechanisms for them <u>in advance</u> of weighing the choices.

When looking specifically at the category of organization decision-making, Iyengar and Chua propose that we assess carefully the extent of choice given to followers.[33] Specifically, they note the varying expectations and interpretations that characterize differing cultures and socioeconomic levels of employees in our organizations. Alerting us to the misperception that extensive choice is always better, they note how some may be frustrated by having options at all, others by the inconsistency of available choices over time. So, instead of offering merely a mixed benefit picture, choice may pose problematic empowerment challenges for supervisees and their managers. This contemporary research echoes well the long-standing tenets of the earlier 20th century human resource scholars and later writers mentioned earlier.

Decision-Making that Counts

Another set of thoughts about choice comes from a recent book by a trio of Bain & Company consultants (Marcia Blenko, Michael Mankins and Paul Rogers) titled *Decide and Deliver*.[34] Here are just a few of their insights about perspectives and tools for your consideration re: the title subjects:

First, they suggest use of a five-step process for improving decision abilities. In order, the steps are (1) Assess the speed, efficacy and execution of decisions currently; (2) Sort out the most critical decisions for your group or organization; (3) Spell out who will be involved and in what roles; (4) See to alignment of structure, processes, talent and culture; and (5) Make the RAPID process (see next) an enterprise-wide capacity.

For this, they propose use of a serial decision-making assessment tool called RAPID, that has been a staple of Bain's toolkit for decades. The letters stand for the following altered letter sequence for allocating decision roles: *R*ecommend a decision or action; Invite *I*nput from those who must inform the process or be informed of the decision; *A*gree formally on a recommendation; D means have a point person with the benefit of the other role inputs who is the *D*ecider, the one who chooses what to implement in the end. Finally, s/he must *P*erform the decision once made. The authors argue that having each of these roles clearly agreed to and assigned goes a long way toward making a well-considered, solid decision that has an optimum chance of working.

They also point us to the very real limits of numbers of inputs into a decision-making process. Their data also suggests that seven is the optimal number of participants for a decision-making meeting or group. In fact, they found that, for each person over that number that is added to the mix, there is a roughly 10% drop-off in likelihood of the group arriving at a consensus decision. That dynamic then "zeroes out" at seventeen members! This is insightful food for thought to be sure, as we compose our teams and seek their considered decisions. Another key and often minimized feature of deciding that they point out is measuring a decision's effectiveness. This involves assessing the quality, speed, yield and effort of a decision. Lastly, they argue for embedding decision capabilities throughout the entire organization, creating a truly system-wide approach to decision-making with efficiency and effectiveness.

A final, noteworthy place to see the bigger picture about decision-making is in Richard Thaler and Cass Sunstien's *Nudge*, about the wisdom of what they call "choice architecture," their label for the organization of contexts amid the many influences on choosing.[35] They urge us to consider appreciating human inclinations more clearly, including our regard for loss, as well as the benefits of a series of inventive "nudges" to limit the choices available, and to have the decision better reflect our true personal preferences. They propose a wider consideration of what they call "libertarian paternalism," a philosophical framework that balances individual choice options within a bounded range of considered benefits. Finally, the book offers a handful of strategies for nudging us toward better, more satisfactory deciding. Their website and blog have gathered a growing list of those strategies, mostly disruptive innovations that mirror the traits described.[36] It is all influential, well-grounded input for use in this important realm of choice and selection.

> **STRONGBOX 4-11**: *The evidence for the benefits of a positive outlook is compelling and robust, encouraging and groundbreaking science.*

Positive Emotions

A writer-researcher mentioned previously when first discussing strengths is Barbara Frederickson. Her findings (see her book *Positivity*) about one's mindset offer several crucial understandings: First, the major function of positive emotions—she has identified ten major ones—is to broaden our personal repertoire of thoughts and actions. These ten foundational emotions are joy, gratitude, serenity, interest, hope, pride, amusement, inspiration, awe, and love. And these are not just whimsy, but well-researched tenets of a larger theoretical framework that is very impressive in its scope, simplicity, validation and impact. The resulting mindsets from use of these positive emotions contrast with negative emotional perspectives that promote a narrower, more limiting prospect both for oneself and for relationships of all kinds.[39]

Also, by expanding that cognitive-behavioral mindset, we uncover novel, creative choices and social networks, and amplify our resources in all domains—mental, physical, emotional and social. This provides reserves in all those areas that enhance our coping and adaptive capacities. Thus, she calls the findings and their implications the "broaden-and-build" theory of positive emotions, and it is another major theme that is altering the larger perspectives of behavioral scientists as well as coaching practitioners.

I have found the suggestions from Frederickson's groundbreaking research and clearly articulated lessons extremely useful, and she has a final (pre-summary) chapter that is itself a highly practical Toolkit for practicing positive living and working. A concise summary of the key findings from her research that serves to fortify the strengths approach to coaching includes these:

Positivity . . .

. . . feels good, which enhances well-being and moves us to want more of this good feeling; broadens minds, literally and widely expanding one's view of possibilities; builds physical, emotional, cognitive and social resources, allowing our immediate future experience to be transformed; is associated with better recall, enhanced creativity, greater resilience, better academic performance, more trust, better choices, and improved interpersonal negotiation; fuels resilience by substituting a mindfulness that breaks the ruminative negativity that can easily become a recycling "do loop."

A positive mindset can be cultivated, her research shows, by being genuine, open, kind, curious and appreciative. Further, positivity ratios of <u>at least</u> three positive experiences or thoughts to every negative one forecast flourishing, and people can achieve that more simply than they may think. This ratio, sometimes attributed to her colleague Marcel Losada, is also an echo of earlier work by both James Prochaska and John Gottman.[40] The former cites a minimum necessary 3:1 ratio of reasons to change vs. reasons not to do so in his decisional balance construct to be elucidated shortly, while Gottman's couple findings also reflect a ratio of better than three to one positive to negative exchanges needed for building an enduring and successful relationship.

Frederickson also lists a set of practices for creating what she calls a "positivity portfolio," including an easy 20-question self-survey for daily assessment of the practice of a flourishing life, to enable one to see the benefits such changes can bring about. Even the 2001 NYC World Trade Center attack epilogs gave ample evidence of the benefits of a positive outlook on people's resilience and recovery from extreme traumatic events. In sum, the prospects for positivity are so well established and widely applicable, that deliberately seeking a lifestyle in concert with positive emotions has become, in the popular vernacular, a "no-brainer."

Thriving

Another perspective I want to describe in this section brings us nearly full circle, as I believe the strengths coach seeks to go beyond helping a client just to survive the challenges of modern living and working. At a minimum, I see the dual goal of achieving meaningful and satisfying survival in daily living, <u>and</u> thriving, experiencing optimal vitality, as much more than only surviving. "Thriving" is a true strength, an asset that portends blossoming, more than merely treading water in the flow of life, more than merely eking out an existence. One could rightly view the notions of surviving and thriving as existing at opposite ends of the continuum of striving that we all engage in daily. Note the visual representation of them below, suggesting that the viewpoint of merely *surviving* relates to a minimalist mindset, sees it as a bare and perhaps hollow, though necessary, achievement. In contrast, the idea of *thriving* is a perspective that seeks to realize the very best of what might be; it is the ideal objective of striving.

SURVIVING <————————————————————> **THRIVING**
(Low)   *STRIVING*   (High)

The goal of happiness or whole life satisfaction, often called generalized well being, is viewed by many behavioral scientists today as the nirvana of positive psychology. It speaks of a high level of vibrance and fulfillment, a gratifying and meaningful being in the world, a better health and longevity experience. As Barbara Frederickson noted so well in her research, it leads to a literal shift from languishing to flourishing, with all the gains that entails. The five key strengths of the VIA group—gratitude, optimism, zest, curiosity and ability to love and be loved—offer a well-researched, verified target for achieving that sense of thriving, a desirable goal for the client of any strengths coach. A popular song when I was a twenty-something was titled "Only the Strong Survive." As I now recall that title lyric, I want to change it to "Only the Strong Thrive." See also the PERMA elements that Seligman highlights in *Flourishing*, as discussed elsewhere in *The Guide* for a complementary framework for thriving.

> **STRONGBOX 4-12**: *The universe is change; life is understanding.*
> *- Marcus Aurelius*

The Centrality of Change

Change is the ultimate objective for all coaching! This statement seems on face to be a bit broad, and yet, if we examine it thoroughly, the truth of that comment seems not to be a "reach" at all. For instance, if a client seeks to improve their skills or adopt a more appreciative outlook, this ultimately entails a decision to change. If a client becomes more aware of their strengths and the implications of them for personal and professional living, they are embarking on intentional and targeted changes. Choosing to change something—be it by broadening a perspective or through concentrated practice of either an interpersonal or self-discipline skill—requires a deliberate alteration of behavior or thought. And yet, it is not easy to undertake, let alone complete. The late economist and author John Kenneth Galbraith is often quoted thus, "Faced with the choice between changing one's mind and proving there's no need to do so, almost everyone gets busy on the proof."[41] We'll begin this segment by exploring the many aspects of undertaking change that face us, both individually and collectively.

Stages of Change (TTM)

A collectin of major, informative guidelines for a coaching mindset with change come from James Prochaska and his associates' Transtheoretical Model of Change, also known as the *TTM* or *Stages of Change Model.*[42] Nearly 3 decades of broadly directed research and widely adopted usage have led to a better understanding of how people view changes, and what specific pathways are the surest steps to elective change. This paradigm has been widely applied in health and medical settings globally with over fifty discrete (mostly health promotion) behaviors. It has also been used successfully in other arenas, such as in organization transformation efforts, and with innovative marketing approaches. For over a decade, a number of colleagues at my campus and I employed the TTM with issues of organ and blood donation, so I came to know well the efficacy of the model, and its attendant approaches.

The Stages of Change model as a whole is a departure from many other approaches to behavior change, in that it also views progress from one stage to another as desirable and normal, and the reasonable focus of interventions done in stages toward maintained change. In fact, the TTM is like a large, almost macro-scaffold! This approach also encourages persistence in the face of setbacks, and seeks to help people move in a stepwise, progressive manner toward achievement of their desired goals. Here is a summary of some of its key lessons for coaching:

The core construct of the TTM is the *stages of change*—a largely temporal dimension of the model, which describes ordered categories along a continuum of motivational readiness to adopt, amend or absent oneself from a target behavior. These are described in linear order, although the model is progressively more helical than linear, particularly in the middle stages.

The first stage is *Precontemplation*, defined as "not intending to take action in the foreseeable future." This initial phase is really a measure of awareness and readiness, as some may not have the change on their radar, are unaware of the need for it and are not even having thoughts of it. Just picture the thoughts of most adults up until the mid-1950s re: the hazards of smoking. They (precontemplators) might also just be unwilling at this time to undertake the prospective change, and may put it out of their conscious thoughts. Or they may refuse at the level of active thinking to give it any real consideration. This could be due to lack of exposure, or to prior discouragement about the particular change issue. For instance, some people are truly not aware of their transactional style and its impact on others. Or, for some, habit changing may have been a bruising and unsuccessful prior experience, relegated to a suppressed place in the annals of personal history. While this could be seen as an attitude of avoidance or resistance, skillful coaching probes and useful self-assessment tools often readily uncover both the current thoughts and prior trials clients have had with seeking to alter key behaviors.

Next is *Contemplation*, the stage of intent to change, wherein the awareness of reasons not to change still outweighs any assessment of the positive pull of beginning to act differently. The ambivalence of this period can stall any resolve to take action, and also is seen to recur when early attempts at changing encounter little or no success. To the outsider, this appears to be procrastination, chronic indecision or weak resolve and commitment. It usually is due to inadequate acquisition of reasons to change (the "pros"), the lack of sufficient pathways or support, and/or recall of prior painful pursuits of the particular goal and behavior. Again, this characterizes the majority of change efforts and agents, and moving through this phase is normal, essential progress toward the action sought.

The third stage—*Preparation*—portends fairly imminent action, and is typified by a concrete plan and timetable, as well as enlistment of supportive others and a declaration of intent. This phase is often short, while for some, it can be protracted for many months as they make detailed preparations and experience long, frequent delays till taking the next crucial step of change in the action stage. This is often a pivotal time in the coaching experience when the client needs strong reinforcement and even seeks concrete suggestions for moving ahead.

Action, the fourth stage, means that the person has begun to employ the behaviors necessary for accomplishing the change objective, most often either lifestyle, transactional, or decisional changes. This could mean a series of adopted or modified behaviors, or less often, a single choice point, all of which denote action toward the desired change goal. In strengths coaching relationships, this stage is the focus of selection, implementation, reinforcement and re-assessment, in the latter phases of the 7-D model.

The final stage for most behavior changes that are to persist, as opposed to one-time choices, is *Maintenance,* the application of consistent reinforcement to create a habit or adapt to a choice to modify or discontinue a behavior. The TTM suggests that six months of consistency is a reasonable period to consider the adopted change maintained. This could be very similar in a coaching compact, as the maintenance of desired change also requires support, reward, renewed commitment, countering challenges to change, and constant appraisal of how it all is faring, and what consequences are being noted. Six months is also the most common initial contract period for most reported coaching relationships, including most of my own client compacts.

STRONGBOX 4-13: *The TTM identifies five common, nearly serial stages to change: Pre-contemplation, Contemplation, Preparation, Action and Maintenance.*

Processes and Strategies for Change

Transitions progressing between the stages of change are influenced by a dozen or more fairly universal processes of change, that were originally derived from an analysis of hundreds of behavior change models and techniques, and were later refined through years of application and research to arrive at their current number and content. Three examples of these experiential and behavioral processes are: consciousness-raising to increase awareness in early stages, social liberation, that involve reappraisal tactics to enlarge one's perspective on a change issue, and reinforcement management, a selective rewarding to manage reinforcement and prevent extinction of the changed behavior.

The empirical findings on this construct of the TTM endorse the tailored use of one or more of these twelve-plus processes at each stage somewhat prescriptively. They are well-chosen and empirically validated psychological interventions, many in the literature for decades, and some strategies work better at some stages, yet not so well at others. Not surprisingly, most of these approaches are routinely chosen and used in some form by effective coaches, particularly those emphasizing asset-based formats and stratagems. Below is the full array of primary processes of change, divided into one set of largely cognitive strategies, and another listing of behavioral approaches. It is easy to see these as interventions for the coaching client to experiment with, using the counsel of their coach to guide the process, and to minimize frustrating and inefficient trials, and likely discouraging errors. The website listed at the end of this section on TTM is a source of clear, applicable examples and descriptions of these strategies and tactics that Procahska et al call *Processes* of change. This handful of concrete, specific and tailored processes can be employed beneficially to offer clients real, evidence-based, proven strategies for moving toward desired ends. Timely application of these processes gives the coachee a menu of strategies to use in meeting their own desired outcomes.

Cognitive	**Behavioral**
Consciousness-raising	Self-liberation
Self-reevaluation	Conditioning/Counterconditioning
Environmental reevaluation	Stimulus control/Generalization
Emotional arousal/dramatic relief	Reinforcement management
Social liberation	Helping relationships

The model also employs the leverage of the "pros" and "cons" of change, referred to collectively as "decisional balance." It appears that three to five positive endorsements, or "pros" for adopting a change, are needed to counter the impact of any single discouragement or "con." This is very similar to the finding Barbara Frederickson reported (described earlier) about positive emotions and their threshold of effectiveness. In addition, one's felt confidence in their own ability to change, often called self-efficacy, is a key construct, especially in the face of situational challenges. The TTM also accommodates other psychological, environmental, cultural, socioeconomic, physiological, biochemical, and genetic influences on the target behavior as well.

An additional key lesson for the strengths coach from the TTM research is the recognition that only about one in five of us is truly ready to act on a contemplated change at any point in time. Therefore, coaches need to acknowledge the finding that says graduated stage changing, not just acting on the terminal objective, is reasonable, natural, and desirable progressive change. Ideally, the coach can strive for stages of change over time—building a "learning scaffold", rather than focusing solely on the supposed end goal of adopting the desired change itself. Further, assessment of readiness for change offers a useful early approach to both coaching itself, and to any particular change objective. So-called "readiness rulers", simple Likert scale-type tools frequently used with the TTM, are also helpful gauges of inclination to progress over time.

In summary, this body of "change" evidence and the associated processes for coaching point to the need for individualized assessment of motivation, and selective, almost tailored use of skill and tool applications. Further, it calls for frequently re-assessing client drive and capacity for using different strategies and tactics to pursue their goals successfully. The TTM/Stages of Change framework is a uniquely comprehensive and thoroughly researched model for change that has wide and deep applicability, and therefore its lessons are especially pertinent to the coaching experience. More detail on the TTM, particularly about the Processes or Strategies, can be found on links at the TTM website listed in the chapter Endnotes.[43]

Changing Mindsets

The TTM offers us a step-wise approach to helping clients change that is grounded in understanding where we are about that change over time, and employing stage-matched strategies for changing. A challenging, yet frequently very effective approach focuses on combining our knowledge of how to assist others with change, and their sometimes seemingly fixed mindsets about their worlds—especially differences between how they and their co-workers might see things. Dweck's prescription for doing so is to emphasize the person's self-efficacy, their ability to make changes that could benefit them, then have them undergo a series of learning steps that expose them to some of their own deviations from presumed or measured mindset.[44] Others have successfully employed a range of similar interventions, such as helping them dispute erroneous information, providing evidence of neuroplasticity, or brain pliability, at any age, and reflecting on how they might counter attitudinal and cognitive biases.[45] All of these have proven to be quite easy to do, and very successful in working on mindset change as precursor to behavior change with my coachees. This is very similar to what others have recommended for engendering hope and optimism, other traits that previously had been thought not to be responsive to such interventions. In fact, strengths approaches to these kinds of outlooks and their associated actions have been among the very best coaching targets for demonstrating improvement.

> **STRONGBOX 4-14:** *The TTM research consistently shows that only about 20% of us are open to changing some behavior at present.*

Attention & Focus

In her discerning compilation of arguments for the importance of attitude and focus titled *Rapt*, that I cited earlier when discussing grit, Winifred Gallagher wrote that a wide range of disciplines has endorsed the skillful management of *attention* as key to individuals achieving happiness and fulfillment.[46] In other words, her review of the topic throughout the behavioral sciences led her to posit that our consciousness foretells our experience; what we focus on determines the quality of our life. Gallagher notes that this relative of the expectation thesis called attention is crucial to how we experience life's felt "ups and downs," and she makes the case convincingly for the influence of prior experience and affect on our focusing behavior. For the strengths coach, *Rapt* serves as a well-compiled summary of the importance of especially attentive focus, and particularly so with an outlook toward the very best outcome possible. What she calls the "rapt dynamic" is repeatedly seen to coincide with good outcomes when the focus is toward the positive and optimum. It also veers toward the dysfunctional and dysphoric when turned in the opposite direction toward skepticism and doubt. The multidisciplinary body of work cited in its pages reinforces the positive framework that underlies coaching with a focus on the client's very best, and also gives the coach a set of helpful cues for aiding clients to use that attending behavior to their real advantage.

The Principle of the 5 Es

A final mnemonic will summarize and finish our discussion of this foundational "know why" or mindset segment. I refer to it with clients as a frequent reminder of the yield on investment that their outlook and energy generate. It's couched in a more easily remembered way as the *Principle of the 5 Es*, and is represented thus:

<u>E</u>xpectation + <u>E</u>ngagement <u>E</u>voke <u>E</u>quivalent <u>E</u>ffects

By this I mean that our viewpoints or perspectives, plus our levels of involvement in behaviors reflecting them, lead inevitably to outcomes that mirror their nature. Put another way, if I see the world as abundant and use a lens of appreciation, my likely dedicated actions in support of that mindset will lead to results that reflect the same or similar perspectives, and lead to commensurate positive consequences. If I expect the world to be beholden, and I remain passively aloof, the resulting outcome is an unenthused presence and likely little connection with people or the purposes sought. In 2008, the cable television channel ESPN honored a trio of college women in Oregon with their annual Sportsmanship ESPY, an award recognizing outstanding athletic performance with exemplary regard for others on the field of play. They merited that recognition in others' eyes for an extraordinary gesture that acknowledged both an abundant outlook and a sense of fair play.

Briefly, when an opposing batter hit a home run, her first ever, but tore her knee's anterior cruciate ligament (ACL) rounding first base, two infielders <u>from the other team</u> picked her up and carried her the rest of the way around the bases to ensure she "touched them all"—a fitting metaphor in several ways. The umpire said that having her own teammates assist her was not permissible, and she'd have been ruled "out." Also, using a pinch runner to substitute for her would have reduced the homer to a single. The spirit of generosity shown by her opponents was both allowable and unprecedented. Several versions reporting this remarkable demonstration of creative sportsmanship exist on the website *YouTube*, and offer visual evidence of just what the 5 E Principle embodies. It was still posted for viewing at the time of this writing, so you can type in "Touching Them All," or "Sara Tucholsky" to see this terrific example of character and bigheartedness.

This chapter has attempted to help the strengths coach literally to *Power Up*, i.e., to enlarge his or her range of perspectives and approaches to working with clients. The emphasis has been on the mindsets—the frameworks or mental maps for creating insightful, reflective dialogue with coachees. It offered a helpful template for the coaching process, both by session and overall, in the 7-D schema, and provided a very contemporary summary of applicable behavioral and management science knowledge. These relevant models and their applications should enable coaches to employ client strengths more readily in the service of their coaching goals. Throughout this pivotal segment about "knowing why", there have been numerous descriptions of a variety of alternative perspectives—differing yet complementary frameworks for self-regard, and viewing one's work and relationships, not to mention coaching itself. The next section will explore the "how to" aspects of strengths coaching . . . the skills that are both basic to and necessary for effective and proficient helping as a coach.

> **STRONGBOX 4-15**: *What lies behind us, and what lies before us, are tiny matters, compared to what lies within us.*   *- Ralph Waldo Emerson*

5

"Know How and When": Skill Sets

> **STRONGBOX 5-1**: *Failure is not fatal, but failure to change might be.*
> *- John Wooden*

Lorna had "reached her limit," she said when she called me some years ago in late autumn. It seems the corporate matrix team she had been put in charge of had become a highly dysfunctional, non-productive management nightmare in just three meetings. They had not gotten anywhere near addressing their target goal of crafting a set of recommendations for a new service response format at their industrial plumbing manufacturing and supply company. In fact, team members were nowhere near even being on civil speaking terms in sessions, according to her. For our coaching work, she sought and successfully used a three-month, weekly session arrangement with me that emphasized what, for them, was a novel approach to working together. We aimed at a more inclusive, less formal and certainly more appreciative paradigm for their deliberations, and Lorna ran with it, and they soared in the end. Being able to sort out her feelings about the group, and test out her hunches about what might work proved critical to their coming together collaboratively to deliver an innovative and promising set of proposals to leadership, that were quickly and widely adopted.

The next key ingredient in the coaching repertoire that we'll cover is the collection of capabilities and competencies that the coach can use for working with clients and their strengths. This aspect of inviting coaches to *Power Up!* directly relates to using the pivotal skill sets for an effective coaching dyad. The chapter is intentionally labeled "Know How <u>and</u> When" to reflect the importance of timing in addition to a fitting application of the skill. We'll begin with some general or basic skills, and move then to a consideration of more situational ones, ending with a note about that crucial consideration of timing.

Self-Awareness

The first topic is the fundamental need to be keenly self-aware. By this I mean having a self-knowledge of the influences of changing mood, thought, or behavior, including your attitude toward the particular client, and the session underway or upcoming. This may call for a conscious self-check, a brief canvassing intrapersonally of how you feel, what thoughts dominate or preoccupy at the moment, and how prepared for the coaching exchange you feel. Self-awareness also means knowing and respecting one's own strengths and limitations in coaching, and not trying unwisely to exceed them.

A form of mindfulness—self-awareness that is very existential and in the moment—may serve the coach best here, allowing dismissal of what Buddhists call our busy, distracted, often fidgety "monkey mind." It is usually sufficient to engage in some self-talk to focus attention on the person and task at hand, to set aside our distractions for the time being, and to focus our thoughts on the client and their needs. This also has relevance beyond the moment, as we need to know if we feel in some way predisposed or oppositional toward certain topics or feelings in general, or even have carryover sentiments from a previous session or recent non-coaching experience of our own.

We need always to be aware of the possible value or belief conflicts that may occur, and are inevitable at times in working with other people. Finding objective and relatively dispassionate dispositions from which to conduct a coaching conversation or have a dialogue that keeps the client's interest uppermost sometimes calls for intentional countermeasures. Some call the Zen practice of self-awareness a matter of "centering," i.e., finding one's consciousness in the moment, free of other thoughts. The ability to pay full and dedicated attention to the client and the focus or declared issues of the coaching dialogue go a long way toward ensuring a productive, helpful session occurs.

Basic Transactional Skills

Let me define clearly what I am referring to here as a coaching skill. Basically, it means any developed ability to perform interactively with a client that is fundamental to or adds value to the coach's role as helper. Because the bedrock of an effective coaching experience is the trusting and mutual, collaborative relationship built between the parties, several linked communication skills constitute the basic methods of helping in the strengths coaching dyad. To begin, I want to affirm once more the importance of knowing whether a client is truly open to coaching. This is especially critical when the coachee is sponsored for coaching by a supervisor, even when it is made clear that the issue is not specifically performance based. I also do not participate at all myself in what some like to call outplacement coaching, where the idea is to prepare an employee for being terminated, and perhaps for finding new work. If it is a client's elective decision to leave employment, and they personally seek my assistance, then the process has a less coercive feel to it, and I might be able to offer some coaching help. In my experience, it doesn't work well for the client <u>or</u> the coach to take on a coaching arrangement intended to be evaluative, such as with a classic performance evaluation agenda, or to offer recommendations for administrative change. If the objectives are not solely the client's, and not in some way geared to a developmental or client change goal, then strengths coaching is probably not the vehicle to employ for intervention.

Coachability

In any case, so-called "coachability," the openness to feedback, exploration and behavior change that may be entailed, is a key ingredient in beneficial coaching, particularly with a strengths focus. Here are the seven main aspects of coachability that I look for and will have early dialogue about with my coachees. The prospective client ideally will . . .

- ° See coaching as a *learning opportunity* that is built on their assets
- ° Be willing to share candidly & fully their own *self-awareness*
- ° See our work as a *mutual exchange* of ideas, feelings and contexts
- ° Be willing to give and receive *feedback* non-defensively
- ° Have *basic values* not too discrepant from mine

o   Be open to reasonable *risk-taking*

o   Be able to *commit* the time, energy & effort to coaching

On my website (www.coachingwithstrengths.com) is a self-assessment checklist for prospective coaching clients to complete in order to gauge how likely a match we are at the time for a coaching arrangement. This is actually a three-part process that I find taps earnestness and readiness to begin, or lack thereof. It also puts us well along on the path to informed coaching by helping focus client thoughts, and by gathering preliminary background information. The items are reprinted early in the next (Tool Set) section under the heading "Coaching Interest and Readiness." As with all the tools in *Power Up!*, the reader is free to use them with attribution in their own practice, if they feel they would serve their coaching interests and needs.

STRONGBOX 5-2: *Problems are frustrated dreams and the dreams came first.*
- Peter Lang

---

3 IFs, All Ands, & No Buts

The discussion that follows next charts the major and essential skills I have identified for a baseline of effective (strengths) coaching practice. Not all will be used in equal measure by any coach, but each is a vital arrow in the quiver of an effective strengths coach, and therefore they constitute a necessary skill set. This will be more like a refresher for many coaches who have prior training in formal helping skills, but may serve as a bit of a primer for those from other than behavioral science and counseling backgrounds.

I headed this segment of the chapter with a takeoff of the familiar phrase "no ifs, ands, or buts," an unconditional qualifier statement that dates from the 17th century in English literature. It means there will be no yielding, no other outcomes are acceptable, and no excuses will be taken for failure to deliver. This rather rigid framework for results is memorable as a sort of mnemonic, but is modified and reversed here to compile the half-dozen skill sets that are the major tools of the strengths coaching trade, along with a critical reminder for using them. The turned phrase then becomes "3 IFs, all ands, & no buts," and refers first to the following 3 sets of IF process couplets:

Interviewing & Facilitating

Inquiring & Framing

Informing & Feeding back

They are followed by a word or two about using the conjunction "*BUT!*"

Interviewing and Facilitating

Consider the beginning pair, "Interviewing and Facilitating," that are linked because they enable the coaching dialogue to proceed progressively with maximum ease and mutual self-disclosure. Interviewing is both a skill and an art, as is expert facilitation. And while interviewing is most familiar perhaps from the context of job hunting, the strengths coach's role is more like that of an informational interviewer. The goal of effective interviewing is to ensure both parties share accurate and comprehensive information—facts, ideas or thoughts, and feelings—to enable them to reach a satisfactory conclusion, decision, or communication goal. Interviewing a client in a strengths coaching session entails the ability to do three things well and simultaneously—fully listen, ask effective & useful questions, and help them find perspective.

The major difference between other forms of coaching and that grounded in a strengths approach, is the use of the templates of positive, possibility-focused mindset and strengths-associated dialogue. This means that frequent and recurrent employment of the client's unique strengths is the major frame of reference for coaching context and content. In practice, it could sound like the following kinds of coaching queries and comments: "How do you see that playing to your _____ strength?" Or, "In what ways do you find yourself using that _____ strength to accomplish or improve on that?" Sometimes it can sound like "It seems that your _____ strength might offer a real capability for success there; what do you think?" or "In what ways are you finding this stressor is not calling on your best attributes, and what do you think might be a good or improved response?" Whether stated as a query or a reflective comment, the message is usually weighed against the backdrop of a felt or measured strength, and thereby enables the coachee to redirect or reframe, to broaden and build, to access or mine their very best; this is the real objective of strengths coaching.

The 3 As of Optimal Listening

The cornerstone of effective Interviewing and Facilitating is that understated and pivotal skill of active listening. What constitutes good, effective listening? Breaking it down into its constituent parts reveals that effective listening involves a series of actions that may be more memorably recalled as the 3 As: *Attending, Acknowledging* and *Affirming.*

Attending includes giving the speaker (client) your full attention and focusing on their words and the associated feelings they are conveying. This includes an appreciation for both the context and the message. It does not mean losing the content through allowing distraction by the delivery, but giving a full and attentive hearing to the client's words and intended meaning. This is especially important and more challenging when the dyad is deprived of visual cues, like when the session is conducted electronically rather than in person, as it often is. Attending entails giving a concentrated, 'in the moment' focus to the exchange being made.

Acknowledging involves actively letting the coachee know you heard and understood them. Often, this means paraphrasing their words or restating their message to check for certainty about your grasp of their statement. It also includes encouraging them to elaborate or just to continue with their narrative. The use of what some call "minimal encouragements"—very brief periods or moments of connection that are part of most mutually engaged conversations is helpful here, too. Words like "OK," Uh-huh," or "Yes," inviting them to "Say some more about that," or, if face-to-face, making appropriate, occasional head nods, all help to keep the client going, and indicate to them that you are right there with them. Acknowledging that you are tuned in and that you comprehend, and want more to help with a fuller understanding are vital to the connecting dynamic so crucial to an effective coaching dialogue.

The third component of effective listening for the strengths coach is Affirming, which is adding at the end of their story a short comment that places their input in a fully appreciative context. That may involve asking for reframing of a comment in a more affirmative or positive manner. Or, it may more simply involve you offering a reflection on how the discussion may have given you a sense of their apt use of their strengths, or how they may want to build further on particular ones. Affirmative reinforcement of both direction and perspective are often best realized through a simple restatement of a positive observation, or a short, easy acknowledgement of the client's viewpoint or decision.

> **STRONGBOX 5-3**: *Listen a hundred times. Ponder a thousand times.*
> *Speak once.*   *- Kurdish Proverb*

Facilitate

The word *facilitate* literally means "to ease" for another. While that term is most often used in the context of chairing a group discussion or meeting, a facilitator is someone who is supposed to help bring about the progress desired in a transaction, to help forward that process to its sought ends. So, facilitation in a strengths coaching dialogue is a process skill that seeks to advance the conversation throughout the 7-D schema, and to make sure that learning is occurring. All the while, the coach honors client needs and pace, and pursues their declared goal for the session, aligning with the sought objectives of the entire coaching relationship. It is a process skill that simultaneously allows the client to more readily expound, reflect and choose, while not omitting the critical variables that cover the entire 7-D process and the coachee's agenda thereby. Well-done facilitation is a combination of good listening, administering to the client's needs, ensuring comprehensive analysis and description, as well as reviewing the interactive experience to guarantee improvement and satisfaction for both parties. In effect, facilitation is the quiet monitoring of the session <u>and</u> the relationship—a skill that usually takes both training and practice, and is critical to effective strengths coaching. Central to good facilitation is ensuring the flow and clarity of the client's narrative. That means making minimal intrusions and seeing to it that s/he is able to progress through the 7 Ds in a concise and open manner, interrupting only to clarify and to add perspective. This is usually accomplished through judicious use of brief summarizing and questioning, the next skill set for mastery. No less important than the process is the need for the coach to ensure client learning and growth, helping them stretch their strengths boundaries and applications in new, desirable ways.

STRONGBOX 5-4: *The major coaching skills—the 3 "IF"s—are Interviewing and Facilitating, Inquiring and Framing, plus Informing and Feeding back.*

Inquiry and Framing

The second paired IF refers to **I**nquiry & **F**raming. Inquiry is the technical skill most often called upon to carry out the basic coaching dialogue. The framework for this that I use as a strengths coach is grounded in the stout, twenty-plus year literature of Appreciative Inquiry (AI) that I mentioned in the introductory section.[1] Before examining AI's main contributions to the coaching process, let's explore the nature of Inquiry itself.

The work of long-time MIT consultant, executive career coach, and writer Edgar Schein is clarifying in this regard. Schein's "process consultation" canon for decades has been a beacon to those of us who serve as organization consultants, particularly for his guidance on the basic communication skill set of the consultant. In his pithy 2009 book called *Helping*, he refers to the challenges and elements of the shared, even mutual helping relationship that coaching is, in reality.[2] He regards both the coach and the client as party to transactions that actually involve mutual helping with what each offers the other. Schein feels one can acknowledge that reality best through what he calls "humble inquiry," a basic skill of effective coaching. Both words are central to this concept, as the questioning process has to involve a modicum of humility, a clearly demonstrated respect, even modesty for the client's words, experience and issues, along with skillful questioning. The ability of the coach to establish a relationship that is seen as mutual exchange, not a one-down, authority-delivered expert opinion to the client seeking help, but rather a growing connection using shared trust and reliance that helps the coachee "discover" their own optimal solutions is the ideal. This also includes being able to discern the real versus the purported needs and wants of the client, identifying with them what would be in their best interest. This is rather than helping them find what would remove the anxiety of the anticipated change, yet not help them in arriving at a meaningful and lasting alternative.

This essential skill set involves a realization that expertise is the silent offering of coaches, not the primary spoken currency of coaching. For instance, Schein writes about the contrasts among advice given by consultants, knowledge of how to perform that might come from a trainer, and sharing personal experience, like a mentor might do. He also notes the distinct kinds of assistance with personal issues for which one seeks counseling or therapy, or may be the focus of life coaching. My view of these related role behaviors differs slightly. I tend to see the coaching role as falling somewhere between counseling and consulting. It has elements of each, and yet has its own unique role and skill combination. While there are times when the skills of a counselor are needed, there are also places where the consultant mindset and skill set are desirable. Thus, the coach has aspects of each in their repertoire, yet is neither of them fully, and only a little bit of each most of the time.

There are a number of very useful frameworks and wise warnings in the *Helping* book that lead me to urge the reader to get and thoughtfully consume this excellent publication that also addresses organizational helping. We'll develop that latter topic in the final chapter, when we discuss coaching with groups and teams, leaders and whole companies. A helpful quartet of perspectives on dialogue and inquiry to assist the coach are described next, beginning with Appreciative Inquiry.

Appreciative Inquiry

Schein would also be a proponent of the kind of appreciative inquiry process first devised by David Cooperrider and Suresh Srivasta at Cleveland's Case Western Reserve University, that is so vital to strengths coaching.[3] This adds to humble inquiry the framework of appreciation—a disposition to see possibility and positive prospect, not deficit and weakness to correct. Basic to an AI approach is the following set of attitudes and beliefs:

Inquiring appreciatively . . .

- assumes health, a positive outlook, and vitality
- entails generative cueing, questioning and guiding
- is an affirmative process, enlarging positive traits
- presupposes the client's self-knowledge is sufficient, though sometimes veiled and not obvious to them

- seeks to build on existing capabilities and viewpoints
- sees abundance, not deficiency, in the client and their world
- acknowledges the client's strengths as foundational to growth, development, and desired change·

To repeat, Inquiry is the use of mostly open-ended questioning (not "yes" or "no" queries) that invites the coachee to tell their story. It seeks a first person narrative that is solely the client's construction of contexts and events, and their impacts on them. Just as Schein has referred to it as a "humble" process of inquiry, the AI writers also frame questioning in this vein. Here are seven critical attitude and process thoughts for conducting the coaching conversationion with both optimal appreciation and effective inquiry:

The strengths coach . . .
- adopts an attitude of curiosity—seeks to learn more
- connects through empathy and genuine interest
- listens with third ear & observes with third eye—the intuitive sensorium, seeking patterns & themes
- probes to find out who, what, where, when, why, & how as relevant
- is affirming and positive, encouraging and optimistic
- remembers SILENT is an anagram for LISTEN
- makes sure it's a dialogue, with them and their stories in focus, leading the way, keeping the ball in their court.

> **STRONGBOX 5-5:** *Appreciative: (adj.) expressing or feeling gratitude or approval; Inquiry: (n.) a request for information, facts, data.*

Models for Questioning & Framing

Adding to our recognition of the importance and power of keen, creative and generative questioning are a handful of very instructive insights from the World Café movement described in Juanita Brown & David Isaacs' book of that same title.[4] The World Café is a global network of people organized in the late 1990s to promote better community dialogue, and to create improved processes for those conversations. Some of the book's very helpful considerations for possibility-promoting questions follow:

The authors mention first what they call the "architecture of powerful questions." They describe the three key elements for crafting questions that lead most effectively to actionable conclusions: the *construction, scope* and *assumptions* dimensions.

First, they recommend use of those question frameworks that yield more incisive and meaningful thoughts and responses—those that are open-ended and begin with stems such as "how, what and why," versus "who, when or where"—stems that often lead to closed-ended, 'yes or no' kinds of responses. In other words, the *construction* of an inquiry is fateful, in that it leads to a certain type of response and a determined lens for scrutiny.

They suggest, too, that more reflective responses come from the influence of a query's *scope*, with more fitting and progressively broader inquiries expanding beneficially into wider boundaries only as befits the purpose and focus of the discussion. For example, if the framework is interpersonal, asking about the organization or a wider lens of context seems inappropriate, or at least premature. Therefore, a question asking what might be the impact of a decision would focus first on oneself, and only later on the work unit or family, and then perhaps the larger units of organization, followed by the community or beyond as relevant, to give the client or speaker proper primary interest. Those other contexts are not irrelevant, just secondary at best, and may not aptly mirror the client's true interest.

Third, they recommend that the *assumptions* involved in any question are potent aspects of it, and deserve careful consideration in designing a line of inquiry. Two examples come to mind: I recently heard a taped presentation by a CEO who asked that his audience consider the implications of the prospect of eliminating the "customer service" function of organizations by making them unneeded, by using a comprehensive quality approach to service and product delivery that rendered such a unit or function unnecessary. Contrast that with the usual questions about how to improve customer service, the bane of most service departments, and the focus of much deserved ire! Once embarked on a chosen path of inquiry, others are often disregarded or avoided by default. So, as the AI writers also noted, the questions we ask determine the nature and gaze of our attention, and simultaneously keep us from pursuing other paths.

Finally, patterns and themes yielded in response to powerful questioning often clue in the coach to both underlying beliefs and more promising directions for discussion and action. They end by recommending use of a series of generative questions to focus client attention better, queries that look at connecting ideas and finding deeper insight, and that ultimately create forward movement. This puts me in mind also of Gervase Bushe's complementary techniques mentioned earlier for ensuring candid, truthful learning conversation in any exchange.

The ideas behind narrative and social construction, a third context for this skill subset, and pioneered in the past twenty-plus years by Michael White, David Epston, and Ken and Mary Gergen, and others, also lend us a helpful perspective here.[5] I'll attempt a short and knowingly oversimplified summary of the most relevant aspects of this approach to sharing information of all kinds.

Fundamental here is the notion that we manufacture and acquire knowledge and meaning in social exchanges with others, that such meaning is nonexistent outside shared discourse. Social construction theory notes that each time a topic is expressed or described, even by the same person, it acquires new meaning and often some changed, novel learning, both for them and the listener. The main tool of this learning is the narrative—my telling of my story about my experience. It is the primary way that most of us communicate with each other, and it is the core transaction in the coaching experience. The lessons from this perspective for coaches are mainly these:

The client will tell his or her stories often, doing so in a unique way that only they can, and in the telling, is likely to acquire new understandings. The coach's role in this is to listen well, to accept the constructions presented as real for the narrator. This is so even if it seems objectively changed from before in the ears of the listener, as it still helps them understand themselves better by reflecting anew on those stories. Here the word "story" means anything the client tells the coach about self, relationships, situations or thoughts. There is much more depth in this set of constructs than will find exposition here, and I encourage coaches to explore them in order to strengthen this skill component of their coaching.

A fourth and final framework for exploration with this skill pair is drawn from the Dialogue movement, perhaps best explained in the book *Dialogue*, by authors Linda Ellinor & Glenna Gerard.[6] They offer the coach (Ellinor was an executive coach with the Centers for Creative Leadership beginning in the 1980s) a thoughtful consideration of the importance of structure for a potent and progressive dialogue between two people. Basing much of their framework on the roots of David Bohm's group dialogue work, and emphasizing the centrality of effective *listening* over the speaking role, they posit that skillful listening is the single most creative and powerful act we humans perform!

There are three levels of listening that they highlight—listening to others, to oneself, and, in groups, to the collective, shared voice's meaning. The first has to do with openly valuing and respecting the other (client's) issues and understanding. Next, one (the coach) listens to the internal, often prejudiced—meaning judgmental based on prior experience—voice that asks what the other person means to them. Finally, there is the sense of communing in statements that come from group dialogue, an extension of the one-to-one exchange. Often, this one entails hearing the contextual culture of the speaker, an important framework for understanding deeply and clearly. There is a strong and impressive plea from the Dialogue movement for appreciating and using silence more intentionally and liberally to bring about meaningful, productive, and helpful dialogue. This set of constructs, too, is much like those described by Schein, Cooperrider, Bushe, and others mentioned elsewhere in these pages.

I'll not expand the depiction here of the many excellent strategies and insights Ellinor and Gerard share, but the gains from adopting them are manifold for coaches, leaders of teams and groups, as well as entire organizations. Their subtitle, *Rediscover the Transforming Power of Conversation*, hints at the nature of the gains to be had from effective, facilitated dialogue—a central facet of the coaching skill set.

> *STRONGBOX 5-6: Coaching is not about just conversing, or even a conventional discussion; at its most effective, it is truly a dialogue.*

Analyzing Success

Another pertinent example of an appreciative form of inquiry is one similar to the root-cause-of-success analysis discussed earlier. The traditional take on the analytics of an action suggests we frame learning solely around "what went wrong" as the target of such an examination. This newer thinking urges an approach that seeks instead to discover the best or most successful aspects of an experience in order to replicate them, either in kind or by comparison. This line of questioning encourages inquiry into the best of prior experience as an appreciative gesture that is more promising, and certainly more in line with strengths coaching. In the examples above, challenging the dominant paradigm leads to a radically different line of inquiry and reflection, and usually to an alternative, more satisfying set of conclusions.

Walter Kisthardt has also articulated a thoughtful inquiry model for strengths-based helping, and his approach with this perspective includes a well-considered set of six principles:

1. The initial focus of the helping process is on the strengths, interests, abilities, knowledge and capabilities of each person, <u>not</u> on their deficits, symptoms, diagnoses and weaknesses, *as defined by someone else.*

2. The helping relationship is one of collaboration, mutuality, and partnership; in other words, power *with* another, not power over another.

3. Each person is responsible for him- or herself, and directs the helping effort.

4. All have the inherent capacity to learn, grow and change.

5. Helping activities *in the helpee's own settings* are encouraged in a strengths-based, person-centered approach.

6. The entire community is a font of resources to the helpee.[7]

His analysis of the range of strengths-yielding questions thoroughly describes the arenas for inquiry in strengths coaching, and we shall explore them as well in the Tool Set chapter. The format appearing there is Dennis Saleebey's eight strengths inquiry categories, with my own sample questions suggested for each.

Yet another useful resource is Bob Bertolino, Michael Kiener and Ryan Patterson's recently published workbook titled *The Therapist's Notebook on Strengths and Solution-Based Therapies.*[8] While the framework is mainly solution-focused lines of inquiry in a therapy context, the question categories and roots offer the strengths coach a thoughtful set of topics, question stems, and focal ideas for application in coaching. Finally, *The Encyclopedia of Positive Questions* from AI pioneers Diane Whitney, David Cooperrider, Amanda Trosten-Bloom and Brian Kaplin is an older, very comprehensive resource for the strengths coach seeking to use appreciative inquiry extensively.[9]

> **STRONGBOX 5-7**: *The glass is never half empty: half is filled with liquid, the other half with air!*
> *- Anonymous*

Frame-shifting

If, as I asserted before, "change" is the holy grail of coaching objectives, then "perspective" provides the map for that quest. In other words, the primary stock-in-trade for the coach is her or his ability to help the client see their issue or dilemma from a number of different angles, thereby optimizing their foundation for decision-making. The particular capability of the strengths coach here is their facility with getting the client to see the range of positive influences and consequences to possibility-focused choices, and the corresponding decisions to be made from among them.

Most of us are familiar with the very popular classic science fiction television (and later movie) series created by Gene Roddenberry and called *Star Trek*. A recurrent feature of the stories was the presence of beings that had the capability to assume the appearance of other, usually more compatible creatures and people. They were called "shape-shifters," in a concept reportedly lifted from Celtic mythology. In a similar vein, the lever of frame-shifting allows us to assume an alternative posture toward a perception, shifting from negative regard to positive alternative.

If the client is "waxing negative," the coach can remind them that what they find wrong represents an absence of something they hold as an ideal, and respectfully redirect them to offer "what that might look like if corrected, done better, or solved." Diane Whitney, Amanda Trosten-Bloom and Kae Rader have a version of this frame-shifting process that they call the "the Flip," in *Appreciative Leadership*.[10] In simple paraphrase, this is accomplished through helping the client convert a negative, problem-focused statement into an affirmative question. They urge us to simply (1) acknowledge understanding, (2) solicit true desire—what outcome or alternative experience is really wanted, and then (3) ask if they could reframe the comment into a restatement using positive language that depicts what they really want.

Here's an example: If the client is complaining about someone else's actions, or offering their own pejorative assessment of that person's effectiveness or style deficiencies, try helping them to frame-shift or flip it for reflection in a new, more appreciative paradigm. Or, if s/he says a colleague "doesn't get it," ask what might they be saying and doing differently if they "got it," then coach them toward arrival at how they might cultivate that desired change. As we noted earlier, another commonly heard "deficit diagnosis" by a client is habitual communication breakdowns and lapses. The coach could help them affirmatively reframe that to a more productive exchange, one that leads to clear, mutual understanding. It really is not a complex shift, but it is vital to the enabling flow of a strengths coaching transaction, and comes only after deliberate practice over time—both for the coach, and ultimately for the client. Numerous other writers have described their versions of this kind of gently confrontational reframing or redirecting aid, and it is both a useful skill and an effective device for strengths coaching.

Context

I wrote earlier of "context," which is no small consideration in the coaching dialogue, and bears repeating and some amplification here. A thorough assessment of the circumstance or environment of a situation is necessary backdrop to any decision or choice to change. Contextual influences often determine the significance, meaning or comparability of an event or action. The strengths coach is at her/his best when relating through both the contexts of client strengths and situational characteristics.

Contextual cues provide the essential boundaries of a coaching exchange. These can also include the organization, the people in the scenario under discussion, the history of the principals involved (and often the principles, as well), the unique features of the client and their situation, your relationship with him or her, and literally any other so-called "outside" influences that pertain to the matter being talked about. Context is an amorphous, gray area that defies easy access, yet is an imperative, influential variable for a beneficial discussion with the client. It colors the situation so much that direction, tenor, scale and scope of actions to be taken are all impacted by its consideration. Skilled exploration of context with the client often is a hallmark of the exceptional coaching practice.

Informing

This is a skill that requires application of two different, yet complementary abilities. The first is the compiled wisdom of experience that is sometimes called intuition, and is comprised of the accumulated knowledge of various experiences over time. In a wide-ranging May 2011 article in the Harvard Business Review, this component of practical wisdom was likened to the Greek notion of *phronesis*, one of the three forms of knowledge (along with *episteme*—valid scientific knowledge, and *techne*—skill based technical know-how), that Aristotle originally wrote about.[11] The authors, Ikujiro Nonaka and Hirotaka Takeuchi, defined phronesis as "experiential knowledge that enables people to make sound and ethical judgments," in this article about wisdom in leadership. The acquired ability enables people to be prudent in choosing among alternatives, and also to stay grounded in moral values in the process of deciding. While some of it transcends disciplines, domains of work, or time, the overall "know how" of the coach is brought judiciously to each coaching encounter. Also, the ability to know when to share solicited or timely information so as to enable reflective thought, not uncritical absorption of it, makes information-sharing by a coach an artful skill that allows the client to find their own way to judgment of the information's utility for them.

This skill of informing also begs the issue of whether a coach unfamiliar with a client's specific arena of functioning can be optimally helpful. My experience with this matter says that the commonalities across different professional and business domains far outweigh the contrasts, and also the client is still the one making application of it to their own circumstance. So, while information gained through like experience may argue for a niche match between some coaches and clients, that seems to me to be true only a scant minority of the time.

When employing this skill of informing, it ideally is in the form of a coach's story, or use of a comparative medium so that its lessons are less teaching or tutoring, and more like offering context for reflection and critical thought through the use of narrative. Finally, yet critically, I always urge coaches I train to begin such a sharing with seeking the coachee's permission to offer it as a personal thought, suggestion or alternate viewpoint. Simply asking "Are you open to another perspective?" or "I have another thought about that; would you like to hear it?" will suffice. If the client is not willing to hear an alternative, then it is not only a waste of time, but doing so also can introduce some discord, or at least unwanted "noise" to the exchange, and hint at a need for the coach to control the exchange.

> **STRONGBOX 5-8**: *Intuition will tell the thinking mind where to look next.*
> *- Jonas Salk*

Feedback

This final skill partner is what author and consultant Ken Blanchard long ago called the "breakfast of champions," alluding to feedback's elemental capacity for directing change and action at any level of performing. There are numerous available tip sheets for providing feedback in a discussion, and they exist both in print and on line, although they are frequently articulated as charts stating what *not* to do. So what follows will be an affirmative notation about this crucial communication skill subset for coaching.

The essence of feedback is contained in its two syllables—*feed back* to the speaker or performer what one sees and experiences, particularly in the moment's conversation with them, or across a number of exchanges over time. As such, it is never without the biases of the feedback provider, no matter how objective they may aspire to be. The term derives from a century-old application to electrical systems wiring that has led to the superficial assumption that there are both negative and positive forms of feedback. The negative ones are thought to serve to extinguish repetition by offering non-reinforcement, with the positive feedback leading to a replication of desired behavior, with a sense of approval. Put simply, feedback that is not favorable contrasts with that which is positive, and is thought to result in diametrically opposite outcomes—first motivationally, and then in actions undertaken. For a superb contemporary rendering of the more detailed complexities of motivation, incentives and rewards, see Dan Pink's book *Drive*, referenced earlier.[12]

Let's examine in more detail what happens when feedback comes in each of the common packages or forms it usually does, including that of performance appraisal, that flawed and infrequent, usually once-a-year experience. First, if the research is to be followed, then giving good news or positive feedback first, then issuing the bad news or negative has two results: It ensures the good is heard, and it conveys the impression that the boss is keeping score. If scorekeeping is indeed going on, then the recipient heard both plusses and minuses, and is not exactly sure where they stand, having received both.

Using the reverse sequence of bad before good news means the good is rarely heard, or at least minimized, because the negative opening drowned out any likelihood of hearing the positive and taking it to heart. This sequence also conveys the sense that the bad outweighs the good in the eyes of the giver of feedback. This approach, too, has its obvious limitations for enhancing relationship and promoting desired actions.

The third option, to deliver just the feedback that seeks correction, just the bad news or negative feedback, probably means that each subsequent exchange begins with the expectation (likely supported) that I will only hear from the boss when I've messed up. That would also create a pattern of attempting to avoid conversation with the supervisor, expecting either no encouragement or a paucity of it for going forward.

Next is the prospect of giving only good news, feedback that seeks just to praise, and not find fault. While this may eliminate the blunting effects of negative feedback, it, too, seems to fall a bit short of ideal, unless it also somehow addressed that which might need improvement. Experience shows that an upgrade from that would be the addition of focused coaching that follows positive feedback. In this framework, the coach can help the client to see what works, and to identify ways to harness the characteristics that enabled that to be, in order to assist with improvement. It can be done through further enhancement of the strengths noted, as well as by looking for ways to amplify those positive attributes that may be underutilized or unbidden as lost opportunities.

Then there is the matter of weaknesses. Some will assert that avoiding feedback about those faculties or non-talents that will likely never become stellar traits is the simplest path and the wisest way to deal with them. My experience differs slightly, although I can see the efficiency argument in the former approach. Instead, my belief and personal data support coaching for what the client seeks to improve, with a clear exploration of both the consequences of those choices and of the omission of other asset possibilities. This way, the option of deciding what issues to pay attention to is the client's, where the choice is likelier to align with his or her truer interests and felt capabilities. I see my coaching responsibility as being sure the client sees the picture clearly, and can make choices about what declarations seem most promising to them for future work.

I also like to use the more helpful and appreciative categories of "useful" and "not useful" to describe the nature of the feedback, as opposed to labeling them good or bad, positive or negative. Feedback will not be very useful and likely will be ineffective if it is evaluative, judgmental, preaching, moralizing, admonishing, or demanding. Giving and receiving effective feedback are essential to maintaining and advancing coaching relationships. If the following conditions are met, the probability that feedback will be useful, effective and helpful is greatly enhanced.

- The client is ready for & open to hearing the feedback
- The feedback is descriptive rather than interpretive
- The client is not "overloaded" with information: use frequent, specific feedback, but not too detailed as to overload the mind
- The feedback is timely: as soon as possible for simple tasks, delayed for complex ones, according to research
- The feedback is perceived to be given for the purpose of being helpful, not to allow the coach just to "level" or "vent"
- The information conveyed concerns behavior that the client is capable of changing
- If the coach giving feedback appropriately shares something of himself or herself in doing so, preferably with an "I" message, such as ". . . When you _____, I feel _____., or "What I heard sounds like it was successful."
- The coach doesn't mask a suggestion masked in the form of feedback, such as in this statement, "Do you think it might be better to approach them less demandingly?" This is merely a veiled criticism, not genuine feedback, and really intends to correct or scold rather than coach.

A final consideration for this topic of feedback is executive coach and author Marshall Goldsmith's notion of "feedforward." In his recent book, *Mojo*, he defines the title topic as a powerful, positive spirit toward what you are doing that radiates from the inside to the outside.[13] In earlier writings, this world-class leadership coach has suggested the use of a helpful "tool" for cultivating "mojo" that he calls Feed*Forward*! It was created years ago by Goldsmith and co-author Jon Katzenbach in recognition of the limited nature of conventional feedback with its retrospective focus on what has already happened and is therefore not subject to change.[14] Goldsmith says this approach enables us to look better at the future and to find positive suggestions for our possible tomorrows. It really is a modified multi-rater tool that focuses on positive suggestions for the future, rather than static evaluation of what may have been faulty in the past. Those providing these types of "feedforward" do so in a framework of ideas and suggestions for future behavior, not amending past behavior *per se*, and thus it maintains a strengths focus. This variant of feedback is worth considering for any role in any setting, but especially with teams of colleagues, and for their leaders.

STRONGBOX 5-9: *Feedback is the "breakfast of champions!"*
- Ken Blanchard

All "Ands," No "Buts"

"But" is one of the 7 (surprise!) coordinating conjunctions in common English usage. Its intent is to signal a contrasting point of view, an alternative take on the earlier statement that preceded it. However, in real usage, and even more surely in conversation that involves an audience, the speaker is often using it to negate or nullify the prior statement, not simply to offer a contrasting point of view. Several years ago, Aubrey Daniels wrote in his excellent little book on applied behavioral analysis for managers titled *Bringing Out the Best in People*, that the use of the word "but" serves as a *verbal eraser* in the ears of the listener, effectively countering the previous phrase.[15] So, if I said "You really seem to be able to get a lot done in a short time, <u>but</u> . . ." almost anything that follows will effectively expunge the former comment from the hearer's thoughts, as the second statement seems to be the real message intended, such as ". . . <u>but,</u> your work is often incomplete or sloppy." No one would say "'but," and then add an affirming complementary (and complimentary) phrase. Instead, such two part messages might be conjoined better by the use of "and," signaling an additive statement to follow, and enabling the listener to include rather than cancel out, to build on, instead of eliminating the first observation or opinion, by suggesting an alternative and preferably affirmative view.

While this may seem like a lot of commentary on a small thing, in practice the misguided and highly commonplace use of "but" to convey an alternative feeling or view has negative power, and comes out of a pair of common and related dynamics. The first is often that the speaker wishes not to seem harsh, and just wants to soften the real blow to follow, so they couch it that way. Further, it often appears that such paired contradictions emerge from a "scarcity" mindset, one that implies things are either one way or the other, and they can't be "both/and." In reality, most of our experience entails an abundance of perspectives and experiences, lots of shades of gray. Most of the time, for most people and subjects, there are multiple legitimate viewpoints.

So, these thoughts about the use of the conjunction "but" are critical in both an appreciative inquiry sense, and for the reality of everyday communication dynamics. My advice to coaches is always to forgo the use of "but," and substitute for it the truly additive word "and." Practice till it becomes habitual, and note the improved consequences. You will also find that doing so frequently leads to a client's own easier acquisition of that practice, and also helps them gain some insight about the several competing perspectives their situations or issues actually involve. In summary of this segment then, in addition to the six skills described in the three IF pairs, one might usefully use "all ands, and no buts" in conversation, especially when offering feedback to a coachee.

Resistance in Coaching

Occasionally, even in strengths-based coaching, one experiences a degree of "push back" from a client. In my experience, this avoidance or resistance to either process or topical consideration usually takes one or more of three forms of self-protection: Resistance to wanting to know something not easily admitted, to wanting another to know what I don't know, or to wanting to do something new or differently. The resistance some clients offer to attempts to help them face some unpleasant or recurrent negative personal information or history is the most common of the three types seen. It is best dealt with by a straightforward, non-accusing observation by the coach, such as this: "It appears to me that you may not yet ready to absorb this possible information about yourself; if you agree, why do you think that might be so, and how shall we respond to it?" Such an approach usually frees up the conversation for a more forthright self-examination, although it may take repeated, appropriately timed attempts to do so.

The second form is a furtive cousin to the first resistance type, as it is not really awareness that is being blocked, but shows an unwillingness to admit that some piece of information or knowledge is not actually already known by the client! The ego-laden discomfort of that belief can get in the way of a fuller and more open discussion of important topics, because the client wants to avoid the embarrassment of acknowledging they did not already know something they feel they should have known. A frank suggestion that the item is not known to all, or that it may not be common knowledge, can be liberating. That also can lead to dropping the resistance, allowing a fuller and more insightful exchange about it, as well as a dynamic that readily permits clients to own gaps in their knowledge base.

The final form of resistance is usually due to unpleasant feelings the client anticipates or already is encountering about letting go of something and taking on a changed reality. William Bridges writes helpfully about this in his depiction of change stages and transition, by describing the challenges to the psyche that changes pose, especially unplanned or imposed ones.[16] A good response by the strengths coach to this third type of avoidance is to facilitate a discussion of the feelings that attend the change, including any sense of loss or felt impotence to deal with one that is imminent or already underway. This can lead to a very helpful examination of the emotional feelings that the change is fomenting, and usually will enable the client to regain some perspective and equanimity about the felt threats and reactions to change. Any of these forms of resistance is a natural, even temporarily helpful reaction, and serves as a sentinel for alerting the client to their emotional responses to these perceived threats, so they can deal with them constructively.

STRONGBOX 5-10: *Compassion is the highest form of wisdom.*
- The Talmud

Ethics & Integrity

Address of the integrity of coaching is never out of place or unneeded in practice, and I've chosen to speak of it here briefly in the skills section, although an equally valid argument could be made for ethical behavior beginning with one's mindset for it. Ethics is the part of philosophy that speaks to moral comportment, dutiful behavior, and the exercise of good judgment. A concise application of a set of ethical principles to coaching is provided by an older framework for professional ethics that I was first exposed to many years ago.[17] It was authored by Karen Kitchener, and comprises five focal principles:

1. **Respect**: Clients have the right to decide how they live their lives, as long as their actions do not interfere with the well-being of others. They have the right to act as a free agent, with the freedoms of thought and choice (called Autonomy).
2. **Do No Harm**: The requirement to avoid inflicting either physical or psychological harm on any client (also known as Nonmaleficence).
3. **Benefit Others**: The obligation to improve and enhance the well being of clients, even at times while inconveniencing the coach (Beneficence).
4. **Be Just:** To be just in dealing with others, assuming equal treatment of all, to afford each individual their due portion, and in general, to observe the Golden Rule (Fairness).
5. **Be Faithful:** One should keep promises, tell the truth and maintain respect and civility in human discourse (Loyalty).

This small set of ethical practices, if observed well, will keep the client safe and aptly cared for, by keeping that coach on solid ground as a helping professional. It is vital to reputation and practice building as well. Kitchener also espoused a set of what she called "the 5 Ps" or the 5 Powers of ethical behavior. These are:

1. *Purpose*: Your objective or intention; the goal.
2. *Pride*: The sense of satisfaction you receive from the accomplishments of those you care about.
3. *Patience*: Trust the process.
4. *Persistence*: Maintaining your commitment and making your actions consistent with your guiding principles.
5. *Perspective*: The capacity to see what is <u>really</u> important in any situation.

Approaching the coaching experience and client with a determination to practice ethically, to avoid boundary violations and conflicts, while keeping the client's best interests uppermost, is critical for the strengths coach. Adherence to these two small standards criteria, the practices and powers of ethical transaction, will serve the strengths coach thoroughly and well if used as guidelines for professional conduct.

In coaching, as in most professional service fields, there are usually both *aspirational* and *regulatory* codes of ethics. The two specific to the coaching field that I like are of the former type, aspirational statements that could also serve as regulatory standards for members of each organization, despite the fact that the coaching field has no single or preferred governing body at present. I urge the reader to look at the codes promulgated by the ICF, the International Coaching Federation, the largest such body in the field, whose rubrics can be found at http://www.coachfederation.org/ethics/. Also, you can benefit from a consideration of the statement by the International Association of Coaching, another large global training and certification enterprise (http://www.certifiedcoach.org/index.php/about_iac/iac_code_of_ethics/). They mirror one another greatly, and a coach would be sensible and do well to conform the conduct of their coaching practice to either of them.

> **STRONGBOX 5-11**: *Ethical coaching includes being respectful, just, and faithful, doing no harm, and benefiting others.*   - *Karen Kitchener*

Scaffolding

The strengths coach can benefit, too, from frequently using an approach to gradual goal accomplishment that is borrowed from the education field, and is called "scaffolding". While this sounds like a tool, it really is a skill, in that the coach needs to frame the dialogue using scaffolding in a very precise and gradual manner. Scaffolding involves the provision of a step-wise and supportive interactive structure, and is especially useful at the outset of coaching, as well as with difficult or challenging themes and topics. It can take the form of a "guided participation," as Lev Vygotsky, the Russian educator, called it.[18] Or, it can be seen as what psychologist Jerome Bruner described as "instinctive structures to aid learning."[19]

Scaffolds are gradual, increasingly challenging and focused actions, a sort of staircase or step-wise approach, with the coach employing supportive processes and instrumental tools to enable the client to a measured development of both reflective skills and real learning. It involves experience-born intuition and a relationship-grounded feel for the particular pace and level of interchange with clients around issues that they struggle to change for the better. It simply entails ratcheting up the level of challenge and reframing over time so the client increasingly is using thoughtful reflection to focus their thinking more sharply. Well-done scaffolding practices are a mainstay in the strengths coaching repertoire, and lead to crisper thinking and clearer decision-making. As the dictionary says, "well-done" in culinary parlance means cooked through or finished to the center—a good analogy for the scaffolding process and its objective for being able to say that coaching was done well.

> **STRONGBOX 5-12**: *Those who trust us, educate us.*   *- George Eliot*

Coach & Coaching Development

Finally, the coach using a strengths approach needs to obtain, use, modify and grow their own repertoire of strengths understandings and information, particularly as the research on positive interventions becomes more exacting and plentiful. This is best done perhaps via a consistent vigilance for such publications, and reading pertinent literature as well as using one's strengths themselves with their clients over time. While I don't recommend this specific practice for emulation by all, I have found a select reading of about two-dozen blogs and list-serves each week to be very helpful and informative. Not surprisingly, for me, many of these share the characteristic of having a positive behavioral bent. With frequent perusal of a number of websites, periodicals, and a couple books a month, I feel better equipped to offer my clients the very best and most contemporary, cutting edge information and research knowledge available, and to which I have been exposed. The range of these is somewhat broad and diverse, both as it reflects my own interests and my wish to be somewhat comprehensive. Niche coaches can tailor their sources more narrowly. These pages of *The Guide*, and especially the previous (mindset) chapter, seek to prime the strengths coach's mental pump, offering a collection of highly applicable advisory perspectives and scholarly summaries that will be both affirming and corrective in places, to aid with better, more up-to-date coaching practice.

Timing

The element of timing for applying a particular skill competency is almost as important as apt use of the skill itself. It is, in fact, often more about knowing when <u>not</u> to intervene, as it is discerning what intervention to use for what particular challenge in the coaching dyad. Often, the pregnant pause is as effective as anything the coach might say, allowing the coachee the space to reflect on their own, without a nudge in any special direction. Then, too, the adept application of a well-chosen skill from among the many in the experienced coach's repertoire is as much a matter of timing as it is good choice of tool or skill. Asking "how and when" is a critical part of the internal dialogue of the coach, and thus the two queries are linked in this chapter because they truly are in practice. Elsewhere in the book I referred to intuition as the offspring of the wisdom that experience alone can give rise to, shape and hone. Much of the "Know-How" spoken of in this section is tempered by the partnered skill of knowing "When" to act in a particular manner to best advance the client's reflection and decision-making goals.

While experience is that proverbial best teacher here, some other initiatives can help carve out a parsimonious path to that wisdom. One is the use of coaching as a tool for the coach him- or herself. By having a coach of one's own, the other side of the coaching exchange can be experienced, even as the topic may be coaching role behavior itself. Some colleagues do this as an exchange of bartered service. Another way to refine the coaching practice and build strengths in doing so is to participate in a small group of peers seeking mutual coaching supervision. In this arrangement, a handful of collegial coaches meet routinely to share their general experience and offer support and peer tutoring to one another, all the while respecting the privacy, confidentiality and anonymity of their clientele. I have not done so for some time, though it was a helpful practice when I was participating in it. Geography has limited opportunity to do so of late. Finally, the most practical and individual approach to building that competency set is ongoing education about both strengths and coaching. When I first started this in the 1980s, there was barely a critical mass of people or scholarship to do either of the last two easily. Today, the professional development opportunities and coaching numbers are both abundant enough to make these practices feasible and affordable. I encourage consideration of all three for enhancing lifelong learning as a coach, as each offers a different platform for improvement.

While there are other skill sets that may be pertinent here, most are derivative of those mentioned in this section, and usually fall outside the basic know-how that the strengths counselor needs and uses in their practice. Next, we turn to the fullest chapter in the book, presenting a variety of activities, tools, uses, and technical applications—the "know what" (to use) for coaching in this model.

STRONGBOX 5-13: Enter every activity without giving mental recognition to the possibility of defeat. Concentrate on your strengths, instead of your weaknesses . . . on your powers, instead of your problems.   - Paul J. Meyer

6

"Know What": Tool Sets

STRONGBOX 6-1: *You can tell whether a person is clever by his answers; you can tell whether he is wise by his questions.* - *Naquib Mahfouz*

Myron contacted me to begin coaching him for the dual shift he was making from East to West Coast, and from a military leadership role to a civilian hospital administrator's post. He had a lengthy history with both MASH units and community medical administration, and wanted to be sure this move, hastened by his spouse's shift to a new job, and probably to his last full time position before retirement, was done "well and right," as he stated. After retiring from the Army as a high-ranking officer, he ended up taking nearly eight months to find and land a job that he felt was suitable for his family and fitting for him. It meant giving up a number of staples in his recent life—a favorite New England location, extended family proximity, friendship and professional networks, and a comfortable home and lifestyle. The coaching we undertook in this period was focused mostly on "transition" as William Bridges calls it: the psychological and social aspects of a physical uprooting and change to a new role. In doing so, we made the lens of strengths a constant in his reframing and reflecting on choices and consequences. In the end, he felt comfortable and confident that the time and effort had been worthwhile, and the coaching felt essential to making his best decision, one he affirmed more than once afterwards, until eventual retirement.

—⚬⚬⚬⚬⚬—

My maternal and namesake grandfather was a *railroad telegrapher* in West Virginia, a job title that is now obsolete, due to the electronic revolution late in the last century. Although I had several days at work with him in my youth, my favorite memories to this day have to do with showing me how he did things for leisure and as do-it-yourself maintenance man around their house—a sprawling seven-bedroom boarding house in a very small town. Those shared tasks—some carpentry, some farming, and recreational interests like fishing and hunting—are cherished recollections and ingrained parts of my limited repertoire of handyman and outdoor skills.

He took particular pride in his tool collection, and in his methodical way of going about a chore, whether a day in the river, shop, or field, even while completing an entire project. Two of my lessons from those times that endure today are contained in a pair of his homespun, mountainside mantras: "Take good care of your tools and they will take good care of you." Also, he told me repeatedly, "The most tedious and yet most important part of a job is the preparation. But, if you get that right, you'll be all set." Numerous other lessons learned "at his knee", so to speak, could be germane to this section of the book, but I want to highlight the applicability of just a few.

The coach who does his or her preparatory work for each individual client and session, and who uses the right approaches and tools at the right moments, stands a better chance of succeeding as a guide for their client. The book contains <u>over forty tools for coaching</u>, with the majority of them in this chapter, all with instructions for their use, including debriefing particulars, and variations for most. Wise use of them might best be directed by a third of Grandpa's favorite recitations to me: "Just because you have a lot of neat things, doesn't mean you should show them all off at once." Astute use of these coaching tools, either to help frame dialogue or assist with self-assessment, is important to all in the role of coach. They are clustered in sets of like approaches, or as variant devices used to attain similar ends. We will start with the preface to a coaching relationship.

COACHING INTEREST & READINESS

Previously, I referenced the following three-part instrument for helping both the coach and the prospective client determine readiness for coaching. Most coach training organizations have similar instruments in their arsenals, although they are usually a bit more focused on logistical preparedness. The three-part form I use is reprinted here as edited from my coaching with strengths website, to illustrate the application of an assessment tool for coachability. Readers are free to use it if they wish, citing its source.

Coaching Possibilities Checklist

1. Put a check mark in front of each of the statements below that you can endorse at this time:

___ I feel I could use some help with my work life or "balance".

___ I have an important, complex project to complete or a deadline to meet.

___ I feel the need to make some positive changes in my lifestyle.

___ I am usually open to reasonable feedback and suggestions.

___ I have benefited from the presence of a coach or mentor in the past.

___ I am a firm believer in my own basic capabilities.

___ I feel I have untapped potential.

___ My foundational outlook on life could be described as one of "abundance," i.e., I feel there really is enough to go around.

___ I compete with my own standards of performance more often than I compete with other people.

___ I feel I am "stuck" or "stagnating" at present.

___ I would like to know more about a strengths mindset and making an appreciative inquiry into my growth and development.

Now, count the number of check marks. If you have 7 or more items checked, you probably ought to go on to complete the Client Survey Form.

Client Survey Form

2. Tell me a little about yourself, and your work, as well as your thoughts about coaching. You can use either a single narrative paragraph or distinct, short answers to the following 7 items:

- A brief personal description of me when at my best reads . . .
- My professional highlights during the past 3 years were . . .
- My present thoughts about being a coaching client include . . .
- My hopes for the next phase of my life include . . .
- My specific desired results for coaching outcomes are . . .
- My questions about coaching and the coach are . . .
- My name, best time and contact data:

3. My Readiness to Begin Coaching at this time is best represented on the chart/ruler below as follows (circle a number):

Not Yet Prepared   Ready to
To Begin   Start

0	1	2	3	4	5	6	7	8	9	10

(Usually, I will help a prospective client who selects a value below 7 on the ruler to identify what is holding them back or has them feeling a bit ambivalent, and then help them progress through the stages to readiness before beginning coaching, assuming they want to pursue it further.)

A number of other coaching tools I have found useful over the years will be examined in the rest of this section, as we look into the "Know what" . . . to use, or Tool Set for strengths coaching. These stimulus devices—whether written, electronically conveyed, or material ones—are mostly methods for creating focused dialogue to further the coaching agenda and conversation. These instruments help create momentary data sets for an extended discussion that uses a common language and framework. Surveys, self-report tools of several kinds, and even reading or behavioral assignments of a wide variety can be brought very beneficially into the strengths coaching process at several points in the relationship. While some of these are built on others' creations, most are of my own devising over the past twenty-plus years. The chapter is set up differently than the foregoing narrative ones: I will introduce serially the activities and tools, say a little about how I use each of them, and often provide a verbatim script and document, outlining its desired effects in the coaching exchange.

STRENGTHS ASSESSMENTS

The most widely used tool in strengths coaching is some sort of strengths assessment, often one of the purchased instruments identified in the beginning of chapter three. The real assets of the strengths assessment tools profiled there are the breadth of measurement, quality and depth of research and assessment, and ease of access they bring to the depiction of strengths. They are well crafted, highly useful and readily available instruments that I recommend to the reader's consideration. As noted earlier, there are currently three main instruments for identifying the primary talents from a range of adult strengths. Those are the VIA full and brief strengths assessments, the Gallup StrengthsFinder 2.0 and StrengthsQuest versions of strengths assessments, and the newer British-born CAPP instrument called Realise2. Web links to them are listed in the EndNotes.

Their major assets include ease of access through the internet, detailed profiling for around $20-(US), and the extensive, comparative global databases and psychometrics underlying them. They are the top of the line in strengths measurement at this time. I have used them all in coaching at various times, and find them to be quite user-friendly, as well as facilitative of coaching dialogue about identified strengths and their descriptions, and they give users access to a number of related resources.

The minor drawbacks of these as I see them are the instruments' costs (for some), and the sometimes limited or variable generation of information about strengths beyond the so-called signature, top 5, or key strengths commonplace in many of the profiles received. Some clients have balked at the length of the instrument, too, citing the dozens of paired comparisons of the StrengthsFinder 2.0, while the VIA assessment is even lengthier. Printouts describe categories denoted mainly by *relative* strength, meaning they are arrayed in descending order of measured strength, and although they do provide a thumbnail sketch of each, it is not clear how to use that information without linking to other resources in their vast library. The Gallup instruments are limited to information about the signature/top 5 only, while their publications do address well the developmental and transactional aspects of using them.

The CAPP printout improves some on the Top Five designation, arraying the long list of strengths in their instrument into categories labeled Realised, and Unrealised (read underused) Strengths, plus somewhat unique to their instrument, Learned Behaviors and Weaknesses. All these devices address the relative strength of each, and provide some detailed explanation of the strengths and their manifestations, as well as some further development prospects. It also has a format for team member assessment.

Some of the same critique applies to the new instrument for assessing dominant or strong preferences for work roles, authored by the Marcus Buckingham folks, and called StandOut. It emphasizes just the top two of the nine possible roles available, adding a third description that is a composite style. It is the most vocationally focused, looking concertedly at work role behaviors and leadership attributes. It, too, has a team assessment format.

Since I (and, I find, most of my clients) like to identify and discriminate among the various types or categories of strengths at hand, I often augment use of these measures with a discussion of the remainder of the strengths, using the concepts identified earlier as the client's subjective rendering of Primary/Lead ones, and Auxiliary, Complementary and Contextual strengths, in addition to those that are measured as highest and sometimes also the lowest.

A modified strengths self-assessment tool using a version of the VIA character traits follows. It uses both rating and ranking activities, and enables the full complement of strengths to be viewed and their relative priority assessed and appreciated by the taker. Evidence for the validity, reliability and salience of such a self-assessment is substantial. As Marcus Buckingham says repeatedly in his presentations, we are each the best expert about what our particular strengths are.[1] This expanded and modified "Strengths Self-Rating Scale" is reprinted here below with author permission, along with some suggestions for using it in coaching.

SELF-ASSESSMENT OF CHARACTER STRENGTHS

Jonathan Haidt, the University of Virginia 'wisdom' scholar, has created a short self-scoring scalar variant of the VIA measure, and, with his permission, I have modified it further to accommodate a new typological framework.[2] It is usable as a supplemental or even substitute instrument for an early coaching discussion, and it works well to address some of the reporting weaknesses appraised above, but has not been psychometrically validated in any way beyond the original twenty-four strengths instrument created by Peterson and Seligman, from which it is derived.

My clients often wish to pore over the range of rankings and the remaining strength categories, and this format enables those conversations. It also assists with moving beyond a minimal awareness of top strengths to deepen understanding and development of them, and to explore others in the set. This obviously takes more than one conversation, and I recommend that it be spread out over a few weeks and sessions, making it a topic for a portion of the expected declaration each time, with occasional reference to these findings as appropriate throughout the course of the coaching relationship. The self-rating instrument appears first, and then a ranking and summary form with interpretive cues follows.

Strengths Self-Rating Scale

(From Haidt, 2006, as adapted from Peterson & Seligman, 2002)[3]

Part One: Everyone has a characteristic set of strengths, that is, things that they excel at or are "strong" in, and that strengthen them in use. Research suggests that there are currently 24 common strengths recognized cross-culturally. As you read the descriptions in the boxes, use the following 7-point scale to *rate them as your relative strengths*. Be honest with yourself. This part will take less than 10 minutes.

7 = describes me <u>all the time</u>   **3** = me only <u>some of the time</u>
6 = <u>very frequently</u> me   **2** = <u>rarely</u> me
5 = <u>often</u> me   **1** = <u>not ever</u> me
4 = <u>occasionally</u> me

Strength	Description
Curiosity Rating____	You are curious about the world and you strongly desire experience of it. You are flexible about matters that don't fit your preconceptions. Curious people do not simply tolerate ambiguity but they like it and are intrigued by it. You seek out novelty, and you are rarely bored.
Love of Learning Rating____	You love learning new things, whether you are in a class or on your own. You always loved school, reading, museums—anywhere and everywhere there is an opportunity to learn. There are domains of knowledge in which you are the expert, and others value your expertise. You love learning about these domains, even in the absence of any external incentives to do so.

Judgment Rating_____	You think things through and examine them from all sides. You do not jump to conclusions, and you rely only on solid evidence to make your decisions. You are able to change your mind. You are very good at sifting information objectively and rationally, in the service of the good for yourself and others. You do NOT just think in ways that favor and confirm what you already believe.
Ingenuity Rating_____	When you are faced with something you want, you are outstanding at finding novel yet appropriate behavior to reach that goal. You are rarely content with doing something the conventional way. This strength is also called "practical intelligence" or more bluntly common sense or street smarts.
Socioemotional Intelligence Rating_____	You are aware of the motives and feelings of others, and of yourself, and you can respond skillfully. You notice differences among others, especially with respect to their moods, temperaments, motivations, and intentions, and then you <u>act</u> upon these distinctions. You also have finely tuned access to your own feelings and the ability to use that knowledge to understand and guide your behavior.
Perspective Rating_____	You have a way of looking at the world that makes sense to others and yourself. Others seek you out to draw on your experience, and you are often able to help them solve problems and gain perspective. You have a good sense of what is really important in life.
Valor Rating_____	You do not shrink from threat, challenge, pain, or difficulty. Valor is more than bravery during physical threat. It refers as well to intellectual or emotional stances that are unpopular, difficult, or dangerous. The brave person is able to uncouple the emotional and behavioral components of fear, resisting the urge to flee and facing the fearful situation. Fearlessness, boldness, and rashness are not valor; it is facing danger, despite fear, that marks valor.

Perseverance Rating_____	You finish what you start. You take on difficult projects and finish them, usually with good cheer and minimal complaint. You do what you say you will do and sometimes more, never less. Perseverance does not mean dogged or obsessive pursuit of unattainable goals. Rather, you remain flexible, realistic, and not perfectionistic.
Integrity Rating_____	You are an honest person, not only always speaking the truth but also living your life in a genuine and authentic way. You are down to earth and without pretense. You represent your intentions and commitments to others and to yourself in sincere fashion, whether by word or deed.
Kindness Rating_____	You are kind and generous to others, and you are never too busy to do a favor. You enjoy doing good deeds for others, even if you do not know them well. Your actions are very often guided by other people's best interests, even when these override your own immediate wishes and needs.
Loving Rating_____	You value close and intimate relations with others. You have deep and sustained feelings for others, who feel the same way about you. This strength is more than the Western notion of romance; it is about very deep ties to several or many people.
Citizenship Rating_____	You excel as a member of a group. You are a loyal and dedicated teammate, you always do your share, and you work hard for the success of the group. You value the group goals and purposes even when they differ from your own. You respect those who are rightfully in positions of authority, like teachers or coaches, and you identify with the group.
Humor Rating_____	You like to laugh and bring smiles to other people. You can easily see the light side of life. You are playful and funny.

Fairness Rating_____	You do not let your personal feelings bias your decisions about other people. You give everyone a chance. You are guided in your day-to-day actions by larger principles of morality. You take the welfare of others, even those you do not know personally, as seriously as your own, and you can easily set aside personal prejudices.
Leadership Rating_____	You do a good job organizing activities and seeing to it that they happen. You are a humane and effective leader, attending to getting the group's work done at the same time as maintaining good relations among group members. You are additionally humane when you handle between group relations "with malice toward none and charity toward all."
Self-control Rating_____	You can easily hold your desires, needs, and impulses in check when it is appropriate. It is not enough to know what is correct; you must also be able to put this knowledge into action. When something bad happens, you can regulate your own emotions. You can repair and neutralize your negative feelings, and generate positive emotions on your own.
Prudence Rating_____	You are a careful person. You do not say or do things you might later regret. You wait until all the votes are in before embarking on a course of action. You are far-sighted and deliberative. You are good at resisting impulses about short-term goals for the sake of long-term success.
Humility Rating_____	You do not seek the spotlight, preferring to let your accomplishments speak for themselves. You do not regard yourself as special, and others recognize and value your modesty. You are unpretentious. You see your own aspirations, victories and defeats as pretty unimportant in the larger scheme of things.

Appreciation Rating_____	You stop and smell the roses. You appreciate beauty, excellence, and skill in all domains: nature, the arts, science, and the wide range of abilities that other people possess. You often see or hear things that cause you to feel profound feelings of awe and wonder.
Gratitude Rating_____	You are aware of the good things that happen to you, and you never take them for granted. You always take the time to express your thanks. Gratitude is a reflection on someone else's excellence in moral character. We are grateful when people do well by us, but we can also be more generally grateful for good acts and good people. Gratitude can also be directed toward impersonal and nonhuman sources—God, nature, life—but it cannot be directed toward the self.
Hope Rating_____	You expect the best in the future, and you plan and work in order to achieve it. Hope, optimism, and future-mindedness are a family of strengths that represent a positive stance toward the future. Expecting that good events will occur, feeling that these will ensue if you try hard, and planning for the future sustain good cheer in the here-and-now and galvanize a goal-directed life.
Spirituality Rating_____	You have strong and coherent beliefs about the higher purpose and meaning of the universe. You know where you fit in the larger scheme. Your beliefs shape your actions and are a source of comfort to you. You have an articulated philosophy of life, religious or secular, that locates your being in the larger universe. Life has meaning for you by virtue of attachment to something larger than yourself.
Zest Rating_____	You are a spirited person. You throw yourself body and soul into the activities you undertake. You wake up in the morning looking forward to the day. The passion that you bring to activities is infectious.

Forgiveness Rating_____	You forgive those who have done you wrong. You always give people a second chance. Your guiding principle is mercy and not revenge. Forgiveness represents a set of prosocial changes that occur within an individual who has been offended or hurt by someone else. When people forgive, their motivations and actions regarding the transgressor become more positive (e.g., benevolent, kind, generous) and less negative (e.g., vengeful, avoidant).

Part Two: Categorizing and Ranking Strengths for Understanding & Use

1. First, transfer your strengths above to the appropriate sections below (not all lines will be used).
2. Then, go back through each section, and attempt to rank order them within the section, except for the *Not My Strengths* section. Write the number of the rank order in the parenthesis after listing. This part will take about 5-7 minutes.

7s or Primary/Lead Strengths: Those I use to function at my best & build my capacity to excel.

_____ ( ) _____ ( ) _____ ( )
_____ ( ) _____ ( ) _____ ( )

6s or Auxiliary Strengths: Those I use to fortify my primary talents and abilities.

_____ ( ) _____ ( ) _____ ( )
_____ ( ) _____ ( ) _____ ( )
_____ ( ) _____ ( ) _____ ( )

5s, 4s, & 3s or Complementary Strengths: Those I use to balance and complete how I function; **and Contextual Strengths:** Those I draw on only in certain, infrequent situations.

5s		**4s**		**3s**	
——————	( )	——————	( )	——————	( )
——————	( )	——————	( )	——————	( )
——————	( )	——————	( )	——————	( )
——————	( )	——————	( )	——————	( )
——————	( )	——————	( )	——————	( )

2s & 1s or Not My Strengths: Those I <u>rarely</u> call on <u>or never</u> find expression.

——————	( )	——————	( )	——————	( )
——————	( )	——————	( )	——————	( )

———————

The original, longer and more complete version of this test can be taken without cost at the authentic happiness website at the University of Pennsylvania: http://<u>www.authentichappiness.org</u>, or see Seligman's new book *Flourish* (2011).[3]

For more information about strengths, happiness, virtues, wisdom, and flourishing, see Jonathan Haidt's website at http://<u>www.happinesshypothesis.com</u>.

I AM . . .

A very different, quick and easy way to begin to identify and talk about a client's strengths is the tool below, which can also be used in a group or team context. Although I use this when in front of a group more often than with a single coaching client, I usually probe somewhat extensively with an individual when using this format. As I am trying to get her/him to elaborate on meanings, uses, and relationships among the defined strengths, I do this early on in the coaching relationship. Have participants write large, filling the page, if showing it to others.

I AM . . .

Write the letters of your preferred first name down the left side of this, or a blank sheet, in a vertical column. Then, identify <u>one</u> of your current self-assessed *strengths* <u>for each letter</u>. Share those attributes, talents, or assets with your coach, saying more about each one chosen. (Or, in a small group exercise, go around the room till all have had their say—*sample below*).

G rateful	( )
E thical	( )
N onjudgmental	( )
E nergetic	( )

Sometimes I also ask them to finish by ranking them in the brackets to the right, so that the very best of those can be surfaced as well, and then further sharing and discussion can take place.

NARRATIVE STRENGTHS ASSESSMENT

As coaching uses the medium of constructed narrative as a major tool, another way I gather baseline input about my client's strengths is through use of an uncomplicated, generative strengths interview format. Here the client tells the coach what s/he views as their strongest attributes, using a story-telling approach and a format like the following stem questions, augmented throughout with appropriate probes for details. I always appreciate it when people share their stories—descriptions of how they have come to acknowledge their assets, the talents that are most constant, and those that help them feel most capable of excelling.

1. "Let's start with you identifying a handful of personal traits that you value: What are a couple adjectives you'd say capture your very best traits, and tell me why you feel they describe you well?"
2. "What would others say about you from having experienced you at your best interpersonally?"
3. "Could I hear about what events or people have been the strongest positive influences on you and your acquired beliefs, and how that came about?"
4. "Lastly, could you comment on how you view strengths operating in your life generally, and how you use them specifically when feeling challenged?"

This leads to a very satisfactory beginning personal narrative description of how they perceive their assets and the origins of them, plus their contextual awareness and usage, and does so in less than an hour. For a few of my coachees, it is preferable to an instrumental measurement, and still an effective way of getting at some baseline strengths information with which to conduct further coaching.

STRENGTHS QUESTION DOMAINS

Another framework for early inquiry and strengths assessment with a client uses Dennis Saleebey's "Question Domains for Strengths Helping" taken from his latest (2009) Social Work text.[4] The eight of them are listed here with my interpretation and suggested alternative application of queries for your consideration. This format and these eight domains offer another fertile and comprehensive range of focused questions useful in helping clients assess their strengths through self-inquiry and narrative responses.

POSSIBILITY ?S

What are your hopes and aspirations? What is your personal vision for the future? What specific actions are you taking to realize those these days? In what ways can I/coaching assist you in that quest?

PERSPECTIVE ?S—

What are the lenses you use for viewing your world and the situations, issues and challenges you face? How do you make choices in life? . . . at work? What are the ways you make sense and meaning of your experiences?

CHANGE ?S—

How do you approach the prospect of change? How do you undertake desired changes and transitions? What are your personal lessons about accommodating change? What changes would you like to make for yourself right now?

MEANING ?S—

Can you identify your primary values in life? What are the most prized beliefs you hold? Can you identify where they come or came from? How do you let others know you cherish them?

SUPPORT ?S—

What activities and people in your life provide needed support? How do they do so? Are there groups or organizations you are part of that reinforce & reward you?

ESTEEM ?S—

If our self-regard comes from how we and others regard us, what feedback do you and receive, and how do you view yourself? What are your own sources of pleasure, joy and pride? What matters most to you and why?

EXCEPTION ?S—

What makes a crucial difference in your life, especially when things are at their best? What is special about those times and you in them? How do you go about finding (more of) that?

SURVIVAL ?S—

What have your struggles in life taught you about yourself, relationships and living in general? What particular strengths have come from surviving and perhaps even thriving in the face of seeming adversity?

I use these sometimes in series, or in a modified sequence to help explore the range of strengths and their sources or applications with a client. The full set is a very comprehensive complement of inquiries for a full rendering of the key lines of self-assessment and strengths identification. It can be used in part or full, and usually works best when employed over time. Most often, I begin with the MEANING or PERSPECTIVE questions, and let the flow of the dialogue help dictate the direction to pursue thereafter with the rest of the question categories. A number of my clients have found this was a useful complement to an instrumental approach.

TRIPLE AAs

Two other shorthand tools I sometimes use with clients beyond initial self-assessment of strengths are made more memorable by their identical mnemonic label, each a cycle of what I call the 'Triple AAs'. The first was inspired initially in 1998, and then again in 2006, by seeing the Centers for Creative Leadership sequence for working with their clients.[5] The entry point for this is an *Aware Assessment* of the client vis-à-vis the issue in focus, usually some issue of attitude, perspective or skill application in a work role and relationship. This "data" & feedback is then used to derive an *Abundant Analysis*, that is, a thoughtful and probing, yet appreciative examination of the data in context, and its meanings for the client's desired change. This then leads to an *Adept Application*, meaning an experiment with coaching support into how the changes called for will play out, and what the client's experience is. That leads to a re-cycling of the same three processes using the new data about the application. In some ways, it is an abbreviation of the 7-D model, but with far less comprehensive assessment of the situation that prompted the issue, and mostly focused on the data generated as feedback.

The second tool using that Triple AA label for recall has to do with a mantra-like recitation, a practical, personal mission statement I wrote some time ago to help with my own outlook and acting in concert with seeing the positive. It goes like this: "I Anticipate Abundance, Appreciate All, and Act on my Assets." I regularly share it with coachees, and we discuss those three couplets' meanings, and their reaction to it as an overall purpose statement and guiding personal mission. Each of these is an encouraging nudge to the client to use a lens of strengths rather than deficits for seeing their world, its occupants and life's situational challenges. It urges the selection of actions that mirror the positive, that draw on our very best in response, no matter the context.

DEEPENING THE STRENGTHS DISCUSSION

Another tool to explore with a client harnesses the related processes of *Mining, Assaying and Lod(e)ing*—all references to the richness of optimal performance and strengths usage. I refer to them collectively as "mining." These three related paths to asset enrichment are described thus:

Mining is the process of a coach and coachee together digging deeper in dialogue to identify strengths more clearly, and to fully appreciate how they came to be, how they have been maintained, sustained, and used. Inquiry stems for this process could include "Tell me about how you recall your _____ strength has come about." Or, you might try, for example, "What is an example of how you find yourself using this _____ strength routinely?"

The Assaying tactic calls for the client to have some directed dialogue that subjectively "weighs" both the perceived "relative and absolute" values of those primary, signature, lead or key strengths—however designated, as discerned by the client. Some strengths are more fully realized than others, and some are more frequently used, while still other times see variant strengths more suitably applied. The discussion teases out those points and realizations. Inquiry stems here might include such as "Could you describe for me how you came to regard these top strengths as you do; in your mind, what makes them represent you at your best?" I might also try "Given these primary strengths you've identified as your major assets, what distinguishes them from one another in terms of their relative primacy or order, and why do you feel that is so?"

Finally, in a neologism called *Lodeing,* the compounding of certain strengths in bundles of two, three or more related themes, can be the basis of a helpful dialogue. I use this for greater understanding of how lead or primary strengths can be augmented by others—usually those identified as auxiliary, complementary or contextual ones. *Lodeing* is creating awareness and making actual use of a mutually potentiating admixture of those—a lode or cache of strength, and it can be a terrific lever for enriching the client's abilities to excel. Possible ways of getting at this feature would include asking "How do you see your combination of strengths complementing one another?" Or, perhaps ask "What two strengths you've identified as your Lead ones might work well together to bolster one another, and how have you seen that play out at work or elsewhere?" One client from the electronics industry told me he came to think of these as the opposite of his more familiar power "surge protectors." He called them "surge promoters," suggesting a desire to bring more strength to the topic at hand, rather than prevent a loss of power. These three inquiry directions make a nice trio of dialogue starters for a conversation with the client about deepening strengths.

STRENGTHS SPOTTING

This notion of spotting the strengths of others is widely promoted among those writing about strengths and positive approaches to living and relating. Shane Lopez, and the trio of AI scholars that wrote *Appreciative Leadership* have made specific suggestions for doing so, with Alex Linley's CAPP even having a twenty-item test for assessing how well you assay yourself or others at their best, plus a list of tips for doing so better.[6] All of this is in the name of improving relationships and productivity, helping join with and simultaneously release others to manifest their strengths. The tool below is another framework for doing so, whether for oneself or another, perhaps a co-worker or supervisee.

One of the most frequently used figures or forms in all of education and training is the 4-cell matrix, the so-called 2 X 2 windowpane. To use this version of such a simple tool for strengths spotting, we just need to appreciate the Hi and Lo aspects of both usage and opportunity for employing personal strengths. The resulting four quadrants or areas of comparison are labeled as follows:

"Q1: Sweet Spot," a narrow place referring to the combination of HI strengths usage with LO opportunity, reflecting a maximum use with minimal opportunity, a real achievement against odds and unfavorable circumstance.

"Q2: Spot-On," for the British phrase that colloquially means exactly right or just so, reflecting an ideal combination of HI use and HI opportunity for strengths application.

"Q3: On-the-Spot," consistent with the idea that people unable to find either ready opportunity (LO), or easy usage (LO) of their strengths are at a real disadvantage in both relating and performing.

"Q4: Blind Spot," for the situation of unrealized or LO strengths usage, despite a perceived HI level of opportunity.

```
HI          ┌─────────────────────────────┐
            │    STRENGTHS SPOTTING       │
            └─────────────────────────────┘

            Q1: SWEET SPOT              Q2: SPOT-ON
    U

    S

    A

    G       Q3: ON-THE-SPOT            Q4: BLIND SPOT

    E


        LO          OPPORTUNITY          HI
```

There are (at least) three distinct ways of strengths spotting with this tool. One is by having the client simply identify which of the four quadrants best represents his or her perceived situation at present in any domain—personal, social or business life. Then a coaching conversation about that can proceed, identifying the causal elements and prospective remedies for that using self-knowledge from the relative strong areas or attributes available to do so.

A second strategy would be to use the device as a set of "boxes" within which the client can distribute their strengths of any type: lead, auxiliary, complementary, and contextual ones. The conversation from that four-cell assignment of strengths can provide both insight and direction for the coachee.

A third way of strengths spotting using the matrix is to do either of the first two applications for another, say a partner, follower or co-worker.

Attending to the strengths one has, and their use, as well as the opportunities one can muster for better, more apt usage is an important part of learning to identify and play to one's very best characteristics. This tool is one of several herein to aid with that task.

STRENGTHS INDEX

Another tool I use for helping clients to appreciate how well they are accessing and employing their best assets, their real strengths, in the work setting is the Strengths Index. It is a simple measure that calibrates the relative *utility* and *opportunity* frequencies that a person has for their current work experience. Once completed, the coach can use the findings to guide a discussion about how to increase usage and optimize opportunity for strengths deployment on the job. Directions for it follow:

Complete the self-assessment below and use the several interpretive questions that follow to understand better how you employ strengths in the work setting. This activity presumes you have some knowledge of what your particular key or lead strengths are.

Answer the following three questions about your Usage of strengths:

A. The approximate percentage of time in a typical day that I really Use my strengths currently is . . .
    1. <20%   2. 20 - 39%   3. 40 - 59%   4. >60%
B. The number of my top strengths I use daily is . . .
    1. 0-1   2. 2-3   3. 4-5   4. 6+
C. The percentage of my weaknesses that I use in an average work day is:
    1. >80%   2. 60-79%   3. 40 - 59%   4. <40%
Then sum the numbers in front of those three circled answers; total = _____.
Next, answer the following 3 items about your strengths Opportunities:
A. My supervisor <u>knows</u> my top strengths . . .
    1. Not at all   2. A little bit   3. Somewhat   4. Very well
B. My supervisor <u>assigns/delegates</u> to me in alignment with those top strengths _____% of the time.
    1. <20% 2.   20-39%   3. 40-59%   4. >60%
C. I <u>ask for</u> work in line with my strengths . . .
    1. Rarely   2. Occasionally 3. Usually   4. Always

Now sum the numbers in front of the second three answers; total = _____

Calculating your Strengths Index Scores: SU X SO = SI, i.e. Strengths Usage <u>times</u> Strengths Opportunity = current <u>Strengths Index.</u>

Place the scores here:

Strengths Usage Sum = _____ & Strengths Opportunity Sum = _____.

Now multiply the two sums to get their product total: _____. This is your <u>*Strengths Index,*</u> *and is the main number we are looking at below. You should also note* <u>*the Differential*</u> *by subtracting the Opportunity score from the Usage score, which may yield a negative number: _____.*

Your Strengths Index represents a combination of <u>*opportunity given*</u> *and* <u>*actual usage or opportunity taken*</u> *to work with your strengths currently. The table below indicates the relative valences and interpretative labels for the Index scores that range from 9 to 144, and are arrayed in five groupings, thus:*

Index =>	*< 36*	*36-59*	*60-80*	*81-100*	*101-144*
Rating =>	*Very Low*	*Low*	*Average*	*High*	*Very High*

Scores on each subset can be regarded in the following ways:

1. If they are equal and high, celebrate your terrific work situation!
2. If they are equal and low, both you and your boss need to consider the gains to be had from increasing Usage via increased Opportunity for strengths employment.
3. If Usage is higher than Opportunity, have a conversation with your supervisor about expanding Opportunity, and explore the ways you might seek more of a matched alignment of strengths and assignments, i.e. of your unique talents with your initiatives and delegated tasks.
4. If Opportunity is higher than Usage, work on your own ability to both deepen and expand your strengths usage; you're in a good position to do so.
5. Generally, if there is a Differential, it is a better situation for the Usage score to be higher than the Opportunity score, compared to the reverse.

Take note of the number of times you cited each score, i.e., the number of 1s through 4s, and seek to understand better what contributed to the higher, more favorable scores. Use that to appreciate how you might focus your efforts to enhance those particular strengths, as well as to augment them with auxiliary, complementary or contextual ones.

These two aspects of accessing strengths in the workplace—*usage* and *opportunity*—are not just idle, secondary features of strengths employment. Correlates of higher strengths usage include greater confidence and contentment, lower felt stress/greater hardiness, higher engagement levels and goal attainment on the job, and superior performance, as well as personal development.[7] So, identifying and pursuing greater opportunities for usage of one's strengths at work have real potential for positive outcomes in many ways that can benefit both employee and employer, worker and team, individual and organization.

POWERING UP!

Related to those assessments of strengths above is the following self- or coach-guided inquiry that is also a prod toward enhancement and expansion of one's strengths complement. It could be considered a form of strengths spotting with oneself. The following device emerged from some similar coaching experiences I had over a number of weeks one winter a few years back. I came to note that more than a couple coachees were struggling either to see their own strengths clearly, or to identify which ones were most deeply felt and frequently used. Identifying the standout items in our own pool of potency from which we draw power can be a very meaningful activity. The emphasis here is on finding that which truly moves, enables and excites us to action, in other terms, finding our sources of "up!" These are the ideas or thoughts, acquired through acute self-awareness or ingrained habit that propel us to action. It includes those beliefs and values that push us from within to do our very best by playing to our very strongest selves. It involves a simple set of seven interrogatives that read thus:

1. What is it that gets me off my seat, impelled to doing something about that which matters most to me?

2. What is it that feels exciting, firing off my neurons in ways that cannot be ignored, as I contemplate ways of being and doing that resonate most soundly?

3. What is it that I recurrently remark about to others, that I am nearly eloquent in my passionate pursuit of, and my dedication to, at least conversationally?

4. What is it that stirs me to feel most energized, stirred with eagerness, enthusiasm and drive to undertake?

5. What is it that I sense is me at my most engaged, i.e., attached to, and connected with? (Could be a task, a behavior, a thought, a cause, etc.).

6. What is it that I feel a steadfast, persistent dedication to as a desired outcome for my life at work, at home, in the community?

7. What is it that might cause me to smile, hearing others extol as my strongest suits, those things that are identified with me at my best?

Following a brief compilation of responses to these, several things can be more readily observed to help the client to "Power Up!" For one, the repeated identification of the same or similar things across the seven queries may be a clear sign of a deeply felt strength. For some, it may also represent reinforcement or affirmation of certain talents. Clients also have reported clearer realization of the opposite aspects of themselves through this activity, surfacing those attributes that are not strengths, or may indeed be weaknesses. Another notable gain would be a finding that there could be a real disconnection with one's activities in light of the strengths culled from the seven areas of introspection. Finally, clients doing this activity often recognize their preferred styles of learning, of accommodating change, and of investing in what really counts, both at the moment and over their lifespan. It frequently serves to catalyze clients' efforts to align their actions and roles with those strengths, and to help them achieve breakthrough shifts toward greater strengths usage and opportunity-seeking.

THE 4 Es FOR CHANGE

Similar to that tool in use, but differing in framework, is the "4 Es for Change," a sequential format for helping a client undertake a cycle of planned change using an experimental approach. The first E calls for *Examining* the change issue and context together, followed by *Exploring* possible applications of alternate behaviors, then doing some well-considered *Experimenting*, and finally, *Evaluating* the entire experience. This is similar to a basic problem-solving format, yet differs in that I use a variant of the U.S. Army's classic "After Action Review" process at the end.[8] This is a procedure for examining what the goal was, what actually happened vs. what was intended, what caused that outcome, and how might improvement be achieved next time.

This prototypical model has been around for nearly thirty years and has seen wide application. Its roots go back over a half century to Edward Deming and Joseph Juran's introduction of the Total Quality Movement (TQM), first popularized in Japanese manufacturing settings post-WWII.[9] The difference in the use of it here is that we shift focus critically, to identify the positive elements and drill beneath those aspects to understand what led to success. Then those lessons are discussed as a way of finding the building blocks of affirmative behavior. In their recent book on *Appreciative Leadership*, Whitney and her co-authors describe a similar strategy they call "root-cause-of-success analysis."[10] It is a fundamental approach to understanding what went right and why, and how to do more of that, to paraphrase the After Action Review's core questions. It can be a powerful tool for gleaning insight for coaching both individuals and teams or groups.

THE FIVE "WHYS?"

Related to the 4 Es is this variant of a tool originally devised by a Toyota engineer in the 1980s to ensure thorough analysis of design problems in automobile manufacturing. The original simply asks for at least five consecutive, deepening levels of inquiry as to why a problem or issue has occurred. An example follows:

My ATM (automated teller machine) card isn't functioning (issue or problem).

Why . . . might it not function? *Magnetic strip is not being read.* (1st response).

Why . . . does a magnetic strip become unusable? *It has somehow become demagnetized.* (2nd response).

Why . . . could its place in my wallet affect its usability? *It is near other magnetic cards.* (3rd response).

Why . . . might another smart card affect it? *One magnetic strip may alter another.* (4th response).

Why . . . does my office door access card erase the ATM stripe's data? *Their proximity causes one to demagnetize the other.* (5th response, a probable root cause).

Therefore, I probably need to get my ATM card replaced or renewed, and store it away from another smart card hereafter (solution or conclusion).

An Appreciative Alternative: While that is a useful and often very effective problem analysis procedure, it seems a bit limited. Instead of solely using it to analyze a problem situation at five levels of inquiry, consider turning the focus to a series of reframed "why" queries that examines <u>the root causes of success</u>. This can be done with a positive situation or outcome, perhaps a problem solved, or a project that succeeded. This approach can enable all involved to appreciate better and to replicate the process elements that enabled that success. Try it below with a recent situational example of your own:

Issue successfully resolved:

1st "why" response:

2nd:

3rd:

4th:

5th:

Conclusion:

This exercise of a multi-tier analysis of the roots of a successful effort can yield insight on several levels: First, it can help the client to appreciate the necessity for avoiding superficial acceptance of surface answers to questions. Next, it can assist in cultivating a habit of analyzing at nearly a half dozen levels of possibility. Third, it offers a deeper understanding of how and why different successful elements of a process contribute to its desired outcome, or perhaps even better. Bob Laliberte of Innovation Partners International has written of a more formal and extensive approach to this same kind of analysis, and details its steps and the gains to be had from use of it as a variation on the Five Whys. It employs a framework based in Appreciative Inquiry, seeking what works best and how to apply it.[11] He does so with a full team, using a four-step process moving from reframing on through Kim Cameron's notion of "positive deviance," and then designing improvements in all areas, and finally, to implementing and analyzing the results, all using a dedicated team endeavor.[12] He calls it "Success Cause Analysis," and notes that it is both more expedient and broader in scope, lending additional insights not typically found in root cause analytic efforts, and handles complexity particularly well. A form of the same strategy is also recommended in the oft-cited (here) *Appreciative Leadership*.[13]

OUR FIVE NONPHYSICAL SENSES

The traditional learning we all experience as kids about our Five Senses provides good lessons for the physical part of our functioning. A cardiologist, Scott J. Deron, wrote about a similar notion in his 2004 book about heart health, titled *C-Reactive Protein*.[14] Below is my own revised list of *the 5 most important senses* for our psyche and our spiritual selves—the aspects of us that we really need to grasp in order to feel we are fully functioning, thriving, and living abundantly. They are in no particular order, as their relative rank or importance will vary at different times, and differ from one of us to any other. Take stock of your own "sensorium" as follows, using the chart provided after reading about them below:

Sense of Purpose—This idea of a clear and motivating personal mission, what Stephen R. Covey says is a necessary part of an inside-out approach to effective leadership, is also linked with longevity by a number of gerontologists, especially for those no longer partnered.

Sense of Awe—This sense is an appreciation of the wonder of creation, of people's ideas and courage. Others' compassion and dedication can serve as both model and motivator. It includes an embrace of the esthetics of the cosmos, the spectacular aspects of the daily, and the "taken-for-granted," that can be even more powerful than a regard for that which society might view as extraordinary!

Sense of Perspective—This is a realization that we are all in a "social sandwich"—people on both/all sides to whom we are accountable, and that there really is a graded order to things in the universe, and to what we experience. This sense is that device by which we find our true place in the world near and far, and the "correct" place of events on our emotional appraisal scale. Abraham Maslow wrote of this as requiring at least a modicum of age-borne experience beyond our youthful adventures.

Sense of Humor—This entails finding the light amid the heavy, the funny alongside the serious, and most of all—having the ability to laugh at oneself routinely, to plumb for one's deeper humanity and one's own foibles. This sense, as the credit card company ad says, is *priceless*!

Sense of Self—Last, but hardly the least, is the 'vessel' wherein the other four reside—our own self-regard and appreciation for the entire package of our "selves." This is the composite sense of what we are about, how we view the world, where we look to assess its meaning. It sources what keeps us vital and flourishing, and capable of knowing what we could do at all times in order to be true to the rest . . . fully in tune with all our senses!

The chart below is in a format that simultaneously allows for assessing how valued each sense is in one's life at present, and how much it is felt to be in play, active and thriving at this time. The differences, i.e., the distance linearly between the numbers assigned to each, help visually expose the variances between them as well as their individual value and felt vitality. Minimal filled space in the center of each bar is seen graphically as ideal. This is a worthwhile tool for a discussion in a later coaching session, after the coach and client have gotten to know one another better, and when it fits within the client's agenda.

Sensory Self-Assessment

Assess these "Five Senses" using the bars below, where 7 is high, 1 is low. Write the number in the box under it that best describes your **value** of that sense, and then again, indicate your appraisal of the level of that sense's current activation or **vitality** in your daily life. Then darken the space between those two assessments for each 'Sense'. Small, i.e. narrow, and centered darkened spaces are ideal, depicting both high value <u>and</u> high vitality.

Example

Value   **Vitality**

| 1 | 2 | 3 | 4 | 5 | 6 | 7 | 6 | 5 | 4 | 3 | 2 | 1 |

5XXXXXXXXXXXXXXXXXXXXXX3

Sense of Purpose

Value   **Vitality**

| 1 | 2 | 3 | 4 | 5 | 6 | 7 | 6 | 5 | 4 | 3 | 2 | 1 |

Sense of Awe

Value   **Vitality**

| 1 | 2 | 3 | 4 | 5 | 6 | 7 | 6 | 5 | 4 | 3 | 2 | 1 |

Sense of Perspective

Value   **Vitality**

| 1 | 2 | 3 | 4 | 5 | 6 | 7 | 6 | 5 | 4 | 3 | 2 | 1 |

Sense of Humor

Value   **Vitality**

| 1 | 2 | 3 | 4 | 5 | 6 | 7 | 6 | 5 | 4 | 3 | 2 | 1 |

Sense of Self

Value											Vitality
1	2	3	4	5	6	7	6	5	4	3	2	1

Cueing Tools

The items that follow are of a similar fashion to one another. They are what I refer to as "Cueing" tools, in that they offer the coach simple, yet diverse descriptive sets of cue letters and words for the extended coaching dialogue. In particular, they enable the client to look at words that hint at expanding their own strengths and their views of them.

DESCRIBING MY STAR

I have put the acronym *STAR*—the 4-pointed, not 5-tipped variety—to use for some time now in discussing the various elements of positivity and personal faculties with clients. The activity using this tool calls for a dialogue where the coach conducts a series of inquiries framed by the notion of "filling in the blanks," or narrating as s/he describes the four elements of the acronym *STAR* below. Queries can be made using the meanings of the terms, having the client elaborate on each in turn.

The S is for Strengths, which are the empowering personal features one has developed to a high level, and they include both viewpoint and a positive propensity. What are 1 or 2 of your perceived personal or professional strengths? Would your closest associates agree or cite others?

The T is for Talents, the capabilities and skills one possesses as a complement of inherited and developed abilities, and which often originate from genetics and/or social habituation. What 1 or 2 of these do you feel are your particular talents and how do you recognize them?

The A refers to Assets, one's special enabling characteristics, including facility with certain 'tools', such as electronic, oratorical, musical, artistic, or mechanical ones. What are your capabilities in this regard? How did they come about?

Finally, the R refers to <u>Resources</u> that are available to a person, such as economic means or physical access to particular material goods. What are your particular resources and how do you maintain them?

This can lead to a number of insights and help focus further inquiry, as well as facilitate a greater appreciation of the unique assets the client possesses and prizes. It is a worthwhile template for an early self-discovery conversation in the coaching relationship. Most of the time, I reinforce this with another, usually more instrumental assessment of strengths at another point in the relationship.

EMPOWERing WITH STRENGTHS

One of the more important aids for the strengths-coached client is the ability to help her/him deepen their knowledge and use of their Primary or Lead strengths. The approach outlined below may be of some help with this objective. It is a seven-step process for opening up or liberating both their awareness and available concrete opportunities to further strengths engagement. It is called *EMPOWER*, and each letter of the acronym stands for the beginning letter of this portal for deepening strengths identification and implementation. This process tool assumes an initial determination of strengths has already been made.

E is for Excavating—This letter activity calls for the coach to assist the client to "dig" deeper in understanding his/her strengths through a collaborative probing of their measured or self-described strengths. This includes more expansive description of those strengths and their applications and impacts. Asking close colleagues and friends to offer feedback and appraisal of one's strengths is an easy and reliable way to begin this.

M is for Maximizing—Another approach to deepening strengths is to focus on how the client can enlarge their use of lead strengths in <u>all</u> the role settings of their life. Maximizing involves seeking out better uses of their top talents and knowhow. An experiment worth trying here is to use strengths to push the boundaries of usual activities at work, perhaps with a short trial of a voluntary assignment that matches your strengths better.

P is for Potentiating—The coach can also assist a client to find small ways to enlarge their opportunities for strengths usage and thereby increase their potency. This could include finding new places in and outside of work to add even minimal time or focus, or even just a new effort at use of a single primary strength to begin.

O is for Optimizing—This leveraging of strengths seeks to identify the most useful and surest of them, to bring the very best strengths more into play in their routine undertakings. One way to do so is to seek more expansive behavioral expression of the primary strengths, perhaps by enlarging the reach of those strengths already in play at work or elsewhere.

W is for Waving—The dictionary meaning of this word as intended here is ". . . a sudden increase in an emotion or phenomenon," and uses quick, even impulsive exercise of one's strengths to achieve a new positive effect. For instance, clients might try a period of orienting their work to their top strengths instead of the other way around.

E is also for Engaging—This calls for full and consistent use of a targeted strength in the service of ongoing fortification of it and its user. Sharing discussion of one's practical attempts at doing so with others—coach or colleagues—is one good means of reinforcing those focal strengths, and gaining both deeper engagement and support for doing so.

R is for Realizing—By reflecting on the effects of using the other six empowering tools, this pondered understanding both of one's strengths and what types of efforts bring them to full and vibrant use, appreciation and growth is the capstone process that empowers through reflection and dialogue with one's coach, peers or supervisor.

THE TIGER

For a few years now I have been a regular practitioner of Qigong, the Chinese movement and breathing exercise routine that is like T'ai Chi—designed to enhance energy and flexibility, among other espoused benefits. It has certainly been an enjoyable practice, along with providing some of those gains. One of the movements in the program is call the TIGER, and it is designed to help us feel the strength and power of our inner tiger. The flexion and muscle movement that is felt in repeatedly "raking the air" with hands and arms as we crouch down and then rise up, help create that sense of empowerment and nimble, tensile strength.

One day after a Qigong session a couple years ago, I came to think that my coaching clients might benefit from cognitively identifying their "inner tiger." So, I jotted down the word's 5 letters and identified the assets of a strong sense of self that the letters of the word "tiger" could convey as an acronym. Here's how I use it: After a brief introduction of its history, I share it with the client one letter description at a time, and use it as a set of stimulus words to help her/him relate thereby to their own strengths. I do so in an extended discussion of about ten to fifteen minutes of guided inquiry and client narration. Here is my set of meanings for this quintet of powerful assets; others may want to vary the stimuli by substituting different words they may deem more fitting, or just for variety's sake, even with the same client over time.

T is for Thriving, being dedicated to more than merely getting by, seeking to flourish in every domain of engagement. What are your areas of most realized strengths, and how do you exhibit them?

I is for Inviolate, the quality of feeling safe and secure. Like the tiger that stakes out their domain, in what areas do you feel that kind of power, self-reliance and solid standing, and how do you convey that to others?

G stands for Growing, the areas of enhancement that you seek to enlarge, building on what are your best assets at present. What are your most sought areas of further growth?

E is for Excelling, the practice of outdoing one's previous best to augment felt strengths. In what arenas do you excel? Do you appreciate how that has come to pass, and can you recruit strategies from that knowledge to enhance your other strengths?

R is for Resilient, your ability to bring a hardiness to challenges, a capacity for endurance and resilience to potential setbacks, an expectation of pliancy and suppleness in your response to others and life's vagaries.

STRENGTHS SEARCH

I have had good success using the following framework for assisting clients to see the flow of strengths engagement from identification on through application to expansion of them. It allows the client, either on their own, or in a coaching dialogue, or using both in sequence, to access and augment their particular strengths in any context. This is a seven step model that has two main uses: First, it gives the client a clear and linear flow chart for how to begin assessing their strengths complement, and for moving stepwise through a series of phases for using and amplifying them further. The second use is as an agenda tool for dialogue about the same process, whether done all at once, or (more often) over a couple sessions. I have found it helps for the client to keep some running notes in a journal, electronic file, or small notebook for the various parts of this process. Here is the sequence of often recursive phases for strengthening one's repertoire of assets:

1. *Assessing*—This is the beginning step of self-examination that seeks to identify what intrapersonal and interpersonal traits are most clearly one's strong suits, the very best qualities and capacities one possessed and practiced with some noticeable regularity. These are often innate and/or developed talents that may be frustrated in their manifestation, yet seem and feel like truly extraordinary features of one's repertoire and persona.

2. *Identifying*—While that initial step of self-assessment is usually a cursory inspection of strengths, the next phase of the process looks to use a more formal, perhaps even instrumental method of discovering those 'best' qualities and talents. This is usually accomplished readily by using one of the several tools identified earlier in the book that are evidence-based, have sizable sets of norms for comparison, and can offer a reliable yardstick for surfacing those traits.

3. *Verifying*—This stage in the process involves looking at one's daily endeavors over some time—usually a couple weeks—to seek validation of those previously identified strengths as they are seen and felt in action and through repeated behaviors across a number of roles and relationships, both professionally and outside one's work situation.

4. *Corroborating*—A step that is too often omitted in appraising our strengths base is seeking from others, mainly in trusted relationships, feedback about that "data." This entails literally soliciting a handful of close contacts' impressions of the use and impact of those strengths as they may have witnessed their deployment. This could involve a listing of suggestive features, however, I have found it fully sufficient and most spontaneous to get substantiation simply using an informal discussion, with little need for cues or descriptions for one's corroborators to react to in the exchange. It can then be summarized in notation. In leadership

training and classes, I sometimes use a modified multi-rater format, a 360° strengths assessment arrangement to accomplish this.

5. *Applying*—This phase calls for trial and error learning to validate the utility of the strengths in daily efforts. A tool like the Strengths Index or the Strengths Spotting activities found elsewhere in this section can provide a method for doing this, and also clients find it fairly easy to merely talk it through with me in focused and ongoing coaching sessions. Helping them figure out the places and ways that they make recurrent and appropriate use of the opportunities for optimizing their particular strengths can be a very rich and compelling experience. Helping them to explore where missed opportunities may lie is also a fitting use of this phase of the process.

6. *Amplifying*—Thus is the place where the direction and the frequency of application of one's strengths are sought, looking for evidence of growth in the use and application of those qualities and behaviors. Here, we are seeking to enlarge the contextual use and even intensification of the application of those identified strengths. Often this is accomplished through use of mutually planned experiments in doing so, discussing the outcomes and applying a success analysis framework to that effort in a later coaching session.

7. *Expanding*—This final phase looks to enlarge the range and character of one's strengths, again using the lessons from appreciating how those 'best' qualities already in use came to be. Carefully scoping out what areas are most accessible for expansion can be accomplished by looking further into the auxiliary and complementary strengths one can identify as secondary to their primary or lead, key or signature strengths. And, most find that some assets lend themselves more readily than others to a ready expansion.

Once that process has been completed, the way is paved for a renewed cycle of examination of one's best qualities, revisiting these seven steps, beginning with a re-assessment, though not more often than every 6 months or year. Again, this can also be a model for a fairly self-directed client to pursue on their own. More often, it gives the coach a helpful tool for framing some progressive dialogue about the client's particular strengths, and their usage and augmentation over time.

COACHES OF MY LIFE

Another tool worth considering is a focused extension of the early recall of coaching experience mentioned in the Introduction, and represented in the verse there about a lifetime of coaches. This particular activity is a fun, retrospective analysis in narrative form that has the client look back on their life from their youth up till now, and identify the coaches in their life—people who literally coached them for some skill activity, or perhaps even a prior professional coach. Beginning with the purpose statement below and then using the question set that follows, coaches can have their clients do a focused mini-life review to recall the people who served such roles previously, including those they might consider longer term mentors. Then the questions for each coaching experience and person can help clients tell the stories of standout experiences that will aid them in identifying the strengths that evolved from those relationships. By directly reflecting on the experiences, the learning done in or after them, and the contributions made thereby to whom they have become and how they think and conduct themselves now, insight and even perhaps some further direction may be gleaned.

Purpose: This activity is a fun reflection on the experiences you might have had with a tutor, teacher, coach or mentor in any endeavor in your past. The directions are simple and literal: first think back to when you had your first coaching experience of any kind. Recall who it was with, what you were trying to learn or do better, and what the context for coaching was. Jot down those details of it for each of the coaches you can recall having after that initial one, going right up to now. Your list may be long or short, depending on your recall of unique developmental and work experiences. Take a few moments to compile that list using this format to gather the information:

Coach	*Dates*	*Topic & Context (for what goal, where, how)*
Mr. Martin	9/88–2/89	Basketball in junior high—fundamentals & team play . . . after school 4x/week in season

Ms. Jordan	1994-97	Supervised activities while working part-time as reservations agent for hotel chain
Mr. Dixon	1998-2000	Mentor during transition from employee to supervisor in Training Unit

Once the list is compiled, I have the client do several things, directing them in this order: "First, identify the best of them at what they sought to do. Next, pare down to a handful of those coaching experiences you recall having enjoyed most out of all of them. Then, try to compile what you believe were the lasting lessons of each experience. For that, we'll go over the culled list starting with those first two types identified—the best and the most enjoyable. As we go through your brief stories about each of them, I'd like you to say whether you have learned anything that you bring today to your interpersonal work, whether in supervision, coaching, or whatever role." This should take about 3-5 minutes per coach identified, once you have the list documented on the basic form, and depending on your work and developmental history.

The dialogue involved in this activity is usually quite fertile and often extensive, as most coaches doing such focused recall will pause to identify recollections of the quality and tenor of the experience in addition to the data asked for. This activity also yields a lot of thematic points for comparison and further discussion in subsequent coaching exchanges.

BOARD OF TRUSTEES

As a former university administrator and faculty member, I was regularly exposed to meetings of Boards of Trustees—appointees from outside the school charged with helping oversee and govern it. Several years ago, I began experimenting with a small activity that has proven to be much more useful and profound than I expected, and than it seemed it could be on its face. The tool is called "Board of Trustees," and the instructions I give for use of it go like this:

"Think about the people in your life with whom you genuinely share a bond of trust. Sociologists tell us that is probably just a small handful of people that you find worthy of your trust. As such, you might be more likely to accept their advice and value their inputs on a variety of matters. These are a set of people you can call your *Board of Trustees*, with the accent on their *trust* relationship with you."

"After you identify some possible candidates for this role, about 4 or 5, approach each of them with the idea of this "Board" that would never meet, but might serve as a set of individual consultants or advisors for occasional issues or questions. You might even consider whether an online group communication arrangement might be desirable and feasible for this. You can determine how to involve them, and may choose to do it without always using the full complement of your Board. Be sure to tell them the trust criteria you have used to select them, and why their counsel might be particularly helpful. You might even consider "staffing" the Board with Trustees of varying strengths themselves, seeking diversity and some balance, by soliciting people with differing backgrounds or areas of expertise. Their use to you will be maximized if they have a number of different attributes. I'd suggest you moderate your use of the Board so you don't wear them out or overuse their inputs."

When I initially tried this out for myself, after experiencing the gains it can yield, over time I have made it a suggestion for a number of clients to consider. It has been a quite successful positive strategy for most of them, with particularly good fits for C-suite executives and people with more than a modicum of years' experience.

DESCRIPTIVE RULERS

In addition to the numerical rulers commonly employed to scale and rate concepts and feelings, I like to harness the power of language by frequently asking a client to use a descriptive, non-numerical ruler. This tyoe of device from the solution-focused therapy paradigm and the Transtheoretical Change Model, uses a continuum of words that, while imprecise, nonetheless can be very helpful in prompting portrayal of a situation or affective assessment by the client. It always is followed by probing further for the meaning and origins of the word chosen from the ruler/ scale, as well a soliciting a narrative example of how that view originated.

It can lead to deeper understanding and to additional exchanges, as well. They do not have to use alliterative or similar roots, nor do they need to be of a certain length, although an odd number of choices, usually five or seven words, seems to work best. Adding a numerical anchor for a sequential frame of reference also can be helpful to some. There is a degree of flexibility with the selection and wording of the question stem and this, too, is important for understanding and stimulation of further remarks. Here are 4 examples; a later one will appear as potentially useful in the team coaching section in chapter seven:

"My readiness to adopt this prospective change to _____ right now is . . ."

Not at all	Thinking about it	Getting prepared	Taking action	Steadily changing	I'm there

I_____I_____I_____I_____I_____I

Another example might assess the here-and-now:

"Could you indicate where on the following continuum of words you'd find the best description of your present feeling about your work life?"

Despairing	Depressed	Disinterested	Delighted	Dazzled

I. I

1   2   3   4   5

Or, how about a question stem such as . . .

"Which word or location on this array of descriptors best captures your current feelings about the effects of your best moments at work?"

| Ennui | Engagement | Enthusiasm | Elation | Ecstasy |

I I

| 1 | 2 | 3 | 4 | 5 |

And, finally, a fourth example:

"Using the descriptive scale below, depict your present appraisal of how you are able to use your strengths at work these days?"

| Not a bit | Barely | Inconsistently | Usually | All the time |

I I

| 1 | 2 | 3 | 4 | 5 |

Just a final footnote should be added here about this form of data description: I use a fair amount of restating and translating of narrative inputs, often asking clients to rate, rank, scale, score, or grade an experience verbally, though usually with just numerical or letter equivalents. For example, if a coachee described an experience as horrible, I might then ask them to scale it on a 1 to 7 basis, with 7 being "not really too bad" and 1 being "worst ever." Or, I could also ask for a grade of A to F for an experience's perceived outcome, using a frame like the scholastic norms of A for excellent and F for failure. These impressionistic evaluations serve a couple purposes in my coaching: I ask for clarity or reinforcement of a statement, particularly one that seemed "loaded" emotionally, or to depict an extreme that was not the usual descriptor for that person. Also, it serves to give the client a second pass at evaluating an experience, and that often yields a modified assessment, after which I will seek to pin down the issue's impact more precisely for further discussion. These are simple, yet highly helpful gambits that are a regular part of my practice toolkit. I feel they are economical and cogent ways of furthering the dialogue, and urge their frequent usage by coaches I train.

SEVEN HOLISTIC ATTACHMENTS

This activity is a form of rating/ranking descriptive ruler, but centered on one's comprehensive view of self and life. Many years ago, psychiatrist Norris Hansell described a set of interdependent, holistic "attachment" categories that all humans share to varying degrees.[15] I have used his framework often over the years in a number of settings and contexts. Clients can follow the directions for using the form for coaching purposes below:

1. After reading their meanings, next to each term and on the first line of the left margin, write your current personal assessment of its <u>Importance</u> (the I list) to you, using *7 for most important, 6 for the next, all the way to 1 for least important.*

2. Then repeat the assessment, this time for the <u>level of Satisfaction</u> (S list) you have with that aspect of yourself and life today, using the same non-repeating numbers (1-7) on the second line in front of the item.

3. Next, compare the two lists—current <u>importance to you</u> and <u>satisfaction</u> at present—for variance, and discuss with your coach the thinking behind those current ratings and observed discrepancies between the two rankings.

4. It might also be useful to reflect on what events or situations have colored those ratings. Nobel Prize awardee and behavioral economist Daniel Kahneman has noted that our *experiencing* selves yield every moment to our *remembered* selves, which have necessarily biased recall, made so by how our minds function in those processes.

This can be a helpful self-assessment at any point in the coaching compact, or even outside it on one's own to assay and reflect on changes over time.

    I   S

_____ _____ Biochemical & data *Basics*: food, oxygen, and information of requisite variety.

_____ _____ A clear concept of a self, i.e., my *Identity*, held with conviction.

_____ _____ *Relationships*: more than one, in persisting, interdependent contact, with some occasionally approximating intimacy.

_____ _____ *Belonging* to groups, more than one, which offer a sense of attachment and social inclusion.

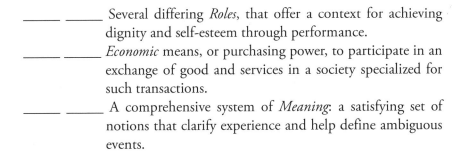

_____ _____ Several differing *Roles*, that offer a context for achieving dignity and self-esteem through performance.

_____ _____ *Economic* means, or purchasing power, to participate in an exchange of good and services in a society specialized for such transactions.

_____ _____ A comprehensive system of *Meaning*: a satisfying set of notions that clarify experience and help define ambiguous events.

The coaching conversations using this collection of perspectives can mine a fundamental and important cache of self-awareness, as it speaks to some very basic aspects of living. Insights can be gathered here through recognition of the interdependent nature of the "Attachments," such that a loss or gain in one almost always impacts some of the other areas of attachment. Another commonly appreciated perspective with this assessment is to compare and contrast the differences between and among the seven on either "importance" or "satisfaction," relative to one another. I often find meaningful conversations emerge around understanding the discrepancies between importance and satisfaction levels on any one key attachment, too. Also, there appear to be some shifts in priority for us as we age, mature, change ambitions, or change jobs and roles in our communities of inclusion.

For example, one client in his mid-50s spoke at some length of the changing importance of relationships relative to means or wealth as he aged. Another focused our conversation on the way that being less responsible for other family members as they left the nest allowed her to shift her attention to more personal objectives and attachments. A third coachee spent our dialogue time after using this tool looking extensively at his new awareness of the holistic connections among the seven categories of the tool. Whether considering the entire set and their links to one another, or focusing on just one or two of the seven attachments, this conversation starter has become a favorite tool in my coaching arsenal, particularly with older clients, those whom I've coached more than once over a number of intervening years, and those in transition in either their professional or personal lives.

"STOP" & "GO" FOR IT

In the mid-1990s at the university where I worked, I found myself teaching several semesters in a row to large classes held in auditoriums and sizeable venues to accommodate the numbers enrolled, usually a few hundred students. This challenged me to create some unique ways to get them all more actively learning and to keep them involved. Since we had not yet evolved into the electronic ubiquity of present day society, and before "friend" became a verb, so the classroom technology was still somewhat basic. I did not have the advantage of harnessing today's tools, such as the remote entry gadgets students can now access, or the capability to use their own handheld electronic devices for registering inputs during class.

So, one of my early and primitive approaches was to give each student a pair of 3 X 5 inch index cards—one red and one green. These were used primarily for a pair of purposes: first, to get a mass, quickly readable signal about their understanding of a segment just covered: showing the red card meant I needed to pause or slow down, as the topic was not quite grasped yet, and showing green meant it was OK to proceed as students felt they had comprehended it well. The other use I commonly made of the two cards was simply to register group preferences visually, or use a closed-ended, yes or no/true or false question, or a survey item with two choices, or just to get a quick impression of the sentiment of the majority on some question. I soon started stapling, and eventually gluing the cards back to back, for a green and a red side on one card. It was a minimally involving tactic, but proved popular and easy to do.

In those large classes, I often had the assistance of a handful of TAs—Teaching Assistants. These TAs were grad students who served as recitation or discussion facilitators for small groups of registrants, and they also assisted with managing the large classes in other ways. One day, a sharp psychology grad named Linda, who was one of those TAs that term, suggested another use for the two cards. That autumn she was also in an interpersonal helping skills course with me, and asked in that seminar whether it might be useful to assign a bit of counseling homework to clients by borrowing the two colored cards idea from the large lecture class to help sort and record events of the week that were appraised as negatively stressful or beneficial and enjoyable—red or green card matter, respectively. From there, it was not much of a leap for a fledgling strengths coach to apply this same format to helping an individual coaching client discern her/his work assignments, tasks or duties by sorting them into those that either reinforced or diminished their sense of strength and productivity. I have used a version of that tactic with many clients since, graduating to 5 X 8 inch colored cards in the interim, and referring to them as "Stop and Go" or "No and Yes" cards at various times.

Marcus Buckingham later described a similar device identifying things "loved" or "loathed," using whole sheets of paper, in his *Go Put Your Strengths To Work*, a very worthwhile 2007 book.[16] I recommend using the approach in whatever form works for you, and suggest you give the client a minimum of two or three somewhat normal weeks to compile the data on the colored cards or pages. After examining together the findings for both their general and more specific gleanings, the ensuing dialogue can help work toward a restructuring of one's work life more in accord with that new awareness. In my experience to date, it has been a very telling and helpful way for clients to identify whether and how they are using their strengths. In tandem with the strengths index or strengths spotting matrix, it can provide a complementary approach to examining and revising strengths usage and opportunities.

MINDFUL ABUNDANCE

Back in 1989, Stephen R. Covey took his synthesis of the extant wisdom literature, that he reported was an offshoot of his doctoral work, and penned the highly successful book, *The 7 Habits of Highly Effective People*.[17] This self-help treatise has been a perennial bestseller on business booklists, and the associated training programs and spinoffs from it have helped make his company, now merged with Hyrum Smith's Franklin Quest into FranklinCovey, a global leader in its product genre. While there are many worthwhile concepts and tools in the company's arsenal, one that Covey coined about mindset is a notion I like to use in my coaching work. It is the idea of the *Abundance Mindset* or *Abundance Mentality*, described earlier in the mindset section.

The ability to see life as non-competitive, and to seek constantly to share the wealth of success and its resultant resources is a key framework for the asset-based thinker. I try to help clients remain constantly mindful of the gifts and attendant gratefulness that reside in an abundance way of thinking and acting. It is a clear corollary to both positive thinking and the exercise of gratitude with all. Therefore, I urge many clients to try the following mindfulness cultivation experiment for two to four weeks:

Start each day with a meditation using self-talk that expects good things, and admits to a belief that everyone has an equal right to expect and to receive what they need, if not always everything they want. Many will remember the Rolling Stones' tune featured in the opening scene of the classic film *The Big Chill* that makes that distinction so well. I suggest that throughout the day, we can also remind ourselves with short, internally uttered mantras like "there is enough to go around," or "I am grateful that there is plenty for all of us." Clients can also say to themselves exhortations like "My gain does not need to be at others' expense." And, I encourage them at the end of each day to take stock of how the day went, and to note what experiences they had that affirm the abundance viewpoint. I assure them from my own and many others' reported experience that their effort over time will be rewarded in manifold simple ways. This reality will further enable them to adopt the abundance perspective fully. Their sense of serenity and their interpersonal relationships both can profit measurably by doing so for at least a couple weeks at the outset. It is likely to become a habit that reinforces itself thereafter!

GRATITUDE

In the past decade we have seen repeated, impressive evidence for the use of strengths assessment, reflection and experimentation to bring about lasting and desired positive emotions, and to secure more meaningful and engaged private life and work situations. In 2005, Nansook Park, Chris Peterson, Tracy Steen, and Martin Seligman conducted an evaluation of effect and duration for a series of exercises to assist others with achieving personal pleasure. Yoked with engagement and meaningfulness, they have referred to it often and simply as "happiness."[18] One of the two most powerful of those tested was the regular use of one's key, lead or signature strengths as mentioned earlier in the book.

The other was a so-called gratitude or blessings activity. Each calls for at least a week of daily focused work on those two aspects of positive living. Stephen Schueller affirmed the attractiveness of the simple gratitudes tool, and addressed the adherence, efficacy and preference for it, and a handful of others framed in a positive vein.[19] Barbara Frederickson encouraged its use in some form routinely to enhance positive emotional feelings, and Robert Emmons found gratitude to be a pivotal and life-changing strategy. His book, *Thanks,* is a splendid source of research summaries and reflections on gratitude, and he also lists a collection of ten of the best, most effective approaches to incorporating gratitude as a beneficial part of one's daily repertoire.[20] The trio of elements identified as central to gratitude include (1) recognition of a gesture that is a favor or material gift, followed by (2) acknowledgement of its receipt, and then (3) expressed appreciation. Sometimes the latter is not transactional, and even occurs only as a statement to oneself.

The activity called the Three Blessings, is possibly the most widely recommended and used of all positive psychology interventions. It is thoroughly researched, frequently cited, and arguably yields the most "bang for the buck" of all such actions. It calls for a daily acknowledgement to oneself of three or more things for which one is grateful, reflecting on acts that occurred or were brought back to awareness during the day just passed. Reflection on how those came about augments the recognition of the benefaction, too. It is a quick, but high-leverage positive device that, over time, has been shown to alter one's temperament, outlook, and even relationships. Further, the impacts noted in all the studies of this practice were counter to depressive affect and simultaneously enhanced felt gratification.

GRATITUDE FOR BEING . . .

A similar activity that I often encourage clients to experiment with is actually a modest form of meditation on personal gratitude. I suggest they perform it daily, preferably at the close of their waking day. It simply calls for reflection on five focal points for appreciating one's life. In sequence of address, they are . . .

1. *Gratitude for being:* Appreciation for existing, having a life, and the freedom to live it autonomously.
2. *Gratitude for being something:* Acknowledging one's particular roles in life, and their many allowances.
3. *Gratitude for being something special:* Delving more deeply into the roles, this is about felt thankfulness for the opportunities that

have enabled a unique, personal experience when in those roles, and experiencing their positive consequences.

4. *Gratitude for being in relationship:* Thankfulness for the gifts of being with, and connected to, a (usually) small number of people in one's circle, with distinctive intensity, intimacy, and affection. For some, this begins with their worship of a divine being, and includes recognition of those given or chosen to be relatives of some close kind.

5. *Gratitude for being a frequent recipient of others' generosity:* This final one is a summative awareness of all that for which we are thankful, and all that we enjoy as a result of those gifts.

One of the amazing aspects of this seemingly repetitive, daily activity is that it yields <u>different</u> appraisals of thankfulness and appreciation practically <u>every time</u>. One might expect it to be a constant recall of the same things and people, but it rarely is exactly the same. That is one of the reasons why it bears such power and importance for its users. It allows recognition of the varying flow of gifts or blessings that we experience, even in the same roles and relationships! This one economical, yet potent activity may be the single best type of tool in this entire book, and its paradoxical dual benefit makes it even more impressive. By that, I mean it benefits the donee who expresses gratitude as much as the donor who is being appreciated with thanks for it. Robert Emmons' *Thanks*, cited earlier, is a trove of evidence and exercises for this. As strengths coaches, we are agents for individuals to explore, examine and experiment with those kinds of fortifying efforts, and as with gratitude, the outcomes can be more than simply salutary, they can be transformative!

WELL-BEING: OUR PILLARS OF STRENGTH

The phrase "pillar of strength" is a commonly used descriptor for someone whom we deem to be a constant, a stalwart support to a person or cause. This tool is a slight variation on that theme, and coaches can use it beneficially to help clients introspectively get at <u>how they apply their core strengths</u>—those that are basic or foundational, and from which they derive their greatest power—in several key arenas of their life. Ben Dean of MentorCoach first exposed me a few years ago to an activity addressing this kind of assessment in his "Pillars of a Balanced Life."

I tried a new, yet similar format a few months back after reading Martin Seligman's *Flourish*, mentioned previously, in which he re-casts "happiness" as too narrow, and sees well-being as a more proper focus of positive efforts.[21] He redirects our attention to five areas of positive well-being that are personal traits or elements, with the acronym PERMA: Positive emotions, Engagement, Relationships, Meaning, and Accomplishment. After reading that, and then seeing Tom Rath's and Jim Harter's provocative little book about thriving, titled *Well Being*, I chose to revise this activity along the lines their work suggests.[22] Their website gives just a small but intriguing sample of the range and depth of influence these five areas have on our lives, and I share that site with clients before our discussion, so they can get a feel for the elements.[23] The website also has a global index of well being that charts daily fluctuations in standard of living, life evaluation, mood and health, using data collected from 150 countries representing most of the populated world. Purchasers of the book from these two strengths scholars at Gallup can get a data-based website connection to do a more grounded self-analysis and tracking of their well-being in these five domains.

The book's subtitle is the *Five Essential Elements*, and therein lies the latticework of the exercise I offer for your consideration. It is simple to use and also makes it easy to proceed to a number of helpful extended discussions. In the end, it is a way to reaffirm what are the client's very best suits—their true lead or primary strengths, and how those actually make a positive difference in their life. I begin with a brief explanation of what I understand to be the book's thesis, briefly defining the nature of the five elements, and framing them as the five pillars of life strengths. Then, there are twelve questions I pose in what Rath & Harter say is the descending order of importance, encompassing the five "Well Being Elements" they describe. It's rare that all twelve items get covered in a single session, so they can be spread out as time and preference allow. Those elements (italicized), and the paired (1-10) and closing queries (11 & 12) using them in the order suggested are:

1. What is your current assessment of the strengths and overall health of your *Career* path?
2. How do you see yourself enhancing that element of your well being in the near future?
3. What is your current assessment of the strengths and overall health of your *Social* or relational life?

4. How do you see yourself enhancing that element of your well being in the near future?

5. What is your current assessment of the strengths and overall health of your *Financial* standing?

6. How do you see yourself enhancing that element of your well being in the near future?

7. What is your current assessment of the strengths and overall health of your *Physical* self?

8. How do you see yourself enhancing that element of your well being in the near future?

9. What is your current assessment of the strengths and overall health of your *Community* engagement?

10. How do you see yourself enhancing that element of your well-being in the near future?

11. What is your summary or collective view of the impact of these areas of applied strengths on your life, i.e. your overall well-being?

12. Why do you feel that is so?

Any number of additional discussion points can issue from this tool, beginning with simply looking in more depth serially or singly at the five pillars, the elements of well-being. Further plumbing of these have added ranking and rating perspectives to the self-assessment, including both valuing or importance as well as efficacy or satisfaction statements, as well as looking at the links and resources on the book website for more in-depth exploring of the pillars themselves. This activity also is a reminder that a psychometric assessment is not always necessary to generate valuable, in-depth coaching discussions. The inquiries here have proven sufficient for a thoughtful and incisive plumbing of the client's well being, without numerical assessments. Comparing responses at different times, such as early and later in the course of coaching over some months, has been interesting as well. This has been an activity I have returned to at several clients' initiation, with important learning accomplished each time.

MY 4 STRONG SELVES

Gervase Bushe notes in *Clear Leadership* (2009) that one or more of a quartet of common disagreements in most work relationships constitute the roots of dysfunctional communication that he calls "interpersonal mush." These are *disagreement about goals, roles, procedures or resources.*[24] While the completeness of that list is arguable, I have built on his proposed remedy for the mush, called the four skill selves, to help a client with their own clarity-seeking in communication. The activity follows in a tool called *My 4 Strong Selves*. Basically, Bushe urges the intentional use of the skills of our *appreciative, aware, descriptive* and *curious "selves"* to build open, truly clear learning conversations between co-workers. Here's the coaching dialogue version of the self-assessment of those four vital postures and related behaviors:

We begin with the *appreciative self,* which seeks to look at the world through an abundance lens, realizing that competition and one-upmanship can be counterproductive, and can deflect us from seeing others and ourselves clearly. I ask the client how s/he sees their world in that regard . . . is it a place where one either has to eat or be eaten, or is it a world where there really is enough to go around, to share and find possibility, not scarcity. Here, I press the coachee to elaborate and to narrate a personal example of how the relevant mindset they identify has been established by them.

Next we discuss the *aware self,* the part of our makeup that recognizes that all affect and cognitive interplay begins as an inside process, and only then moves outside us. So, I inquire whether my client feels they are usually fully aware of what they are "observing, thinking and wanting." These are the three related processes that create our experience, according to Bushe, and are necessary for us to know what is another's experience, how it may differ from what is mine, and what I am constructing as a story to make sense of my experience with them, based on my own past, and our particular history together. I find it is often helpful here to use that immediate moment's experience to clarify what I'm asking, so I solicit their description of their momentary self-awareness as we are talking together. Often, this proves challenging, and helps them to see how easily a communication with a colleague can veer away from what was intended or might actually be going on.

The third skill self is the *descriptive self,* that aspect of each of us that depicts the wider parts of our experience, including the awkward, yet important differences and confrontational elements of our exchanges and co-history. I usually have to "push back" numerous times in this part of the activity, because our learned tendency is to "make nice" and not risk conflict, seeming to be tactless, or showing too much pride in our self-descriptions. The key here is to do so in such a way that the other person becomes <u>more</u> willing to hear, not reflexively reactive in a defensive manner, inclined to create an explanatory, but unchecked story about us.

The fourth skill self that Bushe depicts is the mirror of our descriptive abilities that he calls the *curious self.* This is our capacity for helping others fully disclose their own experience with the subject at hand, and with us. This means literally interviewing the other person, often digging a bit to uncover thoroughly and then to accept the complete story of their observations, thoughts, feelings and wants in the moment of transaction with us.

The routine practice of these four skill selves is an ongoing struggle for most of us, one that does not come easy, as you'll recall from the earlier described lessons of change, and from your own experience in conversing with others. I make it a habit to renew this effort in my coaching sessions, and also to urge clients to try being conscious of practicing these in their work, social and at home conversations. Mastering and modeling them can be powerful levers for improving communication and avoiding disagreements, leading us to experience tactful candor and true learning in our dialogues with others. It is a critical skill set as well as a potent tool for coaches to seek command of, one that can yield maximum leverage for improving relationships and even an entire organization's culture. It certainly has pertinence to leader communications, and as it came from his *Clear Leadership* book, has great utility for those functioning in that role.

STRENGTHS AS A WAY OF BEING

The final tool in this chapter is a summary strengths implementation framework. We all want to change from routinely experiencing TGIF: Thank God It's Friday, and OGIM: Oh God, It's Monday, and instead be able to find genuine engagement, satisfaction, and productivity at work. Perhaps the best way I know personally and from coaching experience to do so is to make strengths a foundational way of being at work. The following heuristic, a list of steps for claiming and renewing use and growth of your best talents, urges adoption of the following seven practices, outlined in sequence briefly. I recommend it to coaches for themselves, and for transmission to their clients as well.

1. *Identify your Best.* Use validated instrumental measures, deep reflection, and feedback from others to find your true strengths.
2. *Learn more about them.* Do so by exploring their applicability and nature in continuing, engaging in focused learning about each of them, and through witnessing mindfully how they play out in your effortful life.
3. *Affirm and prize them.* Allow yourself to see their impacts, including both their best fits and their benefits in your daily and ongoing transactions, appreciating their gifts to you.
4. *Use them and avoid non-strengths.* Seek out and maximize opportunities for their use, and expand the arenas in which you put them to service.
5. *Increase your strengths profile.* Expand your auxiliary, complementary, and situational strong suits, and grow their number and utility through intentional stretching experiments.
6. *Share the wealth.* Become both a model and a tutor for what strengths usage can do for your colleagues and for your shared relationships.
7. *Collaborate to optimize collective strength.* Learn how your combined strengths on teams and throughout whole organizations can be harnessed to achieve shared success.

Those last couple approaches to using strengths in work settings provide a fitting transition to a more concerted exploration of strengths coaching with leaders, their teams, and throughout the full organization in the next chapter. The tools we use with individual coaching clients are versatile and flexible devices for assisting clients in a one-on-one paradigm. However, there are some adaptations and unique features to working as a coach with those in leadership roles. Further, the use of coaching interventions with teams and even whole organizations as a strategy for facilitating communication and planning begs for new considerations that differ from what we use with individual clients. The next and final chapter of the book addresses this complementary type of coaching, and offers both tools and strategic approaches for achieving these special objectives for coaching success. It will begin, however, with a focused exploration of the role of leader that a few of the tools were aimed at in this chapter.

> **STRONGBOX 6-2**: *The expectations of life depend upon diligence; the mechanic that would perfect his work must first sharpen his tools.*
>   — *Confucius*

7
Leader, Team & Organization Coaching

> **STRONGBOX 7-1:** *Leadership is the ability to align strengths (toward a purpose) such that weaknesses are irrelevant.*   *- Peter Drucker*

Nadine was the newly chosen Executive Director of a very large international association of allied health educators, and was aware coming into office of a stormy previous leader-board history, and the remaining turbulent governance situation. She sought me out to help her think through and implement a new start. Nadine was determined not to replay old scripts or revisit old negative issues, and had some thoughts about how to ensure that. We knew each other from serving together on a higher education task force several years before, and she knew I was a consultant and a coach, and wanted to get some outside aid for a critical time in her and the association's life. Drawing on her splendid leadership skills and positive planning mindset, she was able to put together a strategic framework and to assemble the resources to carry it off with a minimum of negative input and felt rancor. My primary coaching role was helping her think about alternatives and comprehensiveness, as she had a solid blueprint for the goals and processes needed at the outset of her term. Over the ensuing three months as we talked weekly, she got things jump-started, cultivated a new ethos, and instituted an infrastructure that was appreciative and asset-focused. She also began to identify staff strengths and to restructure their governance arrangements accordingly, all without rehashing the angst in the system from before.

―――᭜ᦡᦡᦡᦡᦡᦡᦡᦡ――――

Coaching for Leadership, Teams & Organizations

This chapter of *Power Up!* is a description of some of the unique issues for coaching that emerge when addressing the collective strengths of a group or team. First, we will explore some approaches to leadership that clients often have been exposed to with my coaching process in the past decade. Then, this section looks into the use of coaching as an intervention with groups and teams. Finally, we will examine the challenges and prospects of enterprise-wide implementation of a strengths coaching focus, and suggest some issues to examine prior to launching such an initiative. As the dynamics of coaching individual leaders, and those of coaching more than one person simultaneously call for different approaches and logistics, this section has its own box of tools with descriptions of their usage, as they vary from the individual coaching paradigm.

Leader & Leadership Coaching

First, let me make an elementary and yet critical distinction between leader development with coaching, and leadership development with coaching. The former is mostly about coaching to identify high potential leaders in the making, to assist with finding people who possess those desired traits and show exceptional promise. In other words, this is to identify people who are prospectively good candidates for leadership roles and positions. Then, once identified, coaching such "Hi-Po" people takes aim at helping those individuals identified as leaders-in-process to become stronger in those key areas that distinguish leadership from management and followership. Coaching for either often uses some similar constructs and frameworks, and the description below elaborates on their use.

The majority of my coaching experiences have been with what some call C-suite level professionals—"chief" officers in charge of or overseeing a major organization function, such as executive, operating, financial or information functions. In other words, I have worked primarily, but not exclusively, with senior level leaders and entrepreneurs over the past couple dozen years. Inevitably, in those relationships, we come to discussions of their role and relationships as heads of that major function or overall entity. In doing so, we often engage in some intentional dialogue about the leader behaviors they are called on to exhibit.

THE 7 ESSENTIAL TALENTS OF LEADERSHIP

In those discussions, I often have found it useful to introduce one or all of what I refer to as *the 7 Essential Talents of leadership*, derived from a leadership course I have taught several times a year for over a decade now. They are called that for a couple reasons: First, they are indeed talents, in that the majority of leaders seem to rise and fall, excel and fail, based on their ability to demonstrate consistently that they possess and aptly use these talents. These 7 capabilities are often found in a raw version in some leaders, and over time, can develop into solid strengths. The talents are abilities or skills, powers of mind and social engagement to perform exceptionally well. They include what usually are a few *primary* capabilities, and the balance are *auxiliary* and *contextual ones* (as needed), talents that are lesser capacities, often away from one's main strengths. Further, these are called "Essential" for a pair of reasons: first, they are necessary, i.e., they are absolutely fundamental and basic to the organization's (and the leader's) success; and second, each of the seven also begins with the letter "E", thus the label "Essential." Finally, the seven of them collectively represent a comprehensive and thorough, complementary and memorable collection of talents. Here is the list of these seven defined, followed by an instrument to assist with self-assessment of both the essential attitudes and the key behaviors for coaching about leadership strengths using the 7 Essential Talents framework:

Enlightening: Sharing knowledge and ideas, teaching, coaching, tutoring, and using feedback from reviewed experience to strengthen future endeavors at individual, team, and organization levels. Creating a true learning organization at all levels.

Empowering: Enabling followers to exhibit their capabilities, to stretch their capacities, and to deliver on commitments, all the while using emotional intelligence in transactions.

Entrusting: Modeling and reinforcing principle-based behaviors that are ethical, transparent, respectful and goal-focused for others to emulate.

Enrolling: Providing a clear prospectus for the desired future and the pathways to its realization so that others want to enlist their very best efforts to add value and commitment.

Engaging: Bolstering and capturing the passion that followers have for providing what coworkers, clients, customers, and other stakeholders seek from the organization.

Executing: Bringing about the chosen and consensus means of achieving the organization's purposes. This includes matching talents to tasks, people to processes, and enabling optimal performance throughout the organization.

Ensuring: Exhibiting the decisional qualities of transformational leadership, including exceptional leading in both the routine and the extraordinary aspects of organizational conduct.

STRONGBOX 7-2: *Few things help an individual more than to place responsibility upon him, and to let him know that you trust him.*
- Booker T. Washington

The 7 Essential Talents of Leadership
Self-Assessment

This 35-item self-test is focused on your beliefs, roles, behaviors and perspectives as a leader in your organization, regardless of position or experience. It examines those from the shared viewpoints of both leader and follower, and solicits your responses across seven overlapping arenas of activity essential to leader success. Each item has a 7-point range of agreement reflecting degree of similar feeling and thought (1 is low and 7 is high). Do not mull over your answer at length, but circle the number that best corresponds to your current level of agreement with the statement. As these items seek your opinions about their functioning in your life, the scoring of them is not on a "right or wrong" basis, but rather is a measure of your own unique collective ideas about essential leader capabilities. Once you have finished all the items, a short set of scoring directions below will complete the instrument for analysis and coaching discussion.

1) Now, sum the numeric totals for the 5 items for each of the 7 "**Es**" in the sub-total box beneath each section.
2) Next, add all 7 of those sub-scores and place that total here _____.
   (Range = 35 to 245).

3) Then, go back over the scores for each item and <u>circle any "6s & 7s"</u> from all the items of the instrument.

4) Finally, mark each of the seven subtotal scores onto the lines below for later comparison. In terms of relative strengths, the following ranges and descriptors apply for each of those graphed totals:

<14 = *has room for growth,*
          15-28 = *an adequate talent, and*
                    >28 = *an area of strength*

Enlightening

| 0 | 7 | 14 | 21 | 28 | 35 |

Empowering

| 0 | 7 | 14 | 21 | 28 | 35 |

Entrusting

| 0 | 7 | 14 | 21 | 28 | 35 |

Enrolling

| 0 | 7 | 14 | 21 | 28 | 35 |

Engaging

| 0 | 7 | 14 | 21 | 28 | 35 |

Executing

| 0 | 7 | 14 | 21 | 28 | 35 |

Ensuring

| 0 | 7 | 14 | 21 | 28 | 35 |

THE 7 ESSENTIAL TALENTS OF LEADERSHIP	SELF-ASSESSMENT
Circle your numerical self-assessment for each item below, 35 in all:	1 = <u>low</u> agreement; 7 = <u>high</u> agreement with the item.
Enlightening	
I actively promote efforts to make us truly a learning organization.	1 2 3 4 5 6 7
I encourage coworkers to be open to taking risks that may not always succeed.	1 2 3 4 5 6 7
I seek out and support leadership at all levels of the organization.	1 2 3 4 5 6 7
I regularly urge those in positions of authority to learn from their followers.	1 2 3 4 5 6 7
I try to demonstrate openness to learning opportunities and ensure the same for all followers.	1 2 3 4 5 6 7
	☐ Sub-total
Empowering	
Clear delegation of roles and clarification of responsibilities are key parts of how I lead.	1 2 3 4 5 6 7
Helping followers grow to become leaders is one of my main goals as their supervisor.	1 2 3 4 5 6 7
I encourage others to attempt "stretch" assignments, to innovate without fear.	1 2 3 4 5 6 7
Clearing the way for others to succeed is a major part of my approach to empowering followers.	1 2 3 4 5 6 7

I employ a deliberate strengths-based coaching style to help my colleagues stretch and grow.	1 2 3 4 5 6 7
	☐ **Sub-total**
Entrusting	
My practice of good leadership exhibits high level emotional and social know-how.	1 2 3 4 5 6 7
Personal integrity is essential to securing effective followership.	1 2 3 4 5 6 7
Being ethical and trusting co-workers is a major part of my leader profile.	1 2 3 4 5 6 7
I "walk the talk" routinely, modeling effective behavior for all to see and experience.	1 2 3 4 5 6 7
I help instill a culture of integrity and caring among all in the organization.	1 2 3 4 5 6 7
	☐ **Sub-total**
Enrolling	
I share responsibility for the organization's future focus and investment.	1 2 3 4 5 6 7
As a leader, I am dedicated to creating a positive motivating work climate.	1 2 3 4 5 6 7
As a leader, I seek others' commitment to the organization's goals and strategies.	1 2 3 4 5 6 7
My practice of leadership includes endorsing a set of values all can support.	1 2 3 4 5 6 7

I constantly scan inside and outside the organization for future directions and a changing culture.	1 2 3 4 5 6 7
	☐ **Sub-total**
Engaging	
As a leader, I seek to ensure alignment of work processes, people, roles and resources.	1 2 3 4 5 6 7
My leadership entails seeing that the right people with the right skill sets are optimally positioned.	1 2 3 4 5 6 7
Seeing to clear communication in all directions among all team members is a leader imperative for me.	1 2 3 4 5 6 7
I understand, and optimize the various generational and cultural needs and talents of my co-workers.	1 2 3 4 5 6 7
I feel I am charged with overseeing change goals and processes as my primary leader role and duty.	1 2 3 4 5 6 7
	☐ **Sub-total**
Executing	
I help us set and achieve the organization's key goals through successful implementation of our strategies.	1 2 3 4 5 6 7
I clearly establish accountability standards & expectations with those to whom I delegate and encourage initiative-taking.	1 2 3 4 5 6 7

I see to routine and thorough follow-through & follow-up with others.	1 2 3 4 5 6 7
I use solid lead measures and visible scoreboards to gauge progress.	1 2 3 4 5 6 7
I ensure that all in the organization know both their own and the team's top priorities.	1 2 3 4 5 6 7
	☐ **Sub-total**
Ensuring	
I effectively attend to ongoing day-to-day process and outcome issues with my team.	1 2 3 4 5 6 7
I feel well equipped to facilitate meetings, seeing to preparations, conduct and follow-up of them.	1 2 3 4 5 6 7
I exhibit solid change management skills and engage complexity well.	1 2 3 4 5 6 7
Confident, responsive crisis management is a hallmark of my leadership.	1 2 3 4 5 6 7
Seeing to accountability is an essential and consistent aspect of my leader behavior.	1 2 3 4 5 6 7
	☐ **Sub-total**

(Comparative norms for this instrument exist for a collective data set of several hundred subjects; They can be obtained from the author at gene@ coachingwithstrengths.com.)

> **STRONGBOX 7-3:** *Some people disparagingly refer to non-productive workers as "dead wood." In my experience, there is no such thing, just "killed timber," the result of underwhelming and disempowering leadership.*
> *- Anonymous*

LEADER STRENGTHS

A shorter and quicker format for assessment of leader strengths is the following inventory. The instructions are short and easy to follow, and it often generates substantial amounts of dialogue, leading to useful insights as well. It can also be used as an alternate form to the lengthier 7 Essential Talent assessment.

LEADER STRENGTHS INVENTORY

Directions: There are three steps here: First, read each of the twenty items and decide which statements best match your strengths. Mark each of these personal strengths with a checkmark in the Step 1 column. Then go back over your list, and for each of the items checked off as a strength, rate them from 1 to 3 in the Step 2 column, with 1 = competent, 2 = superior, 3 = masterful. Finally, go to step 3 at the bottom for the final data generation, leading to focused dialogue.

Discussion following the scoring of this instrument usually centers on the higher level (3s) items, and usefully helps the client to see the items' interrelationships with each other, and how they impact the coachee's experience as leader. Clients can also choose areas of the tool to emphasize in a concerted effort at enhancement, using concentrated coaching on that topic or theme in ongoing or subsequent dialogue.

Item #	STRENGTH	STEP 1 (√)	STEP 2 (1, 2 or 3)
1.	Is generally proactive rather than reactive.		
2.	Often takes the initiative.		
3.	Learns easily and with an open mind.		
4.	Communicates clearly with others.		
5.	Is flexible and adapts well.		
6.	Is able to see the big picture clearly.		
7.	Can strategize collaboratively with others.		
8.	Welcomes risk-taking opportunities.		
9.	Has an appreciation for system dynamics.		
10.	Readily acknowledges others as deserved.		
11.	Believes in supporting others' development.		
12.	Delegates often and clearly.		
13.	Brings enthusiasm to all s/he undertakes.		
14.	Helps others to "get on board."		
15.	Is trustworthy and extends trust.		
16.	Is confident of her/his abilities and skills.		
17.	Is respectful of others, prizing differences.		
18.	Sees to alignment of talents & tasks.		
19.	Has a ready & healthy sense of humor.		
20.	Leads others into and through change.		

STEP 3: Circle your "3"s statements—the initial focus of an extended strengths coaching dialogue.

POWER POINTS

For over two decades, many of us have used a globally popular software presentation program called *PowerPoint*, marketed by the Microsoft folks. This coaching activity borrows from that name to represent the identification of pivotal strength-based power elements in the team or organization—the unit's "power points." It focuses on the supervisor or co-worker who would identify colleagues by their strengths and the impacts of regarding them appreciatively. It also can be thought of as helping understand better the group's *assets, assignments,* and *alignments*—a trio of core areas that can represent the positive nucleus. Here's how it goes, using a script to instruct the client:

"First, identify the person or people (limit it to 2-3 maximum) you want to focus on. That could be direct report associates or co-workers on a team or project. Start with one of them and assess the following from observation of their work in role."

1. Begin with one of those associates identified, and list three of their strengths as you've witnessed them (Assets).
2. Next, cite one example of each of those you've experienced, for a total of three. That's one per attribute/asset, not three per asset (Assignments).
3. Finally, write down the witnessed positive consequences of her/his use of those attributes in the workplace, on your team or in your unit (Alignments).

These steps can then be repeated for the other persons identified for the activity. The discussion of these answers with the client can lead to a number of benefits and insights. Typically s/he comes to a new appreciation of each one's individual contributions and *assets* for the group or organization. Further, the coachee often makes sense of the data generated in new lights, such as re-thinking optimal matches for their associates' talents, and the tasks they would address—the *assignments and alignments*. It also may yield an insight about missing strengths for the task at hand.

Another use might be the possible gains to be realized through further dialogue with the rest of one's team or work unit. In other words, I'd urge extending the conversation to a larger collection of associates, ideally even having them do it among themselves as a group activity. That kind of empowering exchange and pooling of assets goes way beyond personal appreciation, and can lead to highly meaningful discussions about collaboration and work relationships. Ultimately, beneficial culture shifts in the work environment can be attained by the telescoping effects of this enlarged dialogue.

LEADER-FOLLOWER STRENGTHS DIALOGUES

Several years of working with execs using an asset focus led to a reflection on my part of what seemed to be the recurring or common themes reported from their conversations with associates about shared work objectives, and their relationships. About ten years ago, this yielded the following list of purposes for ensuring menaingful dialogues between them, initiated by the person in the leader role. It entails both a strengths character, and a deliberate regard for building the relationship between the nominal leader and any/all of their followers in regular, direct contact.

The sequence is not critical, particularly after some time together, where the opportunity for addressing all of them has occurred once. However, I will list them in the initial order I feel they occur most readily, and can build on one another in a natural progression.

1. Recognizing the person—This is the dialogue that seeks to personalize the relationship, access better information and understanding of what makes them each "tick", and acknowledge that both of them are unique and to be regarded as such in most ways.
2. Building trust—This conversation has the ongoing goal of creating a sense of trustworthiness, the attribute that over time leads to comfortable delegation, reliance and mutual truth-telling, as well as basic positive regard.
3. Appreciating the Effort—This repetitive affirming conversation seeks to show gratitude for the consistency of full effort shown, allowing for reasonable risk-taking and productivity, growth and success. Dweck's mindset research as described previously provides a clear argument for its use.
4. Learning and teaching—This conversation targets the reality that an open relationship means at times the "boss" is enlightening the

employee who works under his or her direction, and at other times, it is the reverse, and both are extremely valuable.

5. <u>Making the way clear</u>—Conversations of this type are occasional and can be initiated by either party, but most often come from the supervisee's initiative. They involve the simple, but not always easy solicitation of assistance to facilitate progress when another department, manager or a situation has thrown them a curve or set up a roadblock, knowingly or otherwise. It also is a sign of proactive, positive leadership when the supervisor takes the initiative to engage in this conversation.

6. <u>Coaching for change</u>—Deliberate coaching of one's employee to assist them with a desired or needed change or adaptation is the focus of this dialogue. It usually revolves around the challenge of a psychosocial transition more than a physical or personnel shift.

7. <u>Affirming the process</u>—This is the constant characteristic of conversation that seeks to renew these dialogues, and to affirm their importance and value. It entails both a recognition of people and of their unique sets of needs for communication in the workplace.

In practice, these are not seven discrete conversations or topical dialogues, but a series of ongoing talks that pay heed to these seven types of needs for a flourishing co-worker relationship. Their relative frequency and even formality are very much subject to the nature of the parties, the tasks before them, and their desire to build positivity into the work experience. Thinking of each of these as an essential, yet insufficient part of the relationship will help to ensure the leader pays attention to the holistic quality of the set, and s/he addresses them with every employee in their sphere of direct responsibility. Collectively, they are empowering, engaging, and enabling in the best sense of those terms, and a coach would do well to make this framework a part of their repertoire with leader clients.

EMOTIONAL COMPETENCE ASSESSMENT

The importance of emotional intra- and interpersonal competencies on the conduct of daily life, and especially in the role of leader, is well documented. Some estimates have noted that practice of such skills contribute as much as 60% to 85% of the difference between effective and ineffective leadership. As noted before also, it is the fastest of our somatic response systems, and alerts the mind to needed responses.[1]

The following instrument builds on a compilation of emotional intelligence competencies, using Daniel Goleman's original five-part model of Emotional and Social Intelligence, not his later four-part model.[2] The original motivation items are retained here for this self-assessment tool, as I feel it provides a broader and deeper self-evaluation. It is a very thorough device for use as a coaching discussion topic, often extending to several conversations. The scoring paradigm is simple and easy, and the quiz is fairly quick to take and score, despite its length.

EQ Competency Self-Assessment[3]

Read the 4 statements after each italicized competence, e.g., after Emotional Awareness—and in front of each place a 3 if you feel you usually show a "strong demonstration" of this competence, a 2 for an "adequate demonstration" of the competence, and a 1 for a "weak demonstration" at present. Then add the ratings and divide by 4 for to arrive at a competence average score, placing that score next to that heading in the parentheses. There are 25 EQ Competencies in all here, and the key for rating each follows:

> *3* = <u>strongly</u> *demonstrated competency*
> *2* = <u>moderately</u> *demonstrated competency*
> *1* = <u>weakly</u> *demonstrated competency*

PERSONAL COMPETENCE

Self-Awareness

( ) *EMOTIONAL AWARENESS*: Recognizing one's emotions and their effects. People with this competence . . .
___Know which emotions they are feeling and why
___Realize the links between their feelings and what they think, do, & say
___Recognize how their feelings affect their performance
___Have a guiding awareness of their values and goals

( ) *ACCURATE SELF-ASSESSMENT*: Knowing one's strengths and limits. People with this competence are . . .

____Aware of their strengths and weaknesses

____Reflective, learning from experience

____Open to candid feedback, new perspectives, continuous learning, and self-development

____Able to show a sense of humor and perspective about themselves

( ) *SELF-CONFIDENCE*: Sureness about one's self-worth and capabilities. People with this competence . . .

____Present themselves with self-assurance; have "presence"

____Can voice views that are unpopular and go out on a limb for what is right

____Are decisive, able to make sound decisions despite uncertainties and pressures

____Trust their intuition and experience when making choices

Self-Regulation

( ) *SELF-CONTROL*: Managing disruptive emotions and impulses. People with this competence . . .

____Manage their impulsive feelings and distressing emotions well

____Stay composed, positive, and unflappable even in trying moments

____Think clearly and stay focused under pressure

____Are aware of the impact of extreme behavior

( ) *TRUSTWORTHINESS*: Maintaining standards of honesty and integrity. People with this competence . . .

____Act ethically and are above reproach

____Build trust through their reliability and authenticity

____Admit their own mistakes and confront unethical actions in others

____Take tough, principled stands even if they are unpopular

( ) *CONSCIENTIOUSNESS*: Taking responsibility for personal performance. People with this competence . . .

____Meet commitments and keep promises

____Hold themselves accountable for meeting their objectives

____Are organized and careful in their work

____Think ahead to broad consequences before acting

( ) *ADAPTABILITY*: Flexibility in handling change. People with this competence . . .
___Smoothly handle multiple demands, shifting priorities, and rapid change
___Adapt their responses and tactics to fit fluid circumstances
___Are flexible in how they see events
___Remain open to differing inputs

( ) *INNOVATIVENESS*: Being comfortable with and open to novel ideas and new information. People with this competence . . .
___Seek out fresh ideas from a wide variety of sources
___Entertain original solutions to problems
___Generate new ideas
___Take fresh perspectives and risks in their thinking

Self-Motivation

( ) *ACHIEVEMENT DRIVE*: Striving to improve or meet a standard of excellence. People with this competence . . .
___Are results-oriented, with a high drive to meet their objectives and standards
___Set challenging goals and take calculated risks
___Pursue information to reduce uncertainty and find ways to do better
___Learn how to improve their performance

( ) *COMMITMENT*: Aligning with the goals of the group or organization. People with this competence . . .
___Readily make personal or group sacrifices to meet a larger organizational goal
___Find a sense of purpose in the larger mission
___Use the group's core values in making decisions and clarifying choices
___Actively seek out opportunities to fulfill the group's mission

( ) *INITIATIVE*: Readiness to act on opportunities. People with this competence . . .
___Are ready to seize opportunities
___Pursue goals beyond what's required or expected of them
___Cut through red tape and bend the rules when necessary to get the job done
___Mobilize others through unusual, enterprising efforts

( ) *OPTIMISM*: Persistence in pursuing goals despite obstacles and setbacks. People with this competence . . .

___Persist in seeking goals despite obstacles and setbacks

___Operate from hope of success rather than fear of failure

___See setbacks as due to manageable circumstance rather than a personal flaw

___Demonstrate a belief in the best outcomes at all times

SOCIAL COMPETENCE
Social Awareness

( ) *EMPATHY*: Sensing others' feelings and perspective, and taking an active interest in their concerns. People with this competence . . .

___Are attentive to emotional cues and listen well

___Show sensitivity and understand others' perspectives

___Help out based on understanding other people's needs and feelings

___Recognize that empathy has interpersonal boundaries

( ) *SERVICE ORIENTATION*: Anticipating, recognizing, and meeting customers' needs. People with this competence . . .

___Understand customers' needs and match them to services or products

___Seek ways to increase customers' satisfaction and loyalty

___Gladly offer appropriate assistance

___Grasp a customer's perspective, acting as a trusted advisor

( ) *DEVELOPING OTHERS*: Sensing what others need in order to develop, and bolstering their abilities. People with this competence . . .

___Acknowledge and reward people's strengths, accomplishments, and development

___Offer useful feedback and identify people's needs for development

___Mentor, give timely coaching, and offer assignments that challenge and grow a person's skill

___Practice leader-making "stretch" delegation routinely

( ) *LEVERAGING DIVERSITY*: Cultivating opportunities through diverse people. People with this competence . . .
___Respect and relate well to people from varied backgrounds
___Understand diverse worldviews and are sensitive to group differences
___See diversity as opportunity, creating an environment where diverse people can thrive
___Challenge bias and intolerance

( ) *POLITICAL AWARENESS*: Reading a group's emotional currents and power relationships. People with this competence . . .
___Accurately read key power relationships
___Detect crucial social networks
___Understand the forces that shape views and actions of clients, customers, or competitors
___Accurately read situations and organizational and external realities

Social Skills

( ) *INFLUENCE*: Wielding effective tactics for persuasion. People with this competence . . .
___Are skilled at persuasion
___Fine-tune presentations to appeal to the listener
___Use complex strategies like indirect influence to build consensus and support
___Orchestrate dramatic events to effectively make a point

( ) *COMMUNICATION*: Sending clear and convincing messages. People with this competence . . .
___Are effective in give-and-take, registering emotional cues in attuning their message
___Deal with difficult issues straightforwardly
___Listen well, seek mutual understanding, and welcome sharing of information full
___Foster open communication and stay receptive to bad news as well as good

( ) *LEADERSHIP*: Inspiring and guiding groups and people. People with this competence . . .
___Articulate and arouse enthusiasm for a shared vision and mission
___Step forward to lead as needed, regardless of position
___Guide the performance of others while holding them accountable

___Lead by example

( ) *CHANGE CATALYST*: Initiating or managing change. People with this competence . . .

___Recognize the need for change and remove barriers

___Challenge the status quo to acknowledge the need for change

___Champion the change and enlist others in its pursuit

___Model the change expected of others

( ) *CONFLICT MANAGEMENT*: Negotiating and resolving disagreements. People with this competence . . .

___Handle difficult people and tense situations with diplomacy and tact

___Spot potential conflict, bring disagreements into the open, and help deescalate

___Encourage debate and open discussion

___Orchestrate win-win solutions

( ) *BUILDING BONDS*: Nurturing instrumental relationships. People with this competence . . .

___Cultivate and maintain extensive informal networks

___Seek out relationships that are mutually beneficial

___Build rapport and keep others in the loop

___Make and maintain personal friendships among work associates

( ) *COLLABORATION AND COOPERATION*: Working with others toward shared goals. People with this competence . . .

___Balance a focus on task with attention to relationships

___Collaborate, sharing plans, information, and resources

___Promote a friendly, cooperative climate

___Spot and nurture opportunities for collaboration

( ) *TEAM CAPABILITIES*: Creating group synergy in pursuing collective goals. People with this competence . . .

___Model team qualities like respect, helpfulness, and cooperation

___Draw all members into active and enthusiastic participation

___Build team identity, esprit de corps, and commitment

___Protect the group and its reputation; share credit.

When you have completed the assessment to here, review all 25 competency categories, listing each of them according to score average in the appropriate strengths rating section below:

Demonstrated Strengths (Averages are a 3):

Adequate Competencies (Averages between 2 & 3)

Weaker Abilities (Averages of <2):

Once compiled, one should share the results with the coach in an extended discussion of the competencies of Emotional Intelligence, a Skill Set that some suggest may account for a majority of the difference between outstanding performers and those who are less so, particularly in leadership roles.

STRONGBOX 7-4: *Emotional intelligence isn't a luxury you can dispense with in tough times. It's a basic tool that, deployed with finesse, is the key to professional success.*   - *Harvard Business Review, 2003*

A shorter version of the same kind of social and emotional competency framework assessment follows. It is much less comprehensive than that longer one, is based on the revised four-part Goleman model, and might be used as a start to an emotional intelligence dialogue with a client.[5] The coach might propose a later, second self-appraisal using the longer tool, and it can be used to take an EQ pulse of the client at various times. It is scored both separately by segment, and then the totals of each of those are summed for an overall score. The higher the score, the stronger is one's self-perceived competency set.

The Intelligent Use of Emotions "Self-Rating"

For each of the 20 competency item self-appraisals to follow, use the following scale to rate yourself today:

> *1* = *Just OK; lots of room for improvement here.*
> *2* = *I have a fairly good grasp & practice of it.*
> *3* = *This is well in hand; I'm above average here.*

Self-Awareness

____ a. Reading my own emotions accurately, recognizing their influence, and making wise responses.

____ b. Knowing well my strengths & areas of vulnerability.

____ c. Having a sound sense of my self-worth.

____ d. Possessing a keen sense of personal values.

____ e. Having an abundance mentality; seeing possibilities, even in problems.

____ *Subtotal for Self-Awareness*

Self-Management

____ a. Managing my own disruptive emotions & impulses.

____ b. Displaying honesty, integrity &trustworthiness.

____ c. Flexibly adapting to changing situations & impediments.

____ d. Consistently striving for self-improvement & learning.

____ e. Taking initiative appropriately; seizing opportunities.

____ *Subtotal for Self-Management*

Social Awareness

____ a. Being empathic: sensing others' emotional worlds & being actively interested in them.

____ b. Being savvy about team, organization and field, as well as the broader impacting environments.

____ c. Recognizing & meeting others' needs.

____ d. Having an understanding of generational & cultural differences.

____ e. Challenging instances of injustice, bias & unfairness.

____ *Subtotal for Social Awareness*

Relationship Management

____ a. Providing vision & inspiration to followers and other colleagues.

____ b. "Making the case" for and supporting change when & with whomever necessary.

____ c. Helping others take risks to learn, grow & stretch.

____ d. Building teamwork & collaborating.

____ e. Seeing to routine recognition & reward of others as called for.

____ *Subtotal for Relationship Management*

_____ **Overall Total Score(Sum the four subtotals).**

The range of possible scores for each of the four segments is 5-15, and the total range is 20-60. Norms based on a diverse set of 273 completers provide <u>median</u> scores as follows:

Self-Awareness = 12.5   Self-Management = 13.8
Social Awareness = 14.0   Relationship Management = 11.1
Total Score median = 51.4, with a range of 37 to 58.

Discussion of these, too, can proceed like one might following the longer instrument's administration and scoring, looking at the overall section and total scores compared to norm medians, then looking at the 3s in each set to determine what led to their development. Then, conversation can move to the client's preferred targets for growth, and those that may be ongoing bugbears for him or her. I suggest they may be optimally leveraged by first using each of the four subsets as a focus, and later examining the five items in each of those to identify concrete places to improve.

> **STRONGBOX 7-5**: *Truth is not to be found inside the head of an individual person, it is born between people collectively searching for truth, in the process of their dialogic interaction.*
> *- Mikhail Bakhtin*

Positive Deviance

Kim Cameron of the POS program at Michigan has a small gem of a book called *Positive Leadership*, subtitled *Strategies for Extraordinary Improvement.*[6] Not only does Cameron make the case well and repeatedly for the advantages of the described approach to leading, but he provides some concrete advice for how to go about it. These positive strategies are readily adoptable, make perfect sense, and are encouraging to use.

In addition to a very helpful set of short self-assessments throughout, the book also provides a coherent model of four key aspects of positive leader behavior. These are all complementary elements of what Cameron calls "Positive Deviance," and include appreciative approaches to setting climate, building relationships, communicating affirmatively, and deriving positive meaning in the workplace.

The evidence in support of adopting this approach in all our efforts to secure productive and satisfying followership is more than merely intuitive. It appears to effect gains in health and well-being, as well as in the bottom line and fiscal margin arenas of our work as leaders. Thus, these approaches are not just good for business, but are self-reinforcing, in that employees as well as managers can see and experience for themselves the gains to be had from going in this direction.

Building on strengths in the manner described will provide the leader with an entire arsenal of integrated strategies for creating extraordinary results and highly successful organizations, no matter the environment—product or service, private or public.

In close of this segment of the chapter, and to provide some transition from leader-focused to group and team coaching, I'll make the following recommendation: Some of the best writing and the most useful inputs for coaching leaders and organizations can be found in *Appreciative Leadership.*[7] It offers solid, potent prescriptions and evidence to support the approaches outlined, and I commend it to the reader as a plentiful, contemporary resource for leadership coaching ideas, and thematic organization development assistance. I have used it with a number of individuals and groups or classes, always with positive effects.

Coaching Groups

Next, let me make a key point distinguishing between two similar practices with coaching groups: There are several differences between coaching a group of people who only share the interest in developing professionally, versus coaching a group of individuals who serve a common purpose, such as a project team or ongoing group of common direct reports. In the former, the coach is just using the economical context of shared time and discussion to enable clients to get inputs from the coach and the insights of those sharing the coaching time and focus on a common, usually developmental topic. This is not a frequent format that I use, but several coaches have formed entire practices in this way, often using a phone bridge to a common number for telephone group coaching. This can work especially well with a niche group—say all lawyers, or dentists, or small business owners, or people in transition job- or career-wise. In a common, compact geographic area, this can even be done as a coaching support group with regular face-to-face sessions. This model also works in a single organization where the group format is an economical way of coaching several "Hi-Pos," or functional unit heads or managers of commonly dedicated units in a single session. A very recent helpful and comprehensive writing on the matter is Ginger Cockerham's *Group Coaching: A Comprehensive Blueprint.*[8] Now let's look at how team coaching differs in practice from coaching a group as defined above.

Team Coaching

The same individual assessments of strengths can be done with small teams, and three web-based, private instruments in particular lend themselves to this well: The *Realise2,* the new *StandOut* protocol, both mentioned before, and the *Klein Group Instrument.*[9] The latter, despite its label, is a facile, interesting, well-tested and widely utilized team assessment based in the Jungian typology popularized in the MBTI—the Myers-Briggs Temperament Inventory. They all provide for assessment of intact units of workers, and they generate profiles of those teams that enable unit coaching. If strengths identification is a fundamental departure point for team coaching, these offer a good place to start.

Coaching a team is usually a more concisely focused activity than group coaching, as the membership is often fairly stable, and the focus is on one of two shared main objectives: enhancing team cohesion and productivity, and/or facilitating project completion. The next segment speaks further to an approach to team coaching, and offers a series of approaches and tools for doing so. It begins with a statement of the reasons and approaches to team coaching, and then offers a number of devices for alternative interventions when coaching teams.

Why & How To Coach Teams

Purposes: 1. To enhance the abilities of the team to communicate, collaborate and produce collectively through shared coaching experiences as a unit. It allows for team members to optimize their unique and different strengths in the service of a common goal.

Team Coaching Objectives:

Learning & Information-sharing has as its goal the ongoing use of a coached session to help enlarge the mutual teaching-learning dialogues that help ensure a team has optimized its members' knowledge and planning time together. It is the primary focus of team meetings under the eye of the coach, who usually offers both process feedback and some inputs about additional techniques and approaches for the team's tasks. One pattern for this might schedule monthly "best practice" sharing sessions, led by a rotational list of participants.

Development as a team is really two types of sessions: one in which the sole purpose is coaching around how the members relate, what dynamics are noteworthy, and how to improve on their process of sharing. This sometimes includes instrumental coaching, and also often helps deal with inter-member conflict negotiation. A second developmental pattern often entails an ongoing series of sessions with a single, comprehensive theme or topic addressed, so that members acquire a practical new skill over time. The coach is an applications consultant in this format, versus the earlier process dynamics focus. Developmental sessions are the second most common types of coached team meetings.

Decision-making is a related objective, but is narrowly focused on the determination of a course of action, given a previous sharing of facts and options. The focus for coaching here is the actual decision process and making sure the team has done its best with both input and throughput in order to arrive at the best output. The coach can borrow heavily form the literature about choosing and deciding provided in the earlier mindset chapter. It is the third most frequent type of meeting agenda using coaching assistance.

Creativity & Innovation is a special form of coached session where the goal is to generate a novel set of proposals for altering the way the business is conducted, arriving at a new way of collaborating to deliver services or products. Its sole focus is the use of creative techniques to innovate, aided by the coach who often suggests formats for the session, introduces meeting modifications, and offers some creative strategies.

A combination of two or more of these objectives is the rarest of session types, and usually just emerges as such rather than coming about as a planned multi-focal meeting.

Framework: Team coaching differs from one-to-one coaching in a few ways: first, is the fact that the team's own ongoing or start-up system and dynamic entity is the focus of coaching; then, there is the likelihood that the coaching agenda is initially set by a team leader or their supervisor, rather than the team itself, at least to begin with. However, often the coach starts discussions with the team and finds that the needed focus is different from what was described, and yet it almost always entails one of the five objectives listed above. Third, although confidentiality is almost never able to be maintained in a group, the team members can be asked to honor one another's sense of privacy, and keep discussion of the team's coaching transactions within the group. Ideally, the team members will introduce their difference of opinion and feeling during coaching sessions instead of in what Gervase Bushe referred to as "sidebar conversations that create organizational mush." Finally, as this is in the context of a strengths or asset-based construct, the sessions adopt the principles of appreciative inquiry, seeking to reframe negative experience in terms of the growth and learning potential of a positivist approach.

Format: The team coaching session is usually best conducted on a regular schedule, with weekly sessions the norm at the outset, and possibly moving to biweekly if the team chooses to after a period of time, usually three or more months into a life of the team, and half or full year arrangements. In these sessions, the coach can best serve as a process consultant in the same general sense that Edgar Schein depicted that kind of facilitation—for process not content, for thematic and transactional issues, not decisions themselves, and as a respondent, not a meeting facilitator. There also are usually about three places where the strengths coach to a team offers significant input: First is at the outset, in soliciting a reflection from all members about their individual best experiences with the team or its members since the last session—usually with a gratitude statement citing a noteworthy positive highlight. Next, the coach is responsible for intervening with apt coaching commentary, usually some form of inquiry, whenever during the group session it is prompted by her/his observation and sense of timing. At the end of the session, too, it is useful to have the coach make a final statement in summary of observed progress and dynamics, and to offer a thought or two to ponder between sessions. A brief, whole group appreciative evaluation at the close of the session is always encouraged as well.

STRONGBOX 7-6: *To sustain leadership effectiveness, leaders should emphasize coaching as a key part of their role and behavioral habits.*
- Richard Boyatzis

Team-Building

In *Senior Leadership Teams: What it Takes to Make Them Great*, by Ruth Wageman, Debra Nunes, James Burruss & James Hackman, the authors highlight the main findings of their team research.[10] These are the three *Essential* conditions of senior leadership teams, which are the basic prerequisites for good team performance, and the three *Enabling* conditions of senior leadership teams, which smooth the way to excellence and accelerate a team's movement down that path. The final one of these they listed is team coaching. My experience says these are not limited to senior teams, but provide a good checklist for any team that would function optimally. A brief summary of those findings follows:

The Essentials : Senior leaders need to establish the essential conditions for leadership teams by (1) creating a real team, rather than one that is a team in name only, (2) providing the team with a clearly communicated, concrete, and compelling purpose, and (3) ensuring that the team consists of members who have the combined knowledge, skill, and experience that are required for the team's work. When these conditions are in place, the team has a solid foundation for carrying out its work, and is positioned to set out on a course of highly competent, collaborative teamwork.

The Enablers: The three enabling conditions they identified are having (1) a solid team structure, (2) a supportive organizational context, and (3) competent team coaching. These three conditions together enable a team to take full advantage of the solid foundation provided by the essentials. These enabling conditions are not usually fully present at the outset of a team's work; they can be strengthened as the team gains experience and maturity. Essential to the process, say the authors, is effective coaching of the group of execs as a whole.

In summary, they found that it takes a combination of both basic membership faculties and adept facilitative traits for a team to excel, especially an executive or senior leadership group. Thus, coaching for composition, optimizing the use of differing and complementary strengths, and a use of facilitative process are major contributions in team coaching, as derived from the research cited above. The helpful coach can introduce and apply the principles and processes noted with any team, and gradually use those frameworks to great benefit for them. Having a champion for this process as the team leader also goes a long way toward helping this to be realized.

In other notable research about coaching teams, two of these same authors (Hackman & Wageman) have offered this wise counsel for the team coach: Assuming the design and composition of the team is well done, and the organization is disposed to support and facilitate the team's charge, then the following timely matches of process and focus apply optimally. The agenda for coaching early in a team's life ideally is relational and motivational in focus. At midpoint, where the progress of their collective task is most dynamically in view, there is a greater chance for coaching to benefit the team through a strategy focus. In fact, they cite studies that show such mid-life intervention is also associated with greater financial yield, productivity and cohesion. Late in a team's life, the task cycle aligns best with coaching interventions that address knowledge acquisition, and skill development and transfer.[11] What follows next is a versatile tool for team-building that speaks to these dynamics from a slightly different, yet related vantage point, using a descriptive ruler.

TEAMWORK DESCRIPTIVE RULER

In the previous chapter, I provided a handful of examples of "descriptive rulers," linear rating scales that use words instead of numbers for their relative rankings in response to an evaluative query about a subject of interest to the client being coached. Below is a ruler I created that is adapted from the work of Richard Weaver & John Farrell in their 1997 book titled *Managers as Facilitators*.[12] I have used the ideas from this inventive book many times in training settings and group dynamics classes over the years.

This group/team coaching tool expands on what they called the "6 Cs of Relationship," and offers a useful self- and team member assessment for the coaching conversation about teamwork and an intact group's dynamics. For instance, when used with coaching any individual team member, the dialogue can focus more on what is motivating that perception or feeling, and how to work personally to help achieve better levels of teamwork. Similarly, if the ruler is used for a team coaching session, the (almost always varying) levels described by the members can be the focus of a group conversation about the meanings and consequences of those descriptive variances. Then, too, it can be done as combined self- and team ratings, and the differentials for each rater can be plumbed in turn, both for cause and better understanding. Ideally, such an analysis could use a "success" lever, seeking to discover why and how the achievement of the median or mean level of co-working came about, then looking to use such lessons to enhance the group's functioning and cohesion. It could also be used at several intervals of a couple weeks to a month, to derive a graphic developmental picture of the team's progress together over time. Another way to use it is for a separate assessment to be done by all team members for each of their differing projects, or by individual team members for their different teams, especially where people may function in a matrix or cross-functional manner.

Other possible uses for this self-assessment of group contribution and partnership levels are fairly easy to devise. Asking the entire team to contribute to deciding what would best serve their interest at the time of rating may be the most appreciative way of going, as the exercise feels less imposed when the raters choose their own use and evaluative framework. The instrument and its basic instruction follow:

The Road to True Partnership

This framework suggests a continuum that often can be seen on teams, with behaviors and attitudes demonstrably ranging from complete autocracy to full partnership. As one goes up the list from *Coercion* to *Co-Ownership,* the dynamic also moves away from <u>adversarial</u> relating to true <u>partnering</u>, and simultaneously involves the positive shift from "win-lose" to "win-win" paradigms. Assess the level at which you see your team functioning at present, and use the data as the focus of shared learning conversations.

7. <u>*Co-Ownership*</u>: Reflects fully shared responsibility for the work and its outcome; a truly interdependent "working together" accountability model that creates mutual excitement and finds meaningfulness in the work.

6. <u>*Collaboration*</u>: Having a sense of working in tandem, alongside one another, though perhaps not yet fully engaged or responsible for it

all, and likely to be independent still. May care more for the outcome than the people.

5. *Commitment*: A level of moderate effort that equates minimally to a willingness to see things through to completion together; pleasant but not enthused, and likely to be motivated by external rather than intrinsic prods.

4. *Cooperation*: Working together, yet still regarding one's own considerations above that of the commonweal for the group. This is the first (and least) level where people have crossed a line from "me" to "we" thinking to begin to exhibit leadership qualities.

3. *Coexistence*: An independent "I'll do my thing and you are responsible for yours" mindset, that limits contributions. Members are likely to be compliant without any commitment.

2. *Confrontation*: More like a joust to see who can prevail in a minor power struggle; sees little or none of the overall, shared goal, and may render the group impotent to perform as a whole.

1. *Coercion*: Involves the use of power to effect a personally desired outcome; extremely limiting for the group's shared goals, and usually fosters resentment. May also lead to sabotage or abandonment.

While not a strengths tool *per se*, for team and organization-level readiness, I also like and can recommend using the Change Readiness Gauge available from psychologist Chris Musselwhite's *Discovery Learning* shop in Greensboro NC.[13] It measures four areas of change readiness in an efficient, well-researched 40-item instrument. These include awareness, capacity, reactions, and mechanisms for an organization to have at the ready in order to take on change. There is also an interesting and thorough assessment for exploring personal change inclinations called the Change Style Indicator, and one with a circumplex model assessment of ten leadership categories, called the Discovery Leadership Profile, for coaches looking to assist clients with data-based approaches to those topics. The tests are easy to use and to administer, including online access.

> ***STRONGBOX 7-7***: *To improve the way a product is made or a service is provided, when the job is complex, when customer service and quality are important, or when rapid change is necessary—these are the conditions that create the need for teams.*　　　　　　　　　　　　　*- Daniel Levi*

THE "3 WHAT'S?"

Next, we'll consider a device for informing group members, and securing immediate and pertinent, brief feedback in small teams, called "The 3 What's." I have helped install this appreciative informing practice in more than a dozen organizations to date, and its utility, simplicity and consistently reported benefits lead me to commend it to your consideration. It is a scheme for a quick "check-in" at the outset of the workday for groups of affiliated workers. I have seen it used throughout entire large organizations, and also just with leader teams, as well as with functional groups as diverse as housekeeping units and clusters of tech workers.

It is a daily, short convening of team members—usually not even seated—to achieve four things:

1. An appreciative sharing of what has gone well the previous day.
2. A quick depiction of what is on people's plates—individually and collectively—for the current day.
3. A short, anticipatory mention of what is coming up soon, beyond today, for the participants, and
4. A process goal of face-to-face team-building and inclusive communication and feedback, literally building cohesion and connection while informing one another and sharing appropriate feedback.

The sessions usually take only ten to fifteen minutes, longer with larger groups, while the lesser time allotment usually suffices for groups of seven or fewer. Each question is posed in turn by the designated or chosen group facilitator or leader, and every participant "checks in" as appropriate about the items mentioned, making it a quick and useful strengths-focused informing and feedback process. The leader also keeps track of and adheres to the pre-set time limit. The _ONLY_ three items for it follow:

1. *"What's* one thing that happened in the previous work day that represents a "best", a gratitude or a positive event"—these can be small or big—it doesn't matter, as long as each attendee provides a short positive response. One can ask simply *"What* was good? or *"What* went well?"

or perhaps "*What* was yesterday's/Friday's best?" Answers to this "*What*" don't usually need any responses, although some participants may wish to affirm, reinforce or congratulate the speaker.

2.   After the final person has spoken on that, the leader shifts to the next question: "*What's* Up? (today), sometimes worded "*What's* On?" or "*What's* Happening?" For this and the third inquiry, participants may offer to assist, perhaps to pave the way or clear the path to help ensure success or completion, provide additional input about a statement, or ask a question, and it's always done <u>briefly</u>.

3.   After that second question's responses are exhausted, and replies have been given, the leader poses the final question: "*What's* Coming (Up)?" This may refer to tomorrow, or just someday soon, maybe later in the week or month, or even further down the calendar if it refers to a big or complex project or objective needing a lot of contributions and preparation. It serves as a longer-term "heads up," and completes the temporal cycle of having addressed the recent past, the imminent present, and the near future. One of the groups using this format has chosen to call it their "3H session," which stands for the three questions' time focus: *What's* <u>H</u>appened, *What's* <u>H</u>ere & Now, and *What's* on the <u>H</u>orizon!

After that final question has been responded to, the leader closes the session, saying "Thanks! Have a good day, all," or "Thanks! See you together again tomorrow/Monday at (whatever is the next appointed time)." Group leaders in this meeting also sometimes give a summary reminder before the "sign-off," something like, "Those of you who need to confer further about any of this, today or hereafter, should huddle separately *asap*," then offer thanks and adjourn.

These sessions seem to work best when participants meet fairly early, (i.e., within the first hour or so of the work day or shift), and stand throughout—although some groups do sit, and coffee is sometimes in hand. The meeting should always be held at the same time, and ideally in the same place, usually a large enough office or small conference room. It is not a forum for sharing gossip, or small talk about weather, recent sports events, or other less important, non-work-related items. Sometimes the session leader needs to police that at the outset of using this format, until the routine and its protocol become commonplace.

Although the great majority of the groups I know that are using this do so daily, i.e., each scheduled work day, one group I know of goes on a

M-W-F schedule, and another meets only on all even numbered calendar days, while yet another gathers on Tuesdays & Fridays. The content sharing is certainly important, and when well used, it can become a vital and timely part of a group's communication. However, an equally important gain and use of it is for team-building . . . the process is paramount! Lastly, an occasional short verbal evaluation of the gains from this format is worth assessing; I usually suggest it be done no more often than monthly.

> **STRONGBOX 7-8**: *The mind is not a vessel to be filled, but a fire to be kindled.*
> *- Plutarch*

LEADERS OF THE PACK

In the opening pages of *Power Up!* I described the process and outcomes of an activity I do with groups that has them recall prior coaching experiences from earlier life contexts. Another introductory activity I sometimes use in conjunction with the previous coaching experience review, and especially with teamwork and leadership training, follows here. It can work with both previously intact teams, and a heterogeneous participant group. The notes below offer an example of the directions, variations, sample items, and debriefing topics that could be used. If time allows, I often follow this up with some discussion of a more measured strength set using an instrument to gather comparable depictions, and to provide a common language for describing strengths. The *I AM. Describing My Star,* or *Strengths Self-Rating* activities described earlier can suit this purpose well.

Using a series of quick self- and other identifications, I instruct the group members thus: "Nominate yourself or another from among you here present as 'leader of this pack' for each of the following tasks:"

Who would be *strongest* or *best* among you here present at . . .
- giving an extemporaneous speech on how to sail a boat
- explaining the accounting details of a budget (P & L statement)
- demonstrating how to change an infant's diaper
- mentoring a new employee in a management role
- showing how to build a wooden coffee table
- pairing up to give a dance lesson (name two)
- designing a customer service training program

- selecting wines for a high end restaurant meal
- being able to console a mourner at a funeral
- being featured soloist in a *Glee* spoof
- being able to write a powerful and poignant poem
- cooking at a BBQ for this group
- translating a document written in . . . Spanish, Mandarin, French, German, English, "computerese", as a court brief, etc.

This can also be done with a <u>nonverbal, self-directed</u> "lining up" of all group members in a "strongest to least strong" rank order. Using a combination of the two approaches to identify the differing strengths within the group works also, and provides some variety, helping to get people up and moving, staying energized while illustrating the points described below for debriefing afterward.

Following a rating of the entire list, or even just a sampling of it, I gather the participants for a short discussion. In that discussion, and usually in this order, we reflect on the experience and the "data" it generated:

(1) strengths "self-awareness," having each note their new awareness of relative strengths in the pack, and examining the features of a strength, beyond just skilled performing of it,
(2) recognition of <u>differing</u> types and levels of strengths among the group,
(3) acknowledging that no one is strong in every area,
(4) helping to see the importance of playing to & with those strengths,
(5) acknowledging the power of a *team* of diversely strong members,
(6) sharing their overall reaction, e.g., what are the lessons they have found in this activity, and its ranking "outcomes."

Organization-Wide Coaching

The final approach to be covered in this last chapter is an inquiry-based checklist for planning possible organization-wide adoption of coaching. This actually is a set of questions that will enable an organization to decide about the timing and advisability of undertaking enterprise coaching. These seven inquiry frames that use a mnemonic for "seizing the moment," allow for a comprehensive evaluation of the prospects for doing so. It is part needs assessment, yet mostly an appraisal of the organization's readiness for this critical undertaking—no small consideration. The use of L-E-A-D coaches within the organization as both literal and figurative "pilots" for the initiative, as well as ongoing monitors and promoters of it, is also explained.

> **STRONGBOX 7-9**: *The use of experienced L-E-A-D, i.e., Learning, Enabling, Applying, and Developing coaches, will help implement, catalyze, and accelerate enterprise-wide coaching in an organization.*

"Cs-ING" THE MOMENT

7 Basic Question Sets for Organization-wide Implementation of Coaching

What follows is a set of questions in 7 overlapping categories that can help frame the planning activities for an organization that is contemplating system-wide implementation of a coaching initiative.

Champions
Who can ensure the enterprise-wide endeavor has support? . . . voice? . . . persistence?
What will others—coaches in particular—need (from them) to succeed?

Climate
Is this a good time to launch a coaching program?
Is senior leadership poised to enroll and engage associates in this initiative?

Culture
To what extent are these elements present?
- developmental values & collaborative corporate beliefs
- risk-taking is encouraged
- learning from mistakes is a norm
- regular & positive feedback is given
- basically healthy organization & members
- nonhierarchical atmosphere exists
- key people who are open to growing the coaching process

Coaches
How shall we select, train, and match coaches with coachees?
What will be the L-E-A-D* coaches' roles, who are they, and how shall we make their presence known & used?

Clients
With what levels of employees will coaching be done?
What are the purposes of coaching here? (In terms of desired results and goal-related aims, as well as organizational strategy links).

Communication
How & when should we introduce it as an enterprise-wide endeavor?
How might we propose that coaching be spread within the organization?

Counting
Where will coaching 'reside' administratively?
How shall we keep records & assess coaching's impact, costs, ROI & practice excellence?

    *The reference to **L-E-A-D** Coaches above is the acronym for a feature I've created in organizations that helps ensure the dissemination initiative for coaching has "legs, teeth, acuity and longevity." By that I mean these four things respectively: That it . . .

    . . . can move quickly and concertedly to become enterprise-wide in a reasonable time period
    . . . will be a process that finds both champions and support within the organization
    . . . will be both a strategic and a tactical implementation—linked to organization goals and tailored for desired results, and
    . . . is more than a passing fancy as a program, finding thorough enculturation and continuing development.

    The early addition of a cadre of trained coaching "models" among key operatives, that is built on the following related behaviors, can go a long way toward ensuring those outcomes. The letters in the word stand for the following facilitative goals:

Learning—Teaching skills, sharing insights and info. and co-coaching

Enabling—Clearing the way for coaching success; administrative shoehorning and facilitation for organization-wide impact

Applying—Exploring additional coaching applications specific to the work setting & contexts

Developing—Helping individual coaches to grow in the role of coach

To amplify this framework further, first there is the ready availability for consulting that these L-E-A-D coaches can provide. A quick question and opinion, a reinforcing comment or alternative frame to suggest, a coaching moment itself—all can readily be available for the coach in the organization. Then there is the ability to help navigate the organization's infrastructure to enable coaching to occur more smoothly and without impedance, and to be seen to have value for all involved. In addition, the L-E-A-D coach placement can be a sensor for the organization to determine additional, perhaps more fruitful enlargements of the coaching function in the organization. Such a resource often is more capable than an outside coach of knowing the contexts and broader needs of the organization to optimize the use of coaching. Finally, the ability to assist fledgling coaches to grow in the role and to become better coaching practitioners is a fourth type of asset that a L-E-A-D coach can offer to the organization.

Widely distributed placements and communicated availability of L-E-A-D coaches are a boon to the start-up effort in an organization, and may become even more valuable to furthering coaching goals and smooth dissemination as the enterprise is rolled out more widely. Sufficient numbers of such resource people will go a long way toward ensuring desired outcomes for coaching dyads and for the organization as a whole.

A helpful recent pair of publications speaking to the matter of organization coaching, albeit in other contexts than primarily using strengths, are *Organizational Coaching: Building Relationships, Processes, and Strategies* by Virginia Bianco-Mathis, Cynthia Roman, and Lisa Nabors, plus *Coaching in Organizations* by Madeleine Homan and Linda Miller.[14] These two contemporary resources speak comprehensively to their subject matter, and are quite worthwhile additions to the organization coach's library.

The brief Conclusion to follow that will close the formal portion of *Power Up!* briefly summarizes the key coaching approaches from this book, and invites you go to my website for further resources. It ends with a brief forecast of the immediate future of coaching, and an invitation to join and contribute, if you are not already doing so.

> **STRONGBOX 7-10:** *Be a student so long as you still have something to learn, and this will mean all your life.* - Henry L. Doherty

CONCLUSION

STRONGBOX A-1: *A true friend knows your weaknesses but shows you your strengths; feels your fears but fortifies your faith; sees your anxieties but frees your spirit; recognizes your disabilities but emphasizes your possibilities.*
- William Arthur Ward

This brief Conclusion summarizes the key coaching approaches from this book, and suggests you go to my website for further information, links and perspectives. It ends with a brief forecast of the bright future of strengths-based coaching, and encouragement to the reader to jump in with both feet!

In Summary . . .

The pages of this *Guide* that you have just read have offered a series of observations and reports on what this thing called professional coaching has evolved to of late. It looked at the contexts and practices of coaching, its ongoing challenges, and its promise for tomorrow, with particular use of the lens of personal and professional strengths. The core of the book detailed a range and number of knowledge sets—ways of viewing, knowing, and acting on a client's issues and presentation of interests. These included new ways of regarding the coaching enterprise, the requisite skills and approaches to its conduct, and a number of applications, instruments and activities—tools of the trade, if you will. It included a collection of those same frames for working with teams and their leaders, as well as with whole organizations seeking to integrate coaching into their behavioral repertoires.

The key features described in *Power Up!* include the main reasons for using a strengths lens to aid with leader development—the compelling data for a positivist approach and building on assets, not merely attempting to remedy deficits. A growing body of both research and practical evidence in support of the desirability and even the superiority of an appreciative mindset and the behaviors that follow is portrayed. Thus, a strengths foundation is seen as one of the distinguishing features of the coaching promoted in these pages. It is a model that has a number of evidence-based proponents, and a fast-expanding practice compendium.

Next, we explored a wide-ranging set of mental maps, each relevant to growing the effectiveness of performers in all work roles, as well as that of those who coach them. My twenty-four years of work as a coach have led to identifying these topics and the most contemporary thinking on them, themes such as change, goal-setting and decision-making, as central and recurrent themes. Such mindsets make all the difference in effectiveness for their users, and provide the launching platform for actions and formats for optimal use of strengths with relationship-forming and growth, and for choice-making in a variety of contexts. A broad set of perspectives on the frequent thoughts and actions found in routine, as well as extraordinary challenges, is a strong feature of the chapter on mindset. Coaching prerequisites, principles and values were detailed in this segment of *Power Up!* Highlighting this also was the framework for both single session and fuller relational coaching that I call the 7-D model. It is a thorough and flowing schema that aids both parties to coaching to achieve their goals for interacting successfully.

Following that, the recommended coaching skills, especially using the helping formats of "Three IFs, all ands, and no buts," are explained. Here, too, we examined the various ways of creating a coaching relationship that optimizes inquiry and growth, and ensures an ethical partnership of professionals where dialogue and self-direction are highly prized.

The most practical section of the book, the tools found in chapter six, delivered rationales and activities, measures and means for helping clients access their strengths. It introduced nearly thirty different devices, and showed how to employ them in order to achieve their clients' desired objectives, and to help them to grow those powers for performing to new levels of satisfaction and excellence.

Following that tool set segment, the contexts of team and organization, as well as the roles of leadership of them, were spotlighted for nearly a dozen more implements and applications for strengths adaptation and usage. This final section discussed the unique characteristics of group coaching and provided several formats for doing so, along with measurements of attributes used by team members and leaders. Lastly, organization-wide coaching as an positive intervention was addressed. The narrative part of the book will close next with an Appendix highlighting some recent survey research findings and features of coaching.

In all, the pages of *The Guide* have described for readers the perspectives, tools, and dyadic as well as group and team competencies for a successful coaching endeavor using the strengths template and its advantages.

7 SUMMARY TIPS FOR EFFECTIVE STRENGTHS COACHING

Let me summarize in just seven categorical statements the key aspects of effective strengths coaching as promoted in the Guide:

1. Use the 7-D Format—Declare, Define, Distinguish, Differentiate, Develop, Decide, Determine—both overall and by session.
2. Focus on Strengths—Consciously solicit, draw out, build on, and reinforce stories of what works. Help clients achieve <u>at least</u> a 3:1 ratio of positive to negative talk—research on positive emotions, on undertaking change, and for relationship-building are all compelling on that point.
3. Optimize their "Air Time"—Be a model of respect and good listening, providing scaffolded, appreciative feedback and opportunity for insightful reflection with the 3 IF skill sets.
4. *Stay in the Coach Role*—Check any tendency to be the expert by offering unsolicited suggestions or advice. Use questions to help them find their own wisdom, and help them strengthen their capacity for informed decision-making.
5. *Help Clients Speak from the Inside Out*—Encourage coachees to share the hopes, dreams, and passion they find are rooted in their personal experience, urging them to be candid and generous with their narratives.
6. *Apply Activities & Assessments Wisely*—From the outset and throughout the coaching process, use various formats to create data for dialogue, to help document progress, and to provide feedback. Be spare and timely with them; here less is often more.

7. *Ensure Their Success*—Catch people doing things right, as Ken Blanchard used to say, and recognize them for it. Help them make commitments that they intend and are able to keep. Connect them to useful technical and human resources, including other people or work that can support well what they're trying to accomplish.

Website

This (http://www.coachingwithstrengths.com) is the link to my coaching website, and I urge you to find your way there to explore other aspects of my strengths coaching practice, including some of the major links cited herein. It is updated routinely, and logged articles of pertinent topics for your coaching consideration and personal reflection can be found there. This is also the location of weekly blog items on strengths, positivity, leadership and coaching. You are invited to continue with mutual learning and conversations there.

Hereafter

One of the most exciting and promising applications of strengths awareness and usage is the organization-wide "Master Resilience Training" program that Seligman and others have helped the U. S. Army establish recently.[1] It is not strictly a coaching program *per se,* and is actually more a multidimensional training program using many of the tools, skills and mindsets referenced in these pages. Also, recent reports celebrated the United Kingdom-wide adoption of societal well-being measures and promoting the sharing of these as indices of community health.[2] These two massive interventions using a strengths platform are very promising heralds of a positively transformed society that are both a stimulating and a heartening vision for the near term.

Future developments, including the growth of empirical foundations for using the best practices and tools for both general and specified coaching needs offer exciting prospects for maturation and stabilization of the field. Coaches and their clients, and client organizations will all gain from those incipient and impending improvements. Further understanding of the role of strengths and the surest ways to their development and use will also augment the lessons and perspectives found in *Power Up.* The future looks exciting, indeed, and, as an old African proverb translates, "Tomorrow belongs to the people who prepare for it today." I encourage you to join in getting ready for it; better still, help make it come to be!

> **STRONGBOX A-2:** *I've got my faults, but living in the past is not one of them. There is no future in it.* — *Sparky Anderson*

APPENDIX

I have compiled an extended sketch of the primary findings from several research papers and surveys that detail the recent evolution of coaching to its current state today, in 2011. This will enable those readers who want to delve deeper into the breadth and nature of professional coaching to see more clearly its standing as a contemporary business phenomenon.

Contemporary Survey Data

Let's look first at highlights from some of the several coaching surveys and studies conducted in the past few years to shed some light on how coaching is viewed and used in North America and abroad, in both small and large organizations, and with varying types of professional roles.

In 2006, and again in 2008, the ICF commissioned a global study that highlighted a number of findings for the field.[1] Recalling that those data are now some years old, the relevant key findings included . . .

- o A conservative estimate of 30,000+ coaches worldwide
- o Revenues exceeding $1.5 billion per year (USD)
- o Slightly more females were both coaches & clients
- o Most (4/5) held advanced degrees and were of mid-life+ age
- o Executive, Leadership & Life Enhancement categories accounted for 19%, 18%, and 16% (respectively) of practice niches

Drake, Beam, Morin partnered with the Human Capital Institute in 2008 to survey several hundred coaching clients, most at the senior officer organization level.[2] Their findings include these:

- • Clients mainly sought coaching to address derailing behaviors, extend their already high performance levels, address short-term situations, groom high potential managers ("Hi-Pos") for advancement, or to enhance teamwork, all at 15% to 18% levels

- The most successful coaching focused on grooming those Hi-Po managers, helping raise execs to higher levels of performance, or addressing derailing behaviors, all at 20% to 30% usage
- The reasons coaches cited when low impacts to coaching were noted included poor goal definition (35%), lack of client commitment (27%), or the coachee was too busy to engage in the process (15%)
- When financial impact was measured, 77% estimated a ROI at least equal to the cost/investment, and as high as 500%
- Overall, 78% rated coaching a very good or excellent proposition, and they planned to increase its targeted usage.

That same year, a well designed study of 114 upper level managers and their 42 coaches in a multinational drug company found several key areas of measurable improvement associated with the coaching process.[3] Those were listed as improvements in people skills, co-worker relationships and communication competencies, engagement with the culture and the work, productivity on the job, and goal- and priority-setting. The coaches were experienced external professionals averaging four years' experience at the time of the study. The company has since expanded its commitment to coaching as an organization intervention vital to leadership development.

Also in 2008, the ICF published a second major survey to detail the profile of their members' coaching clients.[4] Three primary findings were noted:

- Clients were generally quite satisfied with the coaching experience. Nearly all (96 percent) queried indicated that they would repeat the coaching experience
- When monetary gains were an expected outcome, coaching generated a very good return on investment (ROI) for clients
- That ROI for organizations can be significant, with 86% indicating that their company had recovered their investment or done even better.

The *Harvard Business Review* published their executive coaching survey summary in 2009, and the key findings from that 23-item inquiry follow[5]:

o   Most coaches reported that they were working with execs on either developing high potential leaders (48%), or facilitating executive transitions (96%), followed by a sounding board role about the organization's dynamics or with strategy (26%), while 12 % had a derailing behavior focus.

o   Coaching went on for 7 to 12 months usually (45%), with 2-6 months (27%), and 1 to 1.5 years (18%) next in duration.

o   The majority (75%) were using F2F transactions, and a sizeable minority (29%) were doing phone sessions, for which they were paid—half the time by a third party that engaged the coach—from $200 to $3500 per hour, with a median of $500.

o   Tools rated as important in the process included interviewing (86%), and 360° feedback assessments (77%), followed by shadowing (48%), peer support groups (46%), cultural assessment (42%), and instrumental evaluation and feedback (39%).

o   Practically all cited the importance of a solid connection in the relationship with the coach, backed up by the organization's support for the process and providing compensation.

o   The coaches polled cited change readiness (32%) as critical to coachability, followed by active engagement (28%) in the coaching dialogue and process.

Late in 2009, the UK-based Chartered Institute of Personnel & Development, a private, broad HR function resource center, took what they called the "Temperature of Coaching."[6] This survey of a range of organization types in Great Britain noted that 90% of their several hundred respondent organizations said they were involved in coaching, most had been for nearly a decade, and the great majority of them planned to increase their investment in coaching.

Primary uses for coaching program interventions were for overall performance enhancement (40%), leadership development (23%), managing poor performance (20%), talent and succession planning (15%), for engagement, change management, or for "on-boarding:" the acceleration of orientation of new employees or new role assumption, especially among senior staff (10%). The total exceeded 100% due to respondents checking multiple purpose categories.

Further, nearly two-thirds were implementing coaching through their line managers, using internal coaching support, while just 15%

were employing external coaches for direct service. However, the majority (60%) often brought in outside talent for help with program development, training, and to facilitate organization-wide deployment of coaching, as well as for direct senior staff and executive coaching. A third of those surveyed said all employees were offered coaching, while a fifth reserved coaching for talent development. Only a third of those queried indicated that certification of coaches was an important issue for them. Finally, 80% reported that they evaluate the coaching process, but only 11% of companies reported actually measuring outcomes against either expectations or investment.

An Ohio-based executive coaching and coach training organization, Sherpa, issued their 2010 annual commissioned field survey of leader coaches.[7] It should be noted that a significant number of their survey respondents were their own certified former trainees, and their process model is decidedly not a strengths framework. Reported findings included . . .

- A continuing trend toward more developmental (53%) than remedial work (29%) with clients
- A coincidental shift to more senior manager coaching (73%) and away from a multi-level focus (27%)
- Coaching on a schedule accounted for the majority of arrangements, with 26% using weekly, 38% bi-weekly, and the balance connecting at 3 and 4 week intervals, or 'as needed'
- While 87% overall and 91% of HR professionals viewed executive coaching as of high value, few (18%) calculate ROI
- The majority of coaching was still via electronic means, but the in-person motif was more common in large organizations and with internal coaching
- Assessments, i.e., instrumental evaluations used for feedback and coaching, were used frequently, most often (28%) in a comprehensive multi-rater (360°) format, while 23% used either the DiSC, MBTI or Enneagram, and 21% of coaches used any of over a hundred, often self-produced instruments, while 8% used no formal assessment tool
- The typical executive coach had an average of 6 to 8 clients/week; life coaches had slightly fewer, and the more experienced coaches had slightly more clients than novices

- Similarly, the average coaching rate reported was $200 to $340 per hour for executive coaches, and about 60% of that for life coaches, while more experience tipped income in favor of a higher compensation figure
- Annual incomes ranged from an entry baseline of nearly $60K to more than twice that for executive coaches, while life coaches garnered from $30K to about $80K per year when working full time in the role.

On that last item, income, there really is a wide range out there, along with what is more like a bimodal, uneven distribution. The relevant report segments above captured well the session costs and income figures for <u>most</u> coaching practices. Yet there are also a number—a relative handful of only a few hundred out of many thousands, it would seem—who work with executives in a number of sectors, and charge $500 to $1000 per session, and earn at least six-figure incomes doing it. Their format is typically biweekly (24+ per year) sessions, and they conduct numerous assessments, especially at the outset. An interesting variant of late used by some of those coaches is the classic attorney billing model, with either a charge per contact with pro-rating of the hourly fee, or a retainer fee model, where a fixed fee is assessed for a period of time's 24/7 availability by phone, text or email. Those latter agreements are usually 6 or12 month arrangements, and again, those high-end compacts are the exception, far from the norm. There are also some group practices, notably in the finance and manufacturing sectors, where coaching is an ongoing contract, having spanned years, if not a decade or more. This too, is extraordinary, and not the convention in the field at present, but is out there as a limited use format.

Another private corporation, HDA, a UK-based global human resources consultancy with a history of coaching since the 1990s, reported the following highlights from their biennial survey completed in 2010.[8] It canvassed over a dozen industries' correspondents, more than half of which were international employers with anywhere from 100 to 50,000 employees.

Nearly 70% of organizations surveyed provide all levels of employees with coaching opportunities, including using line managers as coaches (67%), while the ratio of those doing so overall dropped to just over half from 86% over the past two years

- The majority of those surveyed said they looked for value and ROI, and 88% said they had found it. Nearly all respondents said coaching impacted positively on business performance at either individual or team levels, and led to easier acceptance of changes
- More than 9 out of 10 preferred experienced coaches, and saw the in person mode—a hallmark of larger organization coaching arrangements—as ideal, compared to telephone coaching, and did so primarily for 3 to 6 month periods
- Only 20% of organizations mentioned having cut back some on coaching due to the economy, while some were using coaching as a recruitment, engagement and retention tool, and a sometime substitute for paid outside training courses
- Over half surveyed said they had a formal evaluation of their coaching process in place, although reports of efforts beyond anecdotal data-gathering and monitoring were sparse.

Numerous additional surveys conducted in the past few years have contributed further perspective and a fuller depiction of the coaching client profile. I would summarize those additions—some of which offer important contrasts—as follows:

- Many found their coach through incidental or networked contacts, not via more formal methods
- Nearly all used telephone sessions, while over half also used email, and more than a third were coached in person
- Clients were split about credentialing, with about 2 in 5 reporting certification was important
- Most coaching compacts were for 6 to 9 months' duration
- Coaching roles most often sought were as a sounding board, motivator, friend, mentor, business consultant or teacher
- Reasons for seeking coaching included time management, career development, business decisions, relationship management & family-work balance
- Reported outcomes by clients included self-awareness, better goal-setting, more satisfying lifestyle, less stress, more self-discovery and self-confidence.

Other coaching objectives, such as personal aspirations, overall goal-setting, and creativity, as well as focused behaviors like completing projects, communicating better, and increasing income were also reported.

The limitations of these findings are few, yet consistent ones. Most are self-report, post-hoc data sets, and certainly represent a truly "apples and oranges" kind of mix of both coaches and clients, contexts and settings, approaches and measures. In other words, it is like looking at a recent folio of camera snapshots from a series of unrelated trips. Comparisons are global at best, and the sources vary so much that overall summary conclusions are neither easy nor reliable. Despite those warnings, there is a flow to the various results that gives the reader a fair overview of some of the borders and impacts of professional coaching in the past five years. Along with chapters one and two, it offers a fairly broad, descriptive picture of modern coaching in the business world.

ENDNOTES

Chapter 1

1. http://www.coachfederation.com; http://www.certifiedcoach.org.
2. Global Coaching Survey, 2008/2009, Frank Bresser Consulting Report, July 2009. Accessed July 2011. www.frank-bresser-consulting.com.
3. ICF Global Coaching Client Study, April 2009, ICF archives. Accessed August 8, 2011. http://www.coachfederation.org/research.
4. "Coaching in Organizations," London, CIPD, 2007.

Chapter 2

1. Parker-Williams, Vernita. 2006. "Business Impact of Executive Coaching: demonstrating monetary value." *Industrial and Commercial Training.* 38(3): 122-127; McGovern, Joy, Lindemann, Michael, Vergara, Monica, Murphy, Stacey, Barker, Linda, and Rodney Warrenfeltz. 2001. "Maximizing the Impact of Executive Coaching: Behavioral Change, Organizational Outcomes, and Return on Investment." *Manchester Review* 6(1): 1-9; Wasylyshyn, Karol M. 2003. "Executive Coaching: An Outcome Study." Consulting Psychology Journal: Practice and Research. 55(2): 94-106.
2. Passmore, Jonathan. 2007. "An Integrated Model for Executive Coaching." *Consulting Psychology Journal: Practice and Research.* 59(1): 68-78.
3. IAC Masteries Overview. Accessed July 2011. http://www.certifiedcoach.org/index.php/get_certified/the_iac_coaching_masteries_overview/.
4. Stober, Dianne R., and Clive Parry. 2005. "Current Challenges and Future Directions in Coaching." In Cavanagh, Michael, Grant,

225

Anthony M. and Travis Kemp, Eds. *Evidence-based Coaching.* Brisbane, Australia: Australian Academic Press, 13-19; Flaherty, James. 2010. *Coaching: Evoking Excellence in Others.* Burlington MA: Butterworth Heinemann/Elsevier.

5. Grant, Anthony M., and Michael J. Cavanagh. 2004. "Toward a Profession of Coaching: Sixty-five Years of Progress and Challenges for the Future." *International Journal of Evidence Based Coaching and Mentoring.* 2(1): 1-16.

6. Drake, David B. 2009. "Evidence is a Verb: A Relational Approach to Knowledge and Mastery in Coaching." *International Journal of Evidence Based Coaching.* 7(1): 1-12.

7. Grant, Anthony M. 2009. "The Evidence for Coaching." Harvard Medical School and McLean Hospital Coaching in Medicine and Leadership Conference, September.

8. DeMeuse, Kenneth P., Dai, Guangrong, and Robert J. Lee, 2009. "Evaluating the effectiveness of executive coaching: beyond ROI?" *Coaching: An International Journal of Theory, Research, and Practice,* 2(2): 117-134.

9. Stober, Diane, and Anthony M. Grant. 2006. "Toward a Contextual Approach to Coaching Models." In Stober, Diane, and Anthony M. Grant, Eds. *Evidence-Based Coaching Handbook.* Hoboken NJ: John Wiley and Sons; Franklin, John, and Justin Doran. 2009. "Does All Coaching Enhance Objective Performance Independently Evaluated by Blind Assessors? The Importance of the coaching Model and Content." International Coaching Psychology Review. 4(2): 128-144; Laske, Otto. 2004. "Can Evidence-Based Coaching Increase ROI?" *International Journal of Evidence Based Coaching and Mentoring,* 2(2): 41-53.

10. Pfeffer, Jeffrey, and Robert I. Sutton. 2006. "Evidence-Based Management," *Harvard Business Review,* January: 63-74

11. The Ken Blanchard Companies. 2008. "Managing Coaching for Results and ROI." *Perspectives,* 1-6.

12. Stober, Dianne R., Wildflower, Leni, and David Drake. 2006. Evidence=based practice: A Potential Approach for Effective Coaching. *International Journal of Evidence Based Coaching and Mentoring,* 4.

13. Global Coaching Community. 2008. "The Dublin Declaration on Coaching." Version1.4 Final, September, 1-29.

14. Seligman, Martin E. P. 1998. The presidential address. *American Psychologist*, 54, 559-562.
15. Kauffman, Carol. 2006. "Positive Psychology: The Science at the Heart of Coaching." In Stober, Diane, and Anthony Grant, Eds. 2006. *Evidence Based Coaching Handbook*. Hoboken NJ: John Wiley & Sons.

Chapter 3

1. Linley, P. Alex. 2008. *Average to A+*. Coventry England: CAPP Press.
2. Lopez, Shane, Ed. 2009. *The Encyclopedia of Positive Psychology*. New York: Wiley/Blackwell.
3. Rath, Tom. 2007. *StrengthsFinder 2.0*. New York: Gallup Press.
4. http://www.simplystrengths.com.
5. Saleebey, Dennis, Ed. 2009. *The Strengths Perspective in Social Work Practice* (5th ed.). Boston: Pearson/Allyn & Bacon, 10.
6. Buckingham, Marcus. 2007. *Go Put Your Strengths To Work*. New York: Free Press.
7. Ericsson, K. Anders, et al., Eds. 2006. *The Cambridge Handbook of Expertise and Expert Performance*. New York: Cambridge University Press.
8. Hillyard, Paul. 2007. *The Private Life of Spiders*. London: New Holland Publishers.
9. Clifton, Donald O., and Paula Nelson. 1995. *Soar with Your Strengths*. New York: Dell Books; Clifton, Donald O., and Paula Nelson. 1994. *Play to Your Strengths*. Essex UK: Piatkus Books.
10. Buckingham, Marcus. 2007. *Go Put Your Strengths to Work*. New York: Simon & Schuster; Rath, Tom, and Barry Conchie. 2009. *Strengths-Based Leadership*. New York: Gallup Press; Rath, Tom, and Donald O. Clifton. 2004. *How Full Is Your Bucket?* New York: Gallup Press.
11. Cooperrider, David, and Suresh Srivasta. 1987. "Appreciative Inquiry in Organizational Life, Part One and Part Two." *Research in Organizational Change and Development*, 129-169.
12. Seligman, Martin E. P. 2011. *Flourish*. New York: Free Press.
13. http://positivepsychologynews.com/news/bridget-grenville-cleave/2010042610729. Retrieved April 26, 2010.

14. Peterson, Christopher, and Martin E. P. Seligman. 2006. *Character Strengths and Virtues: A Handbook & Classification.* Washington DC: American Psychological Association.

15. http://www.bus.umich.edu/Positive/Center-for-POS.

16. http://www.viacharacter.org/Articles/MayersonStrengthsterms. aspx.

17. Lyubomirsky, Sonja. 2008. *The How of Happiness.* New York: Penguin Press.

18. Gilbert, Daniel. *Stumbling on Happiness.* 2006. New York: Knopf.

19. Ben-Shahar, Tal. 2011. *Being Happy.* New York: McGraw Hill; 2010. *Even Happier.* New York: Mc Graw Hill; 2007. *Happier: Learn the Secrets to Daily Joy and Lasting Fulfillment.* New York: McGraw Hill.

20. Haidt, Jonathan. 2006. *The Happiness Hypothesis.* New York: Basic Books; Keyes, Corey L. M., and Jonathan Haidt, Eds. 2003. *Flourishing: Positive Psychology and the Life Well-Lived.* Washington DC: American Psychological Association.

21. Diener, Edward, and E. M. Suh, Eds. 2003. *Culture and* Subjective *Well-Being.* Cambridge MA: MIT Press.

22. Diener, Edward, Ed. 2009. *The Science of Well-Being*, vol. 1. New York: Springer; Diener, Edward. 1984. "Subjective Well-being." *Psychological Bulletin.* 35: 542-575; Myers, David G., and Edward Diener. 1995. "Who Is Happy? *Psychological Science.* 6(1): 10-17.

23. Linley, P. Alex, Nielsen, Karina M., Wood, A. M., Gillett, Ralph, & Robert Biswas-Diener. 2010. Using signature strengths in pursuit of goals: Effects on Goal Progress, Need Satisfaction, and Well-Being, and Implications for Coaching Psychologists. *International Coaching Psychology Review*, 5: 8-17.

24. Seligman, Martin E. P. 2011. *Flourish.* New York: Free Press.

25. Diener, Edward, and Robert Biswas-Diener. 2008. *Happiness: Unlocking the Mysteries of Psychological Wealth.* Malden MA: Blackwell Press; and Biswas-Diener, Robert, and Ben Dean. 2007. *Positive Psychology Coaching.* Hoboken NJ: John Wiley and Sons; Linley, P. Alex, Willars, Janet, and Robert Biswas-Diener. 2010. *The Strengths Book.* Coventry UK: CAPP Press.

26. Biswas-Diener, Robert. 2010. *Practicing Positive Psychology Coaching*. Hoboken NJ: John Wiley and Sons.

27. Saleebey, Dennis, ed. 2009. *The Strengths Perspective in Social Work Practice*. 5th ed. Boston: Pearson/Allyn & Bacon,102-3.

28. Cramer, Kathryn D., and Hank Wasiak. 2006. *Change the Way You See Yourself Through Asset-Based Thinking*. Philadelphia, Running Press.

29. http://assetbasedthinking.com.

30. Goleman, Daniel. *Emotional Intelligence*. New York: Bantam Books, 1995; Bradberry, Travis, and Jean Greaves. 2009. *Emotional Intelligence 2.0*. San Diego: TalentSmart.

31. Gentry, William A., Weber, Todd J., and Goinaz Sadri. 2010. "Empathy in the Workplace." Charlotte NC: Centers for Creative Leadership.

32. Frederickson, Barbara L. 2009. *Positivity*. New York: Crown.

33. http://www.authentichappiness.com.

34. http:/ www.strengthsfinder.com & www.strengthsquest.com.

35. http://www.tmbc.standout.com.

36. http://www.cappeu.com.

37. http://www.mbti.capt.org.

38. http://www.corexcel.com.

39. Sugerman, Jeffrey, Scullard, Mark, and Emma Wilhelm. 2011. *The 8 Dimensions of Leadership*. San Francisco: Berrett-Koehler.

40. http://www.strengthsexplorer.com; Fox, Jenifer. 2008. *Your Child's Strengths: Discover Them, Develop Them, Use Them*. New York: Viking Penguin Books; http://www.search-institute.org.

Chapter 4

1. Vaill, Peter. 1996. *Learning as a Way of Being*. San Francisco: Jossey-Bass.

2. Covey, Stephen R. 2007. "Stephen R. Covey on Leadership: Great Leaders, Great Teams, Great Results." Salt Lake City: FranklinCovey Co.

3. Barker, Joel Arthur. 1992. *Future Edge*. New York: Harper Collins.

4. Covey, Stephen M. R. 2006. *The Speed of Trust*. New York: Free Press.

5. http://www.merriam-webster.com.
6. Kellerman, Barbara. 2008. *Followership*. Boston: Harvard Business Press.
7. Dweck, Carol S. 2006. *Mindset*. New York: Ballantine.
8. http://www.celebratetraining.com.
9. Cramer, Kathryn D., and Hank Wasiak. 2009. *Change the Way You See Yourself Through Asset-Based Thinking*. Philadelphia, Running Press, 2009.
10. Pink, Daniel. 2009. *Drive*. New York: Riverhead/Penguin.
11. Ryan, Richard M., and Edward Deci. 2000. "Self-determination Theory and the Facilitation of Intrinsic Motivation, Social Development, and Well-being." *American Psychologist*. 55: 68-78.
12. Peshawaria, Rajeev. 2011. *Too Many Bosses, Too Few Leaders*. New York: Free Press.
13. Thomas, Kenneth W. 2009. *Intrinsic Motivation at Work*. 2nd ed. San Francisco: Berrett-Koehler.
14. Langer, Ellen J. 2009. *Counterclockwise:* New York: Ballantine.
15. Gallagher, Winifred. 2009. *Rapt: Attention and the Focused Life*. New York: Penguin, 178-181.
16. http://www.merriam-webster.com.
17. Gallagher, Winifred. 2009. *Rapt: Attention and the Focused Life*. New York: Penguin, 180.
18. Seligman, Martin E. P. 2011. *Flourish*. New York: Free Press.
19. Moskowitz, Gordon B., and Heidi Grant. 2009. *The Psychology of Goals*. New York: Guilford Press.
20. http://www.heidigranthalvorson.com/goals.
21. Tracy, Brian. 2003. *Goals!* San Francisco: Berrett-Koehler; Tracy, Brian. 2007. *Eat That Frog!* San Francisco: Berrett-Koehler.
22. Miller, Caroline A., and Michael B. Frisch. 2009. *Creating Your Best Life*. New York: Sterling Press.
23. Seligman, Martin E. P. 2011. *Flourish*. New York: Free Press.
24. Gillespie, Richard. 1993. *Manufacturing Knowledge: A History of the Hawthorne Experiments*. London: Cambridge University Press.
25. Rosenthal, Robert, and Lenore Jacobsen. 1992. *Pygmalion in the Classroom*. New York: Irvington.
26. FranklinCovey Company. 2002. *FOCUS Participant Manual*, 45.

27. Koch, Richard. 2008. *The 80/20 Principle*, 2nd ed. New York: Doubleday.

28. Lopez, Shane, Ed. 2008. *Positive Psychology: Discovering Human Strengths*. Westport CT: Prager, 41.

29. Bushe, Gervais. 2010. *Clear Leadership*, 2nd ed. Boston: Davies-Black.

30. Lehrer, Jonah. 2009. *How We Decide*. New York: Houghton Mifflin Harcourt.

31. Iyengar, Sheena S. 2010. *The Art of Choosing*. New York: Twelve/ Hachette Group.

32. Fishman, Raymond, Iyengar, Sheena S., Kamenica, Emir, and Itamar Simonson. 2008. "Racial preferences in dating," *Review of Economic Studies* 75: 117-132; Iyengar, Sheena S., and Emir Kamenica, 2010. "Choice proliferation, simplicity seeking, and asset allocation, *Journal of Public Economics*. doi:10,1016/) j.jpubeco2010.03.006; Hernandez, Miriam, and Sheena S. Iyengar. 2001. "What drives whom? A Cultural Perspective on Human Agency." *Social Cognition*. 19(3): 269-294; Botti, Simona, Orfali, Kristina, and Sheena S. Iyengar. 2009. "Tragic Choices: Autonomy and Emotional Responses to Medical Decisions." 2009. *Journal of Consumer Research* 36: 337-352; Botti, Simona, and Sheena S. Iyengar. 2006. "The Dark Side of choice: When Choice Impairs Social Welfare." *Journal of Public Policy and Marketing*, 25: 24-38.

33. Chua, Roy Yong-Joo, and Sheena S. Iyengar. 2006. "Empowerment Through Choice? A Critical Analysis of the Effects of Choice in Organizations." *Research in Organizational Behavior*. 27: 41-79.

34. Blenko, Marcia W., Mankins, Michael C., & Paul Rogers. 2010. *Decide and Deliver*. Boston: Harvard Business Press.

35. Thaler, Richard H., and Cass R. Sunstein. 2008. *Nudge*. New Haven CT: Yale University Press.

36. http://www.nudges.org.

37. Miller, George A. 1956. "The magical number seven, plus or minus two: Some limits on our capacity for processing information." *Psychological Review,* 63: 81-97.

38. Leo, Jacqueline. 2009. *7: The Number for Happiness, Love and Success*. New York: Twelve/Hachette Book Group; Eastis, David

M. 2009. *7: The Magical, Amazing and Popular Number.* Chula Vista CA: Aventine Press.

39. Frederickson, Barbara L. 2009. *Positivity.* New York: Crown, 37-48; Diener, Ed, and Micaela Y. Chan. 2011. "Happy People Live Longer." *Applied Psychology: Health and Well-Being.* 3(1): 1-43.

40. Prochaska, James O., Norcross, John C., and Carlo C. DiClemente. 1994. *Changing For Good.* New York: Avon Press; and Gottman, John., and Nan Silver. 1999. *The Seven Principles for Making Marriage Work.* New York: Three Rivers/Crown.

41. Galbraith, John Kenneth. 1971. *A Contemporary Guide to Economics. Peace, and Laughter,* New York: New American Library, 50.

42. Prochaska, J. O., Norcross, J. C., and C C. DiClemente. 1994. *Changing For Good.* New York: Avon Press; Prochaska, James O., DiClemente, Carlo, C., and John C. Norcross. 1992. "In Search of How People Change." *American Psychologist,* 47, 1102-1114

43. http://www.uri.edu/research/cprc.

44. Dweck, Carol S. 2006. *Mindset.* New York: Ballantine, 226-230.

45. Heslin, Peter A., and Don Vande Walle. 2008. "Managers' Implicit Assumptions About Personnel." *Current Directions in Psychological Science.* 17(3): 219-223.

46. Gallagher, W. 2009. *Rapt: Attention and the Focused Life.* New York: Penguin.

Chapter 5

1. Cooperrider, David L., and Diana Whitney. 2005. *Appreciative Inquiry: A Revolution in Change.* San Francisco: Berrett-Koehler.

2. Schein, Edgar. 2009. *Helping.* San Francisco: Berrett-Koehler.

3. Srivasta, Suresh, Cooperrider, David L., and Associates. 1990. *Appreciative Management and Leadership.* San Francisco: Jossey Bass.; Cooperrider, David L., and Diana Whitney. 1999. *Collaborating for Change: Appreciative Inquiry.* San Francisco: Berrett-Koehler.

4. Brown, Juanita, and David Isaacs. 2005. *The World Café: Shaping Our Futures Through Conversations That Matter.* San Francisco: Berrett-Koehler.

5. White, Michael, and David Epston. 1990. *Narrative Means to Therapeutic Ends.* New York: W. W. Norton & Company; Gergen, Kenneth J., and Mary Gergen. 2004. *Social Construction: Entering the Dialogue.* Chagrin Falls OH: Taos Press.

6. Ellinor, Linda, and Glenna Gerard. 1998. *Dialogue.* New York: John Wiley and Sons.

7. Kisthart, Walter E. in Saleebey, Dennis., Ed. *The Strengths Perspective in Social Work Practice.* 5th ed. Boston: Pearson/Allyn & Bacon, 51-58.

8. Bertolino, Bob, Kiener, Michael, and Ryan Patterson. 2009. *The Therapist's Notebook on Strengths and Solution-Based Therapies.* New York: Routledge.

9. Whitney, Diana, Cooperrider, David, Trosten-Bloom, Amanda, and Brian S. Kaplan. *2001. Encyclopedia of Positive Questions. Euclid OH: Lakeshore Communications.*

10. Whitney, Diana, Trosten-Bloom, Amanda, and Kae Rader. 2010. *Appreciative Leadership.* New York: McGraw Hill, 35-41.

11. Nonaka, Ikujiro, and Hirotaka Takeuchi. 2011. "The Wise Leader." *Harvard Business Review,* May, 58-67.

12. Pink, Daniel. 2009. *Drive.* New York: Riverhead/Penguin.

13. Goldsmith, Marshall. 2009. *Mojo.* New York: Hyperion Press.

14. Goldsmith, Marshall. 2006. *Coaching for Leadership.* New York: John Wiley & Sons, 45.

15. Daniels, A. 1999. *Bringing Out the Best in People* (2nd ed.). New York: McGraw-Hill.

16. Bridges, William. 2009. *Managing Transitions: Making the Most of Change, 3rd ed.* Philadelphia: DaCapo Press.

17. Kitchener, Karen. 2000. *Foundations of Ethical Practice, Research, and Teaching in Psychology.* Mahwah NJ: Lawrence Erlbaum; Kitchener, Karen S., 1985. "Ethical Principles and Decisions in Student Affairs." In Canon, Harry J., and Ronald D. Brown, Ed. *Applied Ethics in Student Services.* SanFrancisco: Jossey Bass, 17-20.

18. Lev Vygotsky Archive. (No date). Retrieved May 22, 2011, from http://www.marxists.org/archive/vygotsky/.

19. Bruner, Jerome. 1996. *The Culture of Education.* Boston MA: Harvard Press.

Chapter 6

1. Buckingham, Marcus. 2007. *"Trombone Player Wanted."* Los Angeles CA: The Marcus Buckingham Company. (DVD).
2. Haidt, Jonathan. Personal communication, November 10, 2010.
3. Seligman, Martin E. P. 2011. *Flourish*. New York: Free Press, 243-265.
4. Saleebey, Dennis, Ed. 2009. *The Strengths Perspective in Social Work Practice*. 5th ed. Boston: Pearson/Allyn & Bacon.
5. Ting, Sharon, and Peter Sisco. 2006. *The CCL Handbook of Coaching: A Guide for the Leader Coach*. San Francisco: Jossey Bass.
6. Lopez, Shane. Ed. 2009. *The Encyclopedia of Positive Psychology*. (New York: Wiley/Blackwell, 954; Linley, Alex. 2008. *Average to A+*. Coventry, UK: CAPP Press, 72-111; Whitney, Diana, Trosten-Bloom, Amanda, and Kae Rader. 2008. *Appreciative Leadership*. New York: McGraw Hill, 67-70.
7. Linley, P. Alex., Nielsen, Karina M., Wood, A. M., Gillett, Ralph, & Robert Biswas-Diener. 2010. "Using Signature Strengths in Pursuit of Goals: Effects on Goal Progress, Need Satisfaction and Well-Being, and Implications for Coaching Psychologists. *International Coaching Psychology Review,* 5(1): 8-17.
8. Garvin, David A. 2000. "Learning in action: A guide to putting the learning organization to work." *Harvard Business Review,* 106-116.
9. Stamatis, D. H. 1997. *TQM Engineering Handbook*. Philadelphia: CRC Press, 160-162.
10. Whitney, Diana, Trosten-Bloom, Amanda, & Kae Rader. 2008. *Appreciative Leadership*. New York: McGraw Hill.
11. Laliberte, Bob. 2010. "Success Cause Analysis." *IPI Newsletter,* December.
12. Cameron, Kim. 2008. *Positive Leadership: Strategies for Extraordinary Performance*. San Francisco: Berrett-Koehler.
13. Whitney, Diana, Trosten-Bloom, Amanda, and Kae Rader. 2010. *Appreciative Leadership*. New York: McGraw Hill, 78-82.
14. Deron, Scott J. 2003. *C-Reactive Protein. New York:* McGraw-Hill, 12.

15. Hansell, Norris. 1976. *The Person-in-Distress: On the Biosocial Dynamics of Adaptation.* New York: Human Sciences Press.
16. Buckingham, Marcus. 2007. *Go Put Your Strengths to Work.* New York: Free Press.
17. Covey, Stephen R. 1989. *The 7 Habits of Highly Effective People.* New York: Fireside.
18. Seligman, Martin E. P., Steen, Tracy A., Park, Nansook, and Christopher Peterson. 2005. "Positive Psychology Progress: Empirical Validation of Interventions." *American Psychologist* 60(5): 410-421.
19. Schueller, Stephen M. 2010. "Preferences for Positive Psychology Exercises." *Journal of Positive Psychology.* 5: 192-203.
20. Emmons, Robert A. 2007. *Thanks: How the New Science of Gratitude Can Make You Happier.* New York: Houghton Mifflin/Harcourt.
21. Seligman, Martin E. P. 2011. *Flourish.* New York: Free Press.
22. Rath, Tom, & James K. Harter. 2009. *Wellbeing: The Five Essential Elements.* New York: Gallup Press.
23. http://www.wbfinder.com.
24. Bushe, Gervais. 2009. *Clear Leadership.* 2nd ed. Boston: Davies-Black.

Chapter 7

1. Goleman, Daniel. 2006. *Social Intelligence.* New York: Random House.
2. Goleman, Daniel. 1998. *Working with Emotional Intelligence.* New York: Bantam.
3. http://www.wbfinder.com.
4. This generic competence framework is sourced from U.S. Office of Personnel Management. 2002. *MOSAIC competencies for professional and administrative occupations.* Washington DC: USOPM; Spencer, Lyle, and Signe M. Spencer.1993. *Competence at Work.* New York: John Wiley and Sons; Richard H. Rosier, Ed.1994, 1996. *The Competency Model Handbook, vol.1 and 2.* Lexington MA: Linkage; Daniel Goleman. 1998. *Working with Emotional Intelligence.* New York: Bantam.

5. Goleman, Daniel, Boyatzis, Richard E., and Annie McKee. 2002. *Primal Leadership*. Boston, MA: Harvard Business Press.

6. Cameron, Kim. 2008. *Positive Leadership: Strategies for Extraordinary Performance*. San Francisco: Berrett-Koehler.

7. Whitney, Diana, Trosten-Bloom, Amanda, and Kae Rader. 2010. *Appreciative Leadership*. New York: McGraw Hill.

8. Cockerham, Ginger. 2011. *Group Coaching: A Comprehensive Blueprint*. Bloomington IN: iUniverse.

9. http://www.capt.org/KGI.

10. Wageman, Ruth, Nunes, Debra A., Burruss, James A., and J. Richard Hackman. 2008. *Senior Leadership Teams: What It Takes To Make Them Great*. Boston: Harvard Business Press.

11. Hackman, J. Richard, and Ruth Wageman. 2005. "A Theory of Team Coaching." *Academy of Management Review* 30: 269-287.

12. Weaver, Richard G., and John D. Farrell. 1997. *Managers as Facilitators*. San Francisco: Berrett-Koehler.

13. http://www.discoverylearning.com/products/assessments.aspx.

14. Bianco-Mathis, Virginia, Roman, Cynthia, and Lisa K. Nabors. 2008. *Organizational Coaching: Building Relationships, Processes, and Strategies That Drive Results*. Alexandria VA: ASTD Press; and Homan, Madeleine, and Miller, Linda. 2008. *Coaching in Organizations*. New York: John Wiley & Sons.

Appendix

1. ICF Global Coaching Client Study, April 2009, ICF Archives.

2. *Global Trends in Separation Practices Report*. Drake Beam Morin, with Human Capital Institute, 2008.

3. Kombarakaran, Francis, Yang, Julia A., Baker, Mila N., and Pauline B. Fernandes. 2008. "Executive Coaching: It Works!" *Consulting Psychology: Practice & Research*. 60(1): 78-90.

4. "ICF Coaching Client ROI Global Study." 2009. Lexington KY: ICF, June.

5. Kauffman, Carol, and Diane Coutu. 2009. "The Realities of Executive Coaching." *Harvard Business Review Research Report*.

6. "Taking the Temperature of Coaching." Summer 2009. London UK: Chartered Institute of Personnel and Development. 1-9.

7. "2010 Executive Coaching Survey." Sherpa Coaching LLC, Cincinnati OH.
8. "HDA Executive Coaching Survey." 2010. London UK: HDA Associates LLC.

Conclusion

1. Reivich, Karen J., Seligman, Martin E. P., and Sharon McBride. 2011. "Master resilience training in the U. S. Army", *American Psychologist* 66: 25-34; Seligman, Martin E. P. 2011. *Flourish*, New York: Free Press, 163-181.
2. http://www.dwp.gov.uk/docs/hwwb-baseline-indicators.pdf.

Further Reading

Ben-Shahar, Tal. 2007. *Happier: Learn the Secrets to Daily Joy and Lasting Fulfillment.* New York: Mc Graw Hill.

Ben-Shahar, Tal. 2010. *Even Happier.* New York: Mc Graw Hill.

Ben-Shahar, Tal. 2011. *Being Happy.* New York: Mc Graw Hill.

Bertolino, Bob, Kiener, Michael, and Ryan Patterson. 2009. *The Therapist's Notebook on Strengths and Solution-Based Therapies.* New York: Routledge.

Bianco-Mathis, Virginia, Roman, Cynthia, and Lisa K. Nabors. 2008. *Organizational Coaching: Building Relationships, Processes, and Strategies That Drive Results.* Alexandria VA: ASTD Press.

Biswas-Diener, Robert, and Ben Dean. 2007. *Positive Psychology Coaching.* Hoboken NJ: John Wiley and Sons.

Biswas-Diener, Robert. 2010. *Practicing Positive Psychology Coaching.* Hoboken NJ: John Wiley and Sons.

Blenko, Marcia W., Mankins, Michael C., & Paul Rogers. 2010. *Decide and Deliver.* Boston: Harvard Business Press.

Bradberry, Travis, and Jean Greaves. 2009. *Emotional Intelligence 2.0.* San Diego: TalentSmart.

Bridges, William. 2009. *Managing Transitions: Making the Most of Change.* 3rded. Philadelphia: DaCapo Press.

Brown, Juanita, and David Isaacs. 2005. *The World Café: Shaping Our Futures Through Conversations That Matter.* San Francisco: Berrett Koehler.

Buckingham, Marcus. 2007. *Go Put Your Strengths To Work.* New York: Free Press.

Bushe, Gervais 2009. *Clear Leadership.* 2nd ed. Boston: Davies-Black.

Cameron, Kim. 2008. *Positive Leadership: Strategies for Extraordinary Performance.* San Francisco: Berrett-Koehler.

Clifton, Donald O., and Paula Nelson. 1995. *Soar with Your Strengths.* New York: Dell Books.

Cockerham, Ginger. 2011. *Group Coaching: A Comprehensive Blueprint.* Bloomington IN: iUniverse, 2011.

Cooperrider, David L., and Diana Whitney. 2005. *Appreciative Inquiry: A Revolution in Change*. San Francisco: Berrett-Koehler.

Covey, Stephen M. R. 2006. *The Speed of Trust*. New York: Free Press.

Cramer, Kathryn D., and Hank Wasiak. 2009. *Change the Way You See Yourself Through Asset-Based Thinking*. Philadelphia, Running Press.

Diener, Edward, and Robert Biswas-Diener. 2008. *Happiness: Unlocking the Mysteries of Psychological Wealth*. Malden MA: Blackwell Press.

Dweck, Carol S. 2006. *Mindset*. New York: Ballantine.

Eastis, David M. 2009. *7: The Magical, Amazing and Popular Number*. Chula Vista CA: Aventine Press.

Ellinor, Linda, and Glenna Gerard. 1998. *Dialogue*. New York: John Wiley and Sons.

Emmons, Robert A. 2007. *Thanks: How the New Science of Gratitude Can Make You Happier*. New York: Houghton Mifflin/Harcourt.

Ericsson, K. Anders, et al., Eds. 2006. *The Cambridge Handbook of Expertise and Expert Performance*. New York: Cambridge University Press.

Frederickson, Barbara L. 2009. *Positivity*. New York: Crown.

Gallagher, Winifred. 2009. *Rapt: Attention and the Focused Life*. New York: Penguin.

Gergen, Kenneth J., and Mary Gergen. 2004. *Social Construction: Entering the Dialogue*. Chagrin Falls OH: Taos Press.

Gilbert, Daniel. *Stumbling on Happiness*. 2006. New York: Knopf.

Goldsmith, Marshall. 2009. *Mojo*. New York: Hyperion Press.

Goleman, Daniel, Boyatzis, Richard E., and Annie McKee. 2002. *Primal Leadership*. Boston, MA: Harvard Business Press.

Goleman, Daniel. 2006. *Social Intelligence*. New York: Random House.

Haidt, Jonathan. 2006. *The Happiness Hypothesis*. New York: Basic Books.

Homan, Madeleine, and Linda Miller. 2008. *Coaching in Organizations*. New York: John Wiley & Sons.

Iyengar, Sheena S. 2010. *The Art of Choosing*. New York: Twelve/Hachette Group.

Kellerman, Barbara. 2008. *Followership*. Boston: Harvard Business Press.

Keyes, C. L. M., and Jonathan Haidt, Eds. 2003. *Flourishing: Positive Psychology and the Life Well-Lived*. Washington DC: American Psychological Association.

Kitchener, Karen. 2000. *Foundations of Ethical Practice, Research, and Teaching in Psychology*. Mahwah NJ: Lawrence Erlbaum.

Koch, Richard. 2008. *The 80/20 Principle.* 2nd ed. New York: Doubleday.

Langer, Ellen J. 2009. *Counterclockwise.* New York: Ballantine.

Lehrer, Jonah 2009. *How We Decide.* New York: Houghton Mifflin Harcourt.

Leo, Jacqueline. 2009. *7: The Number for Happiness, Love and Success.* New York: Twelve/Hachette Book Group.

Linley, Alex. 2008. *Average to A+.* Coventry UK: CAPP Press.

Linley, Alex, Willars, Janet, and Robert Biswas-Diener. 2010. *The Strengths Book.* Coventry UK: CAPP Press.

Lopez, Shane, Ed. 2008. *Positive Psychology: Discovering Human Strengths.* Westport CT: Prager.

Lopez, Shane. 2009. *The Encyclopedia of Positive Psychology.* (New York: Wiley/Blackwell.

Lyubomirsky, Sonja. 2008. *The How of Happiness.* New York: Penguin Press.

Miller, Caroline A., and Michael B. Frisch. 2009. *Creating Your Best Life.* New York: Sterling Press.

Moskowitz, Gordon B., and Heidi Grant. 2009. *The Psychology of Goals.* New York: Guilford Press.

Peshawaria, Rajeev. 2011. *Too Many Bosses, Too Few Leaders.* New York: Free Press.

Pink, Daniel. 2009. *Drive.* New York: Riverhead/Penguin.

Prochaska, James O., Norcross, John C., and Carlo C. DiClemente. 1994. *Changing For Good.* New York: Avon Press.

Rath, Tom. 2007. *StrengthsFinder 2.0.* New York: Gallup Press

Rath, Tom, and James K. Harter. 2009. *Wellbeing: The Five Essential Elements.* New York: Gallup Press.

Saleebey, Dennis, Ed. 2009. *The Strengths Perspective in Social Work Practice.* 5th ed. Boston: Pearson/Allyn & Bacon.

Schein, Edgar. 2009. *Helping.* San Francisco: Berrett-Koehler.

Seligman, Martin E. P. 2011. *Flourish.* New York: Free Press.

Stober, Dianne, and Anthony M. Grant, Eds. *Evidence-Based Coaching Handbook.* Hoboken NJ: John Wiley and Sons

Thaler, Richard H., and Cass R. Sunstein. 2008. *Nudge.* New Haven CT: Yale University Press.

Sugerman, Jeffrey, Scullard, Mark, and Emma Wilhelm. 2011. *The 8 Dimensions of Leadership.* San Francisco: Berrett-Koehler.

Thomas, Kenneth W. 2009. *Intrinsic Motivation at Work.* 2nd ed. San Francisco: Berrett-Koehler.

Tracy, Brian. 2007. *Eat That Frog!* San Francisco: Berrett-Koehler.

Wageman, Ruth, Nunes, Debra A., Burruss, James A., and J. Richard Hackman. 2008. *Senior Leadership Teams: What It Takes To Make Them Great.* Boston: Harvard Business Press.

Weaver, Richard G., and John D. Farrell. 1997. *Managers as Facilitators.* San Francisco: Berrett-Koehler.

Whitney, Diana, Trosten-Bloom, Amanda, and Kae Rader. 2010. *Appreciative Leadership.* New York: McGraw Hill.

ACKNOWLEDGEMENTS

This book could not have made it to print without the following supporters and their contributions, for which I am exceedingly appreciative.

My wife, Nancy, gave me three things essential to this book's emergence: Time to work on it over the months it was being written, irreplaceable time that mostly was taken from her and being together; encouragement, enthusiastic support, and allowance to make my own way with it; and finally, she even read it over more than once, made helpful suggestions for both style and substance, including the title and cover imagery, and thereby served as my midwife for its delivery.

Deb Mathews provided me with a nudging excuse to advance the book's writing timetable by asking for a training curriculum for my strengths coaching course. She also looked over most sections of the book, offered useful advice, and listened constructively as I proposed uses and changes to a number of the content devices and formats.

Paul Knott and Jerry Schaffran reviewed the near final drafts of the work, giving me both psychological backing and insightful critique, patiently helping me to improve and complete it thereby. Thanks to you both, my academic and blood brothers.

The hundreds of trainees and students who were subjected to numerous experiments with sections of the book as text are all greatly appreciated. They enabled me to amplify the utility of some tools, and to sharpen the clarity of writing. You are all to be thanked for that tolerance, the feedback, and the data generated.

The many coaching clients I have been privileged to work with over these past two dozen years-plus, as well as those whose direct tutelage led to this being a key part of my professional life, have all made me the coach I have become to date. The material in this book is also a direct result of their willingness to work with me and my style and frameworks. Their inputs and time spent with me have been the experiential crucible where this book has come into being, and I am humbly grateful for all that.

Numerous other nameless relatives, friends, colleagues, and publisher professionals helped me realize my goals for this material becoming a book, and I am thankful for the various forms that support came in—it was all gratefully received.

You have all made me stronger, and a better user of those strengths—I cannot say adequately how very appreciative I am.

About the Author

Gene Knott is a psychologist and Emeritus Professor in the Department of Human Development and Family Studies at the University of Rhode Island. He was a university administrator for 27 years at 3 different colleges and universities.

Dr. Knott also taught in the University's MBA program, where his courses included Leadership, and Organization Development. He has been an adjunct faculty member in Psychology, Nursing, and Adult Education, and a Fellow in Gerontology.

In addition, Gene has more than 40 years experience in systems consulting, and group facilitation, as well as in training design and delivery for many public and private sector organizations globally. He has also been an executive coach for twenty-four years.

Gene has worked extensively with six sectors: health care, human services, banking, high tech, professional associations, and higher education. His primary areas of interest include organization change, coach training, leadership development, workforce management and succession planning, team building, and cultural competency.

He is also the author or co-author of four books and dozens of book chapters and articles, and has made several hundred invited presentations internationally about his areas of expertise.

Dr. Knott was a psychotherapist for over thirty years, and specialized in behavioral medicine. He is an American Board of Professional Psychology Diplomate, a board certification honor accorded only four per cent of North American psychologists.

A co-founder and former president of the Association for Death Education and Counseling, he is a frequent presenter on topics of dying and grief.

He and his wife, Nancy, live in Wakefield RI, hosting their out-of-state grandchildren on frequent, happy occasions.

Index

Page number references with italics "n" or "nn" indicates endnote information